T0290474

Mission Matters

AMERICAN ALLIANCE OF MUSEUMS

The American Alliance of Museums has been bringing museums together since 1906, helping to develop standards and best practices, gathering and sharing knowledge, and providing advocacy on issues of concern to the entire museum community. Representing more than 35,000 individual museum professionals and volunteers, institutions, and corporate partners serving the museum field, the Alliance stands for the broad scope of the museum community.

The American Alliance of Museums' mission is to champion museums and nurture excellence in partnership with its members and allies.

Books published by AAM further the Alliance's mission to make standards and best practices for the broad museum community widely available.

Mission Matters

Relevance and Museums in the 21st Century

GAIL ANDERSON

ROWMAN & LITTLEFIELD
Lanham • Boulder • New York • London

Published by Rowman & Littlefield
A wholly owned subsidiary of The Rowman & Littlefield Publishing Group, Inc.
4501 Forbes Boulevard, Suite 200, Lanham, Maryland 20706
www.rowman.com

6 Tinworth Street, London SE11 5AL, United Kingdom

Copyright © 2019 by American Alliance of Museums

All rights reserved. No part of this book may be reproduced in any form or by
any electronic or mechanical means, including information storage and retrieval
systems, without written permission from the publisher, except by a reviewer who
may quote passages in a review.

British Library Cataloguing in Publication Information Available

Library of Congress Cataloging-in-Publication Data

Names: Anderson, Gail, 1954– author.
Title: Mission matters : relevance and museums in the 21st century / by Gail
    Anderson.
Description: Lanham : Rowman and Littlefield, 2019. | Series: American
    Alliance of Museums | Includes bibliographical references and index. |
Identifiers: LCCN 2019000812 (print) | LCCN 2019002612 (ebook) | ISBN
    9781538103494 (electronic) | ISBN 9781538103470 (cloth : alk. paper) |
    ISBN 9781538103487 (pbk. : alk. paper)
Subjects: LCSH: Museums—Planning. | Mission statements.
Classification: LCC AM111 (ebook) | LCC AM111 .A53 2019 (print) | DDC
    069/.068—dc23
LC record available at https://lccn.loc.gov/2019000812

♾™ The paper used in this publication meets the minimum requirements of
American National Standard for Information Sciences—Permanence of Paper
for Printed Library Materials, ANSI/NISO Z39.48-1992.

Printed in the United States of America

My dearest John and Maya

Your love, creativity, and passion for life
sustain and inspire me

Contents

Acknowledgments

This book took a village. The process and final book is the result of many individuals who provided wisdom, ideas, feedback, and support from the earliest days of starting work on the book until it went to the publishers. The depth of gratitude I feel is boundless.

Early in the scouting process of finding inspirational missions, many colleagues sent emails with their mission statements for consideration. The field is better as a result of this generous exchange of examples and ideas. Thank you to the many who responded to calls for examples.

From the earliest moments and throughout the creation of this book were many conversations with museum leaders where I benefited from their experience and wisdom, and who in many cases connected me to leaders who eventually became authors for the perspectives featured in chapter 5. My deepest thanks to Anne Bergeron, Dr. Robert Breunig, Janeen Bryant, Joy Davis, Kippen de Alba Chu, David de la Torre, Georgianna la Goria de la Torre, Sarah George, Elaine Heumann Gurian, Jill Hartz, Dr. Selma Holo, Dan Monroe, Martha Morris, Deborah Pope, Marsha Semmel, Elizabeth Silkes, Greg Stevens, Sonnet Takahisa, Chris Taylor, Beth Tuttle, Lisa Watt, Sally Yerkovich, and many more. A special thanks to Elizabeth Merritt and Martha Sharma, Gretchen Jennings, Randi Korn, and Bob Janes, each of whom spent considerable time providing advice and making suggestions for important museums to include due to their leadership work.

The institutions and individuals who graciously shared tools include Julie Decker of the Anchorage Museum; Kaywin Feldman and Karleen Gardner of the Minneapolis Institute of Art; Karyn Flynn of the Bay Area Discovery Museum; Gretchen Jennings; Micah Parzen of the San Diego Museum of Man; Stephanie Ratliffe and Randi Korn for The Wild Center; Bob Sain of di Rosa Center for Contemporary Art; Salvador Salort-Pons for the Detroit Institute of Art; and Nina Simon of the Santa Cruz Museum of Art and History.

The twenty perspectives in chapter 5 were written by museum leaders who generously agreed to write a piece that relayed the story of change at their museums. With admiration and deep gratitude to Cinnamon Catlin-Legutko; Roberta Conner; Julie Decker; Eric Enos; Kaywin Feldman; Karyn Flynn; Lori Fogarty; Terri Lee Freeman; Kay Fukuda; Karleen Gardner; Jamie Glavic with Dion Brown; Lori Fogarty; Sean Kelley; Emlyn Koster; Erin Carlon Mast; Micah D. Parzen, PhD, JD; Richard Piacentini; Stephanie Ratcliffe; Nina Simon; Julie Stein, PhD; Raegan Swanson; and David B. Walker.

Early in the process, I was fortunate to gain the support of two extraordinary museum leaders and colleagues, David Fleming (United Kingdom) and Charmaine Jefferson (United States), both of whom I hold in the highest regard. Each agreed to write thought pieces for the book. Each of them gave much more than their inspirational essays. I am grateful to David for his collegial support, the brainstorming calls, and his generous offer to connect me with his international network, key to securing most of the international mission statements featured in chapter

6. Charmaine tackled the complex and evolving realities around diversity, inclusion, and museums in her essay. Many long calls allowed each of us to talk about, grapple with, and explore the most effective ways to integrate and present issues about the complex topic of equity. I am deeply grateful for the wisdom and unflagging support of both of these leaders.

My deep gratitude to several trusted colleagues who read drafts of chapters and gave candid feedback. Barbara Henry helped with her insights about public engagement for which I am most grateful, not to mention her wonderful encouragement to keep plugging on the book. Daryl Fischer and Laura Roberts provided both support and candid feedback, helping to ensure that the presentation in the book remained balanced and the ideas clear. Laura was a sounding board at various points during the development of the book, reviewing the mission statements with me, and affirming the new categories for grouping the mission statements that the reader will find in chapter 7. Ellen Hirzy, editor extraordinaire, provided her wonderful touch of editing near the end of the process. The reader will benefit from her magic touch with crisper sentences and a better presentation of clear ideas. Every book I have worked on has had an "OMG" moment and this time it happened with Ellen when we both realized the book needed to be restructured. While the rearrangement triggered quite a bit of work, in the end, the book is better for it.

Chris Benitez of Benitez Design, LLC, a graphic designer in San Francisco, provided the vision to capture the Mission Alignment Framework key to the book and also the cover of this book. Taking a concept and translating it into a visual image is a gift. I am deeply appreciative to Chris for his masterful hand and patience as it was refined over at least several iterations.

With much gratitude to Charles Harmon, my prime contact and editor at Rowman & Littlefield Publishers, Melissa McClellan who oversaw copyediting, and Michael Tan, who masterminded the layout. Together they ensured the editing and rigor necessary for a first-rate publication.

Lexie Smith Kliebe, Research Associate for my company, Gail Anderson & Associates, contributed her keen sense of layout, title hierarchy, and developed the style guide for the book to help organize very diverse chapters that each had distinct qualities and factors. She managed to make sense of it all. She also dove into some specific research at various points critical to the ongoing development of the book.

This publication would not have happened without my dedicated and loyal research assistant and project manager, Samantha Hull. For almost two years she has stayed the course, doing massive amounts of research on mission statements and museums, following up on a myriad of details that come with writing a book, tracking and managing all of the files, and somehow keeping the versions straight, especially when I wasn't sure which draft was the latest despite all the dating and tracking. Always, she was upbeat in spirit and up for whatever the challenge of the moment was. With such a long trajectory of work, there were moments of overwhelm and frustration (mine) which, thanks to Sam, never lasted more than a moment. I counted on her and trusted her unconditionally and with unbridled confidence in her work. What a pleasure to work with her; thanks to her determination, we crossed the finish line. Sam, words escape me. How can I ever properly thank you for your extraordinary assistance on this book? You made this book possible.

This time, my daughter Maya was off at university doing her own writing projects, so she was spared the ongoing demands of being home with her mother writing a book. My dear husband John, however, relived me writing another book. Many weekends and adventures with my dear and beloved husband were put on hold. I missed the hikes, escapes to the ocean, and visits to museums with you. You gave up a lot for me and for us, and never complained, probably when you should have. Your love, support, and numerous pep talks made all the difference. And as they say, this wasn't your first rodeo given my other book projects over the years. From the depths of my heart, thank you, John, for all you do for me and for being my North Star and constant inspiration.

Preface

Mission Matters: Relevance and Museums in the 21st Century is a reframing and significant update of the 1998 edition *Museum Mission Statements: Building a Distinct Identity* published by the Technical Information Series, a prior division of the publications department at the American Alliance of Museums. This new volume on mission statements is published by Rowman & Littlefield, the publisher for the American Alliance of Museums.

The concept of a museum's mission is directly tied to the expanding role for museums in the twenty-first century. Mission and the evolving definition of museums are inescapable partners. If museums, and thus missions, are to be relevant in current times, then museum leaders have to be cognizant of, responsive to, and engage with contemporary issues and diverse publics in ways that tap the inherent potential of each institution using adaptive strategies.

This book centers around refreshed thinking about mission, addresses how missions are defined and used to strengthen institutional impact and relevancy, and emphasizes how missions can guide a museum toward meaningful work on behalf of the diverse public museums serve in a complex and ever-changing world. The Mission Alignment Framework is the central concept used to advance thinking about mission to spur relevancy and impact. At the core of this framework is the belief that each museum has the opportunity to come to terms with the realities and pressures of the external environment that influence their museum, to deconstruct the history and traditions embedded in each museum, and to engage in deep institutional reflection to explore what greater purpose, role, and impact is possible for each museum. An outcome of using the Mission Alignment Framework is to support a robust and relevant role for a museum, and thus a relevant mission statement.

ORGANIZATION OF THIS BOOK

Each chapter addresses and delves into an aspect of the shifting thinking about mission statements. In addition to the narrative chapters, there are institutional transformation perspectives written by museum leaders, examples of mission statements, plus tools and strategies that can be useful to instigate change and refinement for the role of a museum and its mission. It is the goal that each section focuses on or illuminates an aspect of the complexities of issues surrounding the mission, providing different opportunities for an individual, an institution, or the field at large, to grapple with the issues that are germane to making museums as viable, inclusive, and robust as possible in this rapidly evolving world. The examples in this volume, whether an inspiring mission statement or the story of transformation for a museum, demonstrate vision, innovation, and a conviction to make a difference.

Chapter 1: Mission Matters

This chapter sets the stage for the book, addressing how museums and their missions are shifting in focus to heighten relevancy in the twenty-first century. The discussion highlights the need for museums to expand their role in the cultural, social, and natural landscape, and dissects the influences, long-held assumptions, and mindsets that can hinder higher impact. References to specific museums undertaking change in their mission are highlighted to illustrate the urgency for change.

Chapter 2: Relevance in the Twenty-First-Century Museum

This chapter features two cornerstone articles by museum leaders who have each grappled with and championed issues of inclusion, relevancy, and timeliness through their respective leadership roles in museums. The first article, by international museum thought leader David Fleming, professor of public history at Hope University in Liverpool, England, and former director of the National Museums Liverpool, discusses the urgency around addressing social issues using the unique resources and capacity of museums to deliver impact and engage new audiences in meaningful ways. The second article is written by Charmaine Jefferson, who addresses issues of diversity and inequities in museums and discusses the connection between cultural competencies and relevance as central to shifting museums toward inclusive organizations.

Chapter 3: Qualities of Mission Statement

This chapter outlines the qualities of an impactful mission statement and defines mission relative to the components of an institutional strategic framework. Examples are used to highlight different styles of missions, different types of museums, and elements of a strategic framework including vision, values, principles, and so on. Guidelines provide reference for language, recommendations for the timing of re-envisioning a mission, and common pitfalls in writing mission statements.

Chapter 4: Mission Alignment Framework

The Mission Alignment Framework graphic tool depicts the external influencing factors in the landscape in which museums operate, and it highlights the importance of having the internal operations of a museum align with the mission for greatest impact in relation to contemporary realities. The Mission Alignment Framework is described for clarity and supported by strategic questions to guide an institutional assessment leading to the creation of a relevant mission as a core management tool and an understanding of the changes needed.

Chapter 5: Twenty Perspectives from Museum Leaders

This chapter includes twenty perspectives written by institutional leaders sharing the evolving changes in their specific missions and future directions of their respective museums. Each perspective conveys the challenges that instigated their transformative change in relation to mission. The perspectives represent museums from Alaska and Hawai'i to Maine and Tennessee, Toronto to San Diego, and points in between. The perspectives reveal the issues institutions grapple with from supporting community healing to increasing environmental awareness to advancing civil rights to reframing historical stories using many voices. Together, the perspectives convey that there is no singular path to defining a relevant mission. These twenty perspectives provide diverse examples useful to museums of any size, focus, or location.

Chapter 6: Mission Statement Examples

With more than eighty examples of different mission statements, this chapter features museums in diverse locations including urban, suburban, and rural, a range of small, medium, and large institutions, and a wide spectrum of types of museums. There are many examples from the United States and more than twenty-five from different museums from around the world. These missions are categorized into four areas: community-building, content-centered, experience-focused, and issues-based museums. These categories are based on considering museums by a dominant defining characteristic rather than by discipline or type of museum such as art, history, and science. This shift is another reflection of how thinking about museums has evolved in the twenty-first century to be an amalgam of creative ideas, broader positioning, and diverse public engagement beyond the limitations of a discipline-imposed mindset about role, purpose, and operations. Some of the examples are model mission statements due to brevity and clarity explaining why they exist and to what greater purpose. Others are longer mission statements, yet the examples reveal a deep commitment to make a difference with communities, the public, and regions appropriate to their institution's own strengths and capacity, and responsiveness to the external environment in which they exist.

Chapter 7: Development of a Mission Statement

Providing some practical advice, this section outlines some strategies for undertaking an institutional assessment to accompany the strategic questions provided in chapter 4 using the Mission Alignment Framework. The process identifies pivotal decisions for a productive process with wide stakeholder engagement, including reframing and writing a mission statement that in turn reveals areas in the institution for change as a fresh institutional position is declared through a new mission.

Chapter 8: Mission Matters Toolkit

The toolkit section features innovative tools that are grouped into three areas: mission matrices, institution frameworks, and theories of transformational change. Some tools provide examples for shaping or revisiting the mission, some are frameworks for institutional analysis and realignment, and others illustrate an approach to undertaking change. Certain tools have been developed and used by specific institutions featured in chapter 5. Other tools have been identified for their simplicity and clarity illuminating useful strategies in support of relevant missions, and still others have been carefully developed through years of work and research to help museums build new inclusive practices in their museums.

Chapter 9: Final Thoughts

This closing section reveals some reflections from the process of building this book and stresses the urgency for museums to act in order to heighten the impact of their institutions in contemporary times.

Bibliography

This curated list of useful references, articles, and publications for the reader provide some examples of inspirational thinking pivotal to the evolution of thought in the field, and new references found during the research efforts for this book.

Mission Matters

WHY ANOTHER PUBLICATION ON MUSEUM MISSION STATEMENTS? WHY NOW?

Simply put, the confluence of issues in society, the external environment, and the world have created new realities and pressures that require museums and museum leaders to examine and rethink how museums can be relevant and more impactful for our citizens and communities.

Museums are not islands: museums exist within a cultural, social, political, economic, and natural environment in which they must play a part. A museum as an unchallenged, venerable institution is a concept that no longer exists.[1] No institution, whether for-profit or nonprofit, can elude public scrutiny or avoid being the focus of a public outcry. Issues impacting individuals, communities, and nations are interrelated and tie to a range of systemic issues such as immigration, racial inequities, local and global economies, disparaties of the haves and have-nots, wars fought over water, religious rights, resources, and land rights—these are just a few realities happening in and around museums.

This amalgam of contemporary realities presents an unprecedented opportunity for all museums to undertake holistic institutional assessment, examine operational assumptions, leverage their unique resources, and determine the most impactful ways of being that make a substantive difference in their communities and in the lives of a diverse public. It is a moment to envision a more responsive, visionary, and vital role for museums that contributes to healthy, vibrant communities. By virtue of being an organization in service to the public, there is an ethical and moral responsibility to take actions to make the world better.[2] Museums must advance inclusion and equity for people of all backgrounds, present the untold stories and histories, and act and care for the fragile environment of our planet.[3]

Indeed, some museums are uniquely positioned to respond to specific topics and issues in depth by virtue of their content emphasis such as science museums addressing climate change, yet all museums need to do their part to protect the environment regardless of the focus of their institution. This is the time to leverage the role of museums as contributors to a better, stronger, more just world and to become positive agents of change in their communities. Every museum has a responsibility to look at the broader external environment and specific local issues, and to select a path forward that resonates and responds to their geographic location, their communities, and the unique resources of their institution.

A relevant and strategic mission for the twenty-first-century museum has the power to galvanize board and staff around instigating meaningful change in communities and the lives of others.

At its core, a mission explains why a museum exists, how it makes a difference in the lives of others, and how it impacts the future, which implies it explains who it is for.[4] The mission is the heart of the institution, its compass, and the grounding force that guides all that a museum does and inspires the people who work there. The mission forms the foundation from which agreement about the role of the museum is clarified, which is especially important as museums undertake transformative and systemic change. A mission is the anchor within a strategic framework alongside a vision, values, operating principles, and impact statements, to name a few, that guide the museum toward its greatest potential and relevancy (see chapters 3, 4, and 8).[5]

A strategic mission plays a central role in the identity of an institution—it conveys to its public why it is there, and it communicates to audiences the ways that they can engage with the museum. A relevant mission translates how the museum connects with the contemporary world, builds meaning with its audiences, challenges assumptions and the status quo, and invites new voices into the larger conversation and dialogue that each museum can facilitate. A strong clear mission, as a management tool, should be clear enough to inform who will lead and advance the mission, what skills and experiences are needed in the staff who work there, what the nature of the work is, and what impact the museum seeks in service to the public. It is like a pebble dropped in the lake: the mission ripples through all aspects of the museum.

Missions matter. Taking the time to define the right mission for each museum is a collective effort and one essential to being able to state clearly "this is who we are, this is what we stand for, this is who we serve, this is how we make a difference, we want to do this with and for you." If the mission is not crafted and thought through with intent, and there isn't the courage to state the institution's conviction for its place in the world, museums run the risk of being disconnected, marginalized, and irrelevant to their communities and the public at large, even the threat of closure.

In the end, each museum has a direction and a focus it will choose. It is about being deliberate and defining a realm in which it will engage the public in meaningful experiences and ideas. Whether a museum is national in focus, a specialty museum, a historic house, or a science institution, it has an obligation to be clear in its intent and define how everything the museum does advances the mission. Every museum will not appeal to all, but each museum can put its stake in the ground and declare its greater purpose that is right for its location, community, and place in the world, its unique characteristics, and the leadership and capacity to deliver the mission.

QUALITIES OF RELEVANT MUSEUMS IN THE TWENTY-FIRST CENTURY

Museums that exude relevancy in the twenty-first century reflect distinct qualities throughout their operations and their vision for the future. These fundamental assertions about museums and thus their mission statements are tied to the greater impact that museums can have.

Relevant museums in the twenty-first century:

- Place the public, communities, and audiences at the center of what they do through meaningful engagement that makes a difference in the lives of people. This fundamental responsibility upholds the museum's social contract with the public to act for the greater good.
- Balance external realities with internal capacity to find the place of greatest impact for the benefit of others. Tapping into the inherent and unique qualities of a museum must be balanced with understanding how to translate contemporary realities into the work each museum undertakes.
- Reflect inclusivity and diversity at all levels of the museum, including representation on boards and staff, the nature of the work undertaken, the voices and histories included, the balance of content and perspectives embraced, and an inclusive organizational culture. This requires that each museum has named and grappled with

underlying biases, assumptions, practices, and modes of behavior that may have supported elitist and exclusionary practices. This leads to reframing new principles and approaches for greater inclusion and success.

- Act with institutional-wide responsibility to uphold environmentally sensitive actions in support of caring for the fragile planet. All museums must do their part in this urgent reality of climate change facing our world and impacting generations to come. Museums must lead by example and empower the public to do their part.
- Facilitate experiences, dialogues, ideas, and engagement onsite and out in the world that are meaningful, inclusive, and respectful of a diverse public. This requires a commitment to lead with humility and listen attentively as a core tenet of operations, welcoming new perspectives and participation as an ongoing way of working and learning.
- Act with integrity, accountability, and transparency, and uphold legal and ethical standards, and financially responsible practices in support of the mission and nonprofit requirements of operation.

In the end, the challenges for today's museums require leaders to act with conviction, courage, and commitment to ask the tough questions, redefine what no longer works, retain what remains useful, stay the course for the long-term to transform museum practices, and undertake the fundamental changes that will be necessary to achieve and sustain relevancy. Significant change takes time and will evolve as new challenges and realities emerge.

EMBEDDED CONSTRUCTS CREATE BARRIERS TO RELEVANT MUSEUMS

Embedded constructs must be addressed to get at the heart of reframing missions, given that many ideologies are so intertwined into thinking and practices that moving forward could be impaired without rigorous examination. Constructs refer to a range of deeply rooted beliefs, structures, and practices such as unexamined assumptions, academic frameworks, systemic racism, and inherent privilege. The following are a few examples of constructs impacting museums.

Decolonization in Museums

Anthropology museums typically hold collections that are based on an academic anthropology framework focused on studying non-Western cultures. Thus, most anthropological collections reflect cultural artifacts of indigenous peoples from the Americas, Africa, and continents across the globe. These diverse cultures were the subject of research, study, and observation by many of the anthropologists of the 1800s and early 1900s, epitomizing the fascination of studying the "other" and the exotic. Many artifacts were stolen and taken to amass cultural collections acquired with disrespect to the people who created them, used them, and attributed sacred and spiritual meanings central to their identity and cultural vitality.[6] In today's world, a museum that still adheres to the ideology of traditional anthropology advances an imbalanced, racist, and colonial view of the history of humans while sustaining cultural objectification practices.[7]

The San Diego Museum of Man, founded as a traditional anthropology museum of global cultures, has shifted the lens to be about understanding human behavior and interactions rather than using the academic anthropology lens. The museum has initiated a decolonization approach to deconstruct this nineteenth- and twentieth-century exploitive and voyeuristic mindset.[8]

As SDMoM changed its direction in 2010, with exhibitions like "RACE: Are We So Different?" [a traveling exhibition from the Science Museum of Minnesota], it set the stage for . . . a lengthy process of self-examination, and . . . a commitment to institutional decolonization. American and European museums have long been associated with the formation and continuation of empires. Many were created to house and display the material and biological remains, and intangible culture, of colonized Indigenous communities in support of a national narrative predicated upon the concept of white supremacy. As a result, museums have often helped perpetuate many endemic social ills, including that of structural racism.[9]

It should be noted that, as part of reframing the work of the San Diego Museum of Man, the board and staff are planning a name change that reflects all of humanity not conveyed with the current name.

While this is a contemporary example of decolonizing efforts featured in this book, several other institutions such as the Glenbow Museum in the late 1970s initiated a rigorous process of decolonization, where 60 percent of the population are Native born. This effort was evident through featuring first-voice interpretation in exhibitions and mounting the largest repatriation of sacred objects in Canadian history. Similarly, the Museum of Northern Arizona engaged Hopi and Navajo elders in the interpretation and representation of their culture and artifacts also in first voice in a major reinstallation in the late 1970s.

Particularly relevant to museums holding indigenous artifacts is the fact that for many cultures, in particular Native American tribes, the concept of keeping an object in perpetuity is antithetical to tribal customs and beliefs. The remarkable U.S. legislation, the Native American Graves and Protection Rights Act of 1990, acknowledged this disparity in museum and Native cultural concepts resulting in many objects being repatriated to their tribes. In some cases, memorandums of understanding have been established between museums and Native tribes for the safekeeping of cultural objects with the agreement that tribal leaders may borrow sacred and ceremonial objects for use in rituals. As one example, the Museum of Northern Arizona in Flagstaff has such a memorandum of understanding with the Hopi Tribe.

The Complexities of American Art

A museum with American art in its name prompts a different set of questions: How is American defined? Does the art have to be created by an American citizen? Does this include an undocumented immigrant? Is there representation of female artists and the full spectrum of artists of color, male and female? This example points to the importance of addressing the underpinnings, definitions, and assumptions inherent in the history of a museum dedicated to American art or a museum dedicated to a nation's artistic heritage. This can be an opportunity to generate thoughtful, inclusive, and empowering conversations that may lead to a new paradigm of public engagement, efforts to broaden representation in the collections, and a more expansive view of artists of diverse backgrounds, and thus a revised and inclusive mission.

The Influence of the National Narrative

The challenge of confronting historical misrepresentation and untruths in museums is one that some museums have been addressing in order to honor all the voices and experiences of a people, an event, or a place. This challenge is not limited to U.S. museums but is happening with museums across the globe when difficult truths and stories about abuse, racism, human atrocities, and war are not fully told (see chapters 2, 5, and 6).

In 2011, the Colombian Government signed Law 1448 which intends to provide comprehensive reparations to nearly 8 million victims of the internal armed conflict since 1985. This Law founded the National Center for Historical Memory (NCHM) with the objective of "designing, creating, and administrating a Museum of Memory, destined to achieve the strengthening of the collective memory regarding Colombia's recent history of violence, making sure to combine efforts from the private sector, civil society, international cooperation, and the state." The National Memory Museum (NMM) constitutes thus as a symbolic reparation measure aiming to restore the dignity of victims, the public acceptance of wrongdoings, the preservation of historical memory, and guarantee the non-repetition of acts of violence and human rights violations.[10]

In the spring of 2018, the Equal Justice Initiative in Montgomery, Alabama, opened The National Memorial for Peace and Justice to honor the men, women, and children who were brutally killed through lynchings, beatings, burnings, and torture from the 1800s into the 1900s. At the same time, the Equal Justice Initiative opened The Legacy Museum, where the exhibition "From Enslavement to Mass Incarceration," presents the evolving story of this horrific past connecting the history of slavery to contemporary forms of oppression, bias, and discriminatory actions. Bryan Stevenson, an attorney, and the executive director and visionary for both projects, believes the museum and the memorial will help tell the larger story and help "change the national narrative."[11]

CONNECTIONS BETWEEN CONTEMPORARY ISSUES AND MUSEUM PRACTICES

Just as the world changes, so too has the vision of some museum leaders regarding the role of their institution. Through the research for this book, several illustrative examples were found where museum leaders are undertaking transformative change, including new voices, abandoning elitist and exclusionary practices, and addressing contemporary issues (see chapters 5 and 6). Note the categories for organizing the missions and their correlating definitions are outlined in the introduction of chapter 6.

Issues-based Museums

The Coastal Discovery Museum in Hilton Head, South Carolina, leverages the unique setting and fragility of the Lowcountry, the unique natural habitat along the South Carolina coastline, as a springboard into larger conversations about visitors taking responsibility as stewards for the planet. See the Coastal Discovery Museum mission and vision in chapter 6.

The Phipps Conservatory and Botanical Gardens in Pittsburgh, Pennsylvania, embraces environmental consciousness holistically whether evidenced in a LEED building, internal best practices, or programs that help the visitor understand the interconnected relationship between humans and the plant kingdom. See the perspective in chapter 5.

The Anchorage Museum in Alaska is dedicated to addressing the pressing issues in the Arctic and the Circumpolar North. Through agreements with other museums in the other eight Arctic Nations, they have mounted, created, and addressed issues shared across the northern region of the world as vanishing glaciers, changing climates, and communities now underwater plague the North with pending global impact. At the Anchorage Museum the intersection of indigenous peoples in Alaska and the issues of the environment spotlight ways to bring stories long kept separate into an integrated and informative way of thinking about the environment and Native cultures together. See the perspective in chapter 5.

The National Museums Liverpool in England, under the leadership of David Fleming, has leveraged its museums as places for addressing contemporary issues, controversy, social change, and social justice (see chapters 2 and 6). This amalgam of institutions, the International Slavery Museum, the Museum of Liverpool, Walker Art Gallery, and the World Museum, to name a few of them, has focused on contemporary issues and inclusion of the people in Liverpool, the United Kingdom, and beyond to heighten relevancy. Summing up his position, Fleming states:

> I think that if museums wish to remain relevant in today's society they need to make sure that they're dealing with difficult issues—some of the issues that they have studiously avoided dealing with in the past. It's the only way, really, to connect with modern people: we've got to more honest than we used to be.[12]

Community-building Museums

Some museums are inextricably linked to their communities, sometimes creating a vital lifeline for the health and well-being of a community, whether defined geographically or by cultural identification or other self-defined characteristic.

The Tamástslikt Cultural Institute in Oregon focuses on the Confederated Tribes of the Umatilla values, beliefs, history, language, and cultural traditions. It is an urgent endeavor to represent and document the traditions through Elders' voices, especially pressing as Native languages are endangered not just in this Native community but in many other tribes across the United States, Canada, and the world. Roberta Conner, the executive director at Tamástslikt, stated "the greatest sign of our success is when a member of the tribe entrusts us with their families' treasures because they know we will care for those objects and tell their stories for generations to come."[13]

The Anacostia Community Museum of the Smithsonian Institution was born out of a conviction to reflect and connect with an underserved, predominantly black community in Washington, DC, to tell their stories, and celebrate a community that had been marginalized. This organization continues to do groundbreaking work building upon John Kinard's vision and groundbreaking work of the 1960s.[14]

A more recent story of a community-based museum is the Santa Cruz Museum of Art and History, where an institution on the brink of closure was saved through a reframing of purpose and mission to be by, for, and with the community. In Nina Simon's perspective, she chronicles the journey of the reinvention that turned the Santa Cruz Museum of Art and History into a community hub that has enlivened the city and become a magnet for building a vibrant level of public engagement[15] (see the perspective in chapter 5).

Content-centered Museums

For many museums, persistent questions from the public have demanded inclusion in historical accounts, and formerly unheard voices and stories reveal the full story of a community or people.

In September 2017, the long-awaited National Museum of African American History and Culture opened on the Mall in Washington, DC. This Smithonian museum, many years in the making, tells the African American story that in turn tells the broader and more complete story laying bare the underbelly of American history around lynchings, slavery, and racist ideology in the United States. Lonnie Bunch, founding director of the National Museum of African American History and Culture, stated in reference to the goals of the museum:

Understanding race, understanding our tortured history can help us with the world we live in today.[16]

We are in a divided America, where race and issues of white supremacy are at the forefront of our conversations. I think the museum is a place that helps us explore things that are difficult, helps us explore where race matters and how it's divided us. I also think people come because they believe that by looking at the history of America through an African-American lens, they're finding moments of optimism, moments to believe that no matter how bad things are, you can effect change if you're willing to struggle and to demand America live up to its stated ideals.[17]

The Museum of History of Polish Jews in Warsaw vision is to "create a platform for social dialogue . . . offering a profound, transformative experience and promoting new standards of relating to history." Their mission statement is to "recall and preserve the memory of Polish Jews, contributing to the mutual understanding and respect amongst Poles and Jews as well as other societies of Europe and the world" (see chapter 6).

The Kenya Wildlife Service is working against the clock to protect the wildlife within their national parks system. Simply put, their vision is "to save the last great species and places on earth for humanity." This example highlights the urgency with which education and action is required in order to avoid irreparable damage and permanent loss (see chapter 6).

Experience-focused Museums

Experience-focused museums are often attributed to childrens' museums, interactive science museums, and historical sites. More and more, museums in all areas are integrating experiences into their approach for engaging the public.

In children's museums, there is a focus on parent-child relationships, exploratory experiences, early childhood education, and the growth of toddlers and children into responsible and caring human beings. At the Bay Area Discovery Museum in Sausalito, California, their commitment to getting it right translates into the significant allocation of funds to undertake research on childhood education and creativity that informs decisions and strategies, influences programmatic choices, and guides the way staff engage with visitors (see the perspective in chapter 5).

The Tenement Museum offers tours of the living quarters of poor, immigrant families in New York City between the 1860s and 1930s. The experience of walking through this site helps the visitor relive and feel the conditions of the people who lived there while striving to care for family members. With current issues around immigration, this museum is relevant to the issues of the day around immigration, prejudices, and deplorable working conditions (see chapter 6).

The Museo Interactivo Economía in Mexico City focuses on "the use of economics as a lens for people to discover how the world works," using interactive exhibitions and presentation of topics not typically featured in a museum setting (see chapter 6).

All of the examples of leadership described in the prior pages are just a few ways that museums are contributing to the world in which they exist with goals to make a difference—some locally, some nationally, and others internationally.

The Power of Collaboration to Lead Change

Some members of the museum community have come together as leaders to instigate the necessary change that has been slow to manifest in museums. "Museums and Race: Transformation and Justice," a convening organized by The Museum Group, held in January 2016 in Chicago, brought together leaders representing ethnic diversity and generations of museum professionals to discuss and outline strategies to help advance museums and the museum field into reflective and inclusive institutions with meaning and connections to a widely diverse public. One of the predominant discussion points was around the power of collaboration.[18] This convening was followed by workshops and conversations at the American Alliance of Museums meeting in Washington, DC, in the spring of 2016.

At the same time a group of visionaries and activists, participated in MASS Action, a group that has met once a year since 2016 at the Minneapolis Institute of Art, and as a result of a collective effort produced the MASS Action Toolkit.[19] This toolkit is a manifestation of the group's commitment to make accessible new ways of advancing equity and re-envisioning museums as integrated, connected, and inclusive institutions. Janeen Bryant, a participant in "Museums and Race" and MASS Action stated,

> Diversity and its oft-used counterpart inclusion . . . should always be coupled with measurable tactics and a clear strategy for change. Any recommendations for a 21st-century reality require adaptability and recognition that we are no longer sure of where our goal posts are day to day. As a field, our drive, purpose, and curiosity require us to define a way of working beyond assimilation to . . . actualizing what museums could be in the future.[20]

Another collaborative effort is the Coalition of Museums for Climate Justice created and led by Robert Janes, former director of Glenbow Museum in Calgary. The mission of the coalition is "Building museums' capacity to promote awareness, mitigation and resilience in the face of climate change."[21] In a recent address at the Alberta Museums Association/Western Museums Association conference in Canada in 2017, Janes emphatically stated that the urgency for museums to take responsibility, and participate in addressing climate change, is now. Janes opines:

> One challenge is the widely-held belief that museums must protect their neutrality, lest they fall prey to bias and special interest groups. The unspoken argument is that museums cannot risk doing anything that might alienate their audiences or sponsors, real or potential. This claim of neutrality underlies the belief that museums may abstain from addressing societal issues, because they have complex histories and unique missions which absolve them from greater accountability.[22]

In his address, he highlights two essential lessons from the LGBTQ community. The first is the need to have conversations about uncomfortable subjects, like queer rights and climate change, and the second is the need to focus on the *immorality of inaction*.[23]

These examples of collaborations emerged because of inaction in the museum field evident by the avoidance of grappling with the issues of the day, and the uncomfortable reality of abdicating responsibility. The reality is that museums must change.

THE ROLE OF A RELEVANT MISSION

The role of a relevant mission is its alignment with the world in which it exists. A relevant and vibrant institution assumes a leadership position that befits who the museum is, where it is located, and its capacity to hit the right mark, role, and path forward. As the reader moves through the various chapters of this book, many more examples will be revealed with the goal of inspiring other museums to make a difference and enhance their impact.

This book presents a re-envisioned paradigm about missions and museums. The examples and discussions throughout this book highlight the need for inspired and visionary leaders who exhibit the highest level of humility and the courage to dismantle injurious, exclusionary, and outdated practices. The subsequent step is to reframe thinking, re-envision public engagement, and define an approach that makes a difference and by association becomes more relevant in this complex world.

Museums are in the intersection of choices. Choices about what the legacy of a museum will be. Choices about declaring why your museum matters. Choices about how to undertake the work that museums can uniquely do to make a difference. Choices about who the institution is really for and who it serves. Choices about how your museum and mission can impact change. Choices about how you will ensure that your museum remains relevant in the twenty-first century.

Take stock in the many visionary examples in this book and determine what courageous vision will be the legacy of your museum. Envision your museum as an integral player in your community, respond to issues that improve lives, and engage in ways that make your museum a contributor to a better world. The moment is now.

NOTES

1. Brian Boucher, "Outrage at Museum of Fine Arts Boston Over Disgraceful 'Dress Up in a Kimono' Event." *Artnet News* (July 6, 2015). https://news.artnet.com/art-world/outrage-boston-museum-of-fine-arts-disgraceful-kimono-event-314534.

2. Robert Janes, *Looking Reality in the Eye: Museums and Social Responsibility* (Calgary: University of Calgary Press, 2005); Robert Janes, *Museums in a Troubled World* (Abingdon: Routledge, 2009); Robert Janes, *Museums without Borders* (Abingdon: Routledge, 2016).

3. Gail Lord and Ngaire Blankenberg, *Cities, Museums, and Soft Power* (Washington, DC: American Alliance of Museums, 2015); Robert Janes, "Museums and Climate Change Activism" Alberta Museums Association/Western Museums Association International Conference 2017–Museums UNITE to Improve Communities, Alberta, Canada, September 23, 2017; Chris Taylor, "Inclusive Leadership: Avoiding a Legacy of Leadership," *Mass Action Toolkit*, (2017): 73–88; Nicole Ivy (ed.), "Facing Change: Insights from the American Alliance of Museums' Diversity, Equity, Accessibility, and Inclusion Working Group," *American Alliance of Museums*, 2018.

4. Simon Sinek, *Start with Why: How Great Leaders Inspire Everyone to Take Action* (New York: Penguin Group, 2009).

5. Randi Korn, *Intentional Practice for Museums: A Guide for Maximizing Impact* (Lanham, MD: Rowman & Littlefield Publishers, 2018); Gail Anderson, *Reinventing the Museum: The Evolving Conversation on the Paradigm Shift* (Lanham, MD: Altamira Press, 2004); Gail Anderson, *Reinventing the Museum: The Evolving Conversation on the Paradigm Shift*, second edition. (Lanham, MD: Altamira Press, 2012).

6. Michael M. Ames, *Cannibal Tours and Glass Boxes: The Anthropology of Museums* (Vancouver, British Columbia: University of British Columbia Press, 1992).

7. Ivan Karp and Steve Lavine, *Exhibiting Culture: The Poetics and Politics of Museum Display* (Washington, DC: Smithsonian Press, 1991); Ivan Karp, Corrine A. Katz, Lynn Szwaja, and Tomas Ybarra-Frausto, *Museum Frictions: Public Cultures/Global Transformations* (Durham: Duke University Press, 2006).

8. Wendy Ng, "Decolonize and Indigenize: A Reflective Dialogue," *Medium*, June 12, 2018; Amy Lonetree, *Decolonizing Museums: Representing Native America in National and Tribal Museums* (Chapel Hill: The University of North Carolina Press, 2012).

9. Personal communication, Micah Parzen, PhD, JD, chief executive officer, San Diego Museum of Man, July 25, 2018.

10. Personal communication, Michael Andres Forero Parra, architect for the National Museum of Memory, Colombia, March 1, 2018.

11. A conversation with Bryan Stevenson on December 1, 2018, with members of The Museum Group, Montgomery, Alabama.

12. David Fleming, International Council of Museums conference, March 13, 2017.

13. Personal communication, Roberta Conner, executive director, on May 23, 2018.

14. Joy Kinard, *The Man, the Movement, the Museum* (Washington, DC: A. P. Foundation Press, 2017).

15. Nina Simon, *The Participatory Museum* (Santa Cruz: Museum 2.0, 2010); Nina Simon, *The Art of Relevance* (Santa Cruz: Museum 2.0, 2016).

16. Lonnie G. Bunch III, "New Smithsonian Museum Confronts Race 'to Make America Better.'" Interview by Michele Norris, *National Geographic* (September 24, 2016).

17. Lonnie G. Bunch III, "A Place To Come Together On Matters That Divide Us." Interview by S. Goldberg, *National Geographic* (March 14, 2018).

18. Daryl Fischer, Swarupa Anila, and Porchia Moore, "Coming Together to Address Systemic Racism in Museums." *Curator The Museum Journal*, 60, no. 6, (2017), 23–31.

19. Chris Taylor, "Inclusive Leadership: Avoiding a Legacy of Leadership," 73–88.

20. Personal communication, Janeen Bryant, November 8, 2018.

21. Robert Janes, "Museums and Climate Change Activism," 2017.

22. Janes, "Museums and Climate Change Activism," 2017.

23. Janes, "Museums and Climate Change Activism," 2017.

Relevance in the
Twenty-First-Century Museum

INTRODUCTION

Relevance in the twenty-first century is a complex and continually evolving mix of realities and challenges. It is this complex landscape in which museum leaders must navigate and define a path that has meaning for a diverse public and communities, tap the greatest impact possible for any given museum, and relate to the contemporary issues of our time. This chapter features two museum thought leaders who share their perspective based on years of grappling with social justice issues, the complexities of inclusion and diversity, and the responsibility to contribute to the vitality and health of individuals and communities in this place and time. This is inextricably linked to a relevant and impactful mission.

The first article is by international museum thought leader David Fleming, professor of public history at Hope University in Liverpool, England, and former director of the National Liverpool Museums. Fleming discusses the urgency for museums to join the conversation on social issues using the unique resources and capacity of museums to deliver impact and engage new audiences in meaningful ways, which in turn relates to mission and institutional role in society. As the leader of the National Museums Liverpool, a system of twelve museums, these institutions employ diverse strategies designed to engage new audiences and address socially relevant issues well suited to the unique qualities of each museum. Museums in the National Museums Liverpool system include the International Slavery Museum, the Museum of Liverpool, and the Walker Art Gallery, to name three. Fleming, a leader in socially responsible work for museums, speaks around the world about the importance of social and cultural inclusion, the value of relevant missions, and the mandate that museums have a responsibility to make a difference.

The second article is written by Charmaine Jefferson, the former director of the California African American Museum in Los Angeles, current member of the Los Angeles Cultural Affairs Commission, and independent practitioner. In her position paper, Jefferson addresses issues of diversity and inequities in museums, and discusses the connection between cultural competencies and relevance as central to shifting museums toward inclusive organizations. Her piece discusses the complexities and nuances of inclusion and institutional biases inherent in implementing meaningful change and overcoming embedded exclusionary practices. In addition to Jefferson's museum leadership experience, she served as the former deputy director at the New York Department of Cultural Affairs and was former director of the acclaimed Dance Theatre of Harlem.

MISSIONS AND THE TWENTY-FIRST-CENTURY MUSEUM—A PERSPECTIVE

David Fleming, professor of public history at Hope University in Liverpool, England

We write missions to explain our purpose, both to ourselves and to others who are not necessarily closely involved in what we do, but who, for a variety of reasons, may need to be alerted to (or to be reminded of) the importance of museums. Because of this, there are two points that I feel I need to make straight away: first, museums and missions have not always sat together comfortably, because museums have often struggled with agreeing their purpose; second, the twenty-first-century public demands a lot more from museums (and therefore throws up a whole new set of challenges for their missions) than they ever have before.

The essence of a good mission is that it is succinct—and not so long as to become a mere description of activities—and that it does the job of motivating those who read it (whether they be closely involved with the museum as staff or volunteer, or whether they be a museum user or other type of "external"). Gail Anderson's book contains many examples of good missions.[1]

Museums perform a variety of functions. There are the ones with which few disagree, such as research, collecting, and preservation; there are some that cause heated debate, such as the museum's role in helping change society, and what exactly we mean by "education" or "interpretation." The point is that a mission can clarify for all comers exactly what it is the people involved most intimately with the museum think of (or, at least, claim) it's there to do. It is the statement with which others may agree and accept, perhaps even support, or with which they may disagree violently.

I would like to express a few thoughts on the issue of the "neutrality" of museums. It became part of the accepted lexicon of museums that they were "neutral"; that in their research, collecting, and interpretation, they retained a position of expressing no opinions about anything. This was repeated so often by museum people at all levels that the general public probably came to believe that it was true. Of course, this is an entirely bogus position to adopt: whenever individuals are involved in making decisions, they demonstrate bias. This is inevitable, and is a normal part of the human condition, rather than something of which to be ashamed and from which to hide.

Museums are not neutral; they never have been neutral; and it is time that they stopped pretending that they are.

Nonetheless, it has suited some people in museums to keep up the pretense that museums avoid making judgments ; I can only assume that in so doing museums were attempting to claim that they were trusted institutions where only the "truth" could be found, either in order to protect funding or to protect status. This approach has been challenged in recent times, and there has been clearer and clearer acknowledgment that "museums are not neutral" for some time.[2]

The UK Museums Association (so old, founded in 1889 and the world's first museum association, that it calls itself the Museums Association) has created a vision for the UK museum sector at large entitled Museums Change Lives.[3] This arose out of lengthy discussions about what museums should be striving for in future and is an unequivocal piece of positioning with which not everyone working in the UK museum sector agrees, but which nonetheless throws down a challenge to museums to step up their efforts in addressing societal issues, by using their collections and by working in partnership with others (such as health charities and other "third sector" organizations). This is, essentially, a mission for the whole of the UK museum sector.

Museums Change Lives accepts that the world is in the process of rapid change, however much dispute there may be about what museums ought to do about it. We have technological change, which has led to all manner of behavioral changes (think mobile phone technology, the internet, social media, digitization); we have economic shifts; we have climate change (with all sorts of consequences, both on human behavior and on biodiversity); we have profound movements in political terms, which in turn reflect profound changes in belief systems, and which are leading to renewed global tensions; we have myriad ongoing social issues arising out of the continuance of various forms of inequality (of women, of people of color, based on poverty, sexuality, or disability, for example); we have the advent of American English as the global lingua franca; we have globalized behavior and aging populations; we have the spread of exploitation of child labor; we have all manner of enslavements; we have new patterns of migration and of refugeeship.

Change is everywhere, and people are responding in various ways. In the cultural sector, for example, we have the inspiring MuseumsResist movement in the United States. The American Alliance of Museums, traditionally, an avoider of controversy and museum activism, has recently produced the Report Facing Change; when this kind of step change occurs it's clear that something new is going on, and museums everywhere need to ensure that they move with the times rather than adopt a position that pretends that the twentieth century never happened, let alone the twenty-first century.[4] It is the mission of the museum that enables it to position itself in the eyes of the world. The mission of National Museums Liverpool (NML) of which I was director for seventeen years, reads:

To be the world's leading example of an inclusive museum service.

The newly adopted mission of the International Museum for Democracy in Rosario, Argentina (July 2018), reads:

Ser un lugar de reflexión y debate sobre la democracia y los derechos humanos.

(To be a place for reflection and debate about democracy and human rights.)

These missions are short and have been designed to be memorable, which, in my view, helps make them good ones. Both are backed up by a series of "values" that define more closely how the museum expects to operate.

I remember once being part of a panel of museum directors in front of a sizable museum audience, and a member of the audience asked panelists if they knew their respective institution's mission. I believe I was the only panelist who was able to answer in the affirmative (because the others' tended to be too long and descriptive for anyone to remember or to quote). It took a long time and many iterations, of course, before NML was able to adopt the mission here, but it has always felt like a good fit for the museum service because it reflects how we actually behave. It is not merely an empty statement of aspiration, created to make ourselves appealing to government or its agents.

The mission has been created neither to demonstrate value for money, nor to win votes. The best way to create a usable mission that genuinely reflects the personality of a museum is, of course, for the creation to involve as many as possible of the people who are responsible for its delivery. This is certainly the approach we took both at NML and, previous to that, at Tyne & Wear Museums (now Tyne and Wear Archives and Museums [TWAM]). Of course, not everyone can be involved fully, and not everyone will agree, but the process of self-analysis, of contemplation and criticism of the museum's way of behaving, and of the context within which it operates, will always throw up new perspectives, and may, as at Tyne & Wear Museums and NML, throw up a modern, motivational mission.

TWAM's mission was rewritten in the mid-1990s, and it appears to have stood the test of time since then, in that change has been minimal.[5] The emphasis contained within the TWAM mission was on the social impact the museum service could/ought to have. It is almost certain that every museum will end up with a different mission (because the context in which any museum operates is never the same as contexts elsewhere) but it is entirely possible that all museums could adopt missions that make reference to the social impact that is expected (remember, a mission is meant to be an inspirational and explanatory statement of purpose, not a list of activities). The important thing is to write a powerful mission that captures the museum's intent. No half-decent modern museum can get by without such a statement.

SELECTED BIBLIOGRAPHY

Anderson, Gail, ed. *Museum Mission Statements: Building A Distinct Identity*. Washington, DC: American Association of Museums, Technical Information Service, 1998.

Anderson, Gail, ed. *Reinventing the Museum: The Evolving Conversation on the Paradigm Shift*. Second edition. Lanham, MD: AltaMira Press, 2012.

Baldwin, Joan. "Museums and Investing in Social Responsibility." *Leadership Matters Thoughts On 21st Century Museum Leadership by Anne Ackerson and Joan Baldwin* (blog), November 6, 2017. Accessed November 6, 2018. https://leadershipmatters1213.wordpress.com/category/museums-are-not-neutral/.

"Facing Change Insights from the American Alliance of Museums' Diversity, Equity, Accessibility, and Inclusion Working Group." American Alliance of Museums. 2018. Accessed November 6, 2018. https://www.aam-us.org/wp-content/uploads/2018/04/AAM-DEAI-Working-Group-Full-Report-2018.pdf.

Fleming, David. 2013. "The Essence of the Museum: Mission, Values, Vision." In *The International Handbooks of Museum Studies: Museum Practice*, edited by Conal McCarthy, 3–25. Chichester, West Sussex: John Wiley & Sons, Ltd.

Janes, Robert R. *Museums and the Paradox of Change: A Case Study in Urgent Adaptation*. Second edition. London, UK: Routledge, 2013.

Knott, Jonathan. "Mission Critical." *Museums Journal*, May 2018, 27–31. Accessed November 6, 2018. https://www.museumsassociation.org/museums-journal.

"Museums Change Lives The MA's Vision for the Impact of Museums." Museums Association. 2013. Accessed November 6, 2018. https://www.museumsassociation.org/download?id=1001738.

Sandell, Richard, and Robert R. Janes. *Museum Management And Marketing*. London, UK: Routledge, 2010.

Sacco, Nick. "Replacing Mission Statements with 'Why Should I Care?' Statements." In *The Museum Blog Book*, 146–52. Edinburgh, UK: MuseumsEtc.

Weil, Stephen E. *Making Museums Matter*. Washington, DC: Smithsonian Books, 2006.

Professor David Fleming, OBE, MA PhD, AMA, is one of the world's leading authorities on inclusion and diversity in the museum sector. He was director at two multi-award-winning museum services in the United Kingdom: Tyne & Wear Museums (1991–2001) and National Museums Liverpool (2001–2018). He now holds a chair in public history at Liverpool Hope University. Fleming was responsible for massive uplifts in visitor numbers to both services (from 710,000 per year to 3.3 million per year in Liverpool, for example) and for the creation of two globally influential museums: the International Slavery Museum and the Museum of Liverpool. The latter won the Council of Europe Museum Prize in 2013.

Fleming has published extensively and has lectured in more than forty countries on museum management and leadership, social inclusion, diversity, ethics, urban history, slavery, and identity. He has advised governments and municipalities in Argentina, Austria, Belgium, Egypt, Germany, the Netherlands, New Zealand, Norway, and the United Kingdom, and is currently a member of the International Council of Museums Ethics

Committee. Earlier this year, Fleming lectured in New Orleans at the Making New Orleans Home Triennial Symposium. In 2019 he will be working in Italy, Qatar, Singapore, and Taiwan. He is the only person in history dating back to 1889 to have twice been elected president of the UK Museums Association. In 2014, he was invited to give a keynote address at the annual conference of the American Alliance for Museums entitled "Museums for Social Justice."

Fleming sits on a number of governing bodies, including those of the SS *Daniel Adamson* (an early twentieth-century steam-powered tugboat) and of Muzeum Slaskie in Katowice, Poland. He is founder-president of the Federation of International Human Rights Museums, which has its annual meeting in 2019 at the Canadian Museum for Human Rights in Winnipeg. Fleming attended the Harvard Business School program entitled Strategic Perspectives in Nonprofit Management and is a graduate of the Getty Foundation's Museum Management Institute program held at the Berkeley campus of The University of California.

MISSION RELEVANCE AND CULTURAL COMPETENCY: INESCAPABLE PARTNERS FOR THE FUTURE

Charmaine Jefferson

Control and creativity drive our need to build community, share legacy, and have opportunities for self-validation and growth. We form identities and establish institutions, and even countries, in which to codify, document, display, and give mission to our lives, establish place, and extol our values. Our own country, the United States of America, was constitutionally founded on the initiating value that "all men are created equal." Our Pledge of Allegiance calls for "liberty and justice for all." So there should be little surprise that these ingrained values are at the heart of increasing expectations to achieve diversity, inclusion, access, and equity at a faster rate in the world, our country, communities, and even in the public institutions we build like museums. These demands for greater equitable recognition and shared participation are what make mission relevance and cultural competence inseparable partners in museum building. Having a museum that operates within a culturally competent mindset will always require periodically asking if your mission is being broadly interpreted or narrowly conceived, and whether the implementation of that mission carries with it presumptions about who might be interested or have important insights that could contribute to mission fulfillment.

In a climate of previously ignored voices loudly seeking equity, examining mission relevance requires digging deep into what it means to practice and live in a culturally competent environment. "Diversity," "access," "inclusion," "equity," "social justice," "racial justice," "cultural justice," and "civil rights" are all terms that signal historical as well as contemporary aspirations that, not if but, when achieved will represent our highest ideals of how we should value our society and each other. The expectations these terms represent are not new concepts or goals, just new to realities for those who have held the most power. There have always been cries from people of all classes to be recognized and respected. The demand is getting louder, and comes with a growing expectation that within museums such recognition and/or respect will manifest itself in a way that allows the viewer, the staff, the board member, and sometimes even the donor to see themselves in the way your mission is interpreted. Voices that never had a platform for being heard in how and what you do or how you interpret your mission are critical to your museum's ability to determine and judge its own relevance.

These demands are complicated by the fact that our world is in a cycle of trying to ingest old rationales for "protectionism" and "nativism" as part of a resistance to the acceptance of additional voices, cultures, religions, experiences, lifestyles, traditions, etc. These anti-inclusion forces could do much to halt or turn back progress, but they are also abutting new generations expecting faster shifts. There is little interest in accommodating the status quo with the same level of patience as has occurred in the past. The kinds of changes expected in our society, and in turn from our museums, are expected in real time and not over multiple lifetimes. It is in this context that as a former museum director and funder, and current cultural and government policy maker, college trustee, and nonprofit consultant today, that I push myself to surface truth, identify gaps and disconnects, find links between diversity and relevance, promote active institutional reflection, and to be a proactive part of changing mindsets so that all of us can get to the power of inclusion.

Surfacing Truth

TRUTH plays a big part in this equation of achieving cultural competence. Mission relevance expands exponentially when TRUTH is acknowledged and revealed, especially as it inevitably always rises to the surface. A museum collection grounded in objects stolen from a conquered society will always be displayed with an acknowledgment as to their origin and assumed purpose, but a culturally competent environment will also include the truth of the oppressive use of power and/or injustice that authorized the initial theft to take place. We seem to understand this when tackling ownership of the artworks stolen during the German atrocities of 1938 to 1945, but give little or no attention to how the artifacts of hundreds of cultures wound up in vitrines oceans away from the customs and people who made them. Without such truth, the audience, the scholar, the visitor engaging with the objects are never fully informed. Policies that perpetuate imagery in monuments and artifacts that only reflect one belief system or one side of an issue, by their very nature, make value judgments and can create intended or unintended acts of exclusion. Awareness of the truth is a preventive measure to avoiding the injustices of the past. Truthful interpretation cannot be neutral to these kinds of acts of cultural injustice.

Mission relevance and cultural competence expand exponentially when giving voice to truth. It can be both freeing and gut wrenching to listen to the pain that less powerfully placed people have been protesting about for generations. During his presidency, the late Nelson Mandela taught us that hearing and acknowledging outrage is a critical first step toward healing and reconciliation. Truth is integral to the process of understanding what is needed before any institution can fully test its mission for relevance and evolution into an environment that operates within a greater state of cultural competence.

Disconnect Identifiers

Mission and cultural disconnects surface when organizations gain power and become the institutional voice, the highest regarded interpreter for others. Disconnects can occur when mission development processes fail to provide a wider platform for broadening and expanding an institution's mission and vision. Field-wide, the entire system for the existence of museums has, in the past, had little room for the voice of the less powerful and the nonexpert. The ability of a museum to assess its relevance and the relevance of what it presents, who it attracts, and who it hires has grown up around a caste system of wealth, education, and privilege. The wishes and belief systems of those in power, and the interests that wealth could buy, have too often defined who or what we recognize as a museum, a valid mission, who should have access to funding, and who should be in authority to lead it. Even outside stakeholders can perpetuate disconnects when they continue to discount or ignore the voices and existence of others. Reaching out to engage donors and stakeholders to engage in more culturally competent practices supports and furthers the good work and powerful evolution that might already be taking place within your museum.

Creating authentic opportunities for the voiceless to enter your doors for their own reasons, and not just to serve a quota need or because of the dictates of experts or the wealthy, is by itself an uneasy balancing act. Your museum certainly cannot operate without adequate resources and outside stakeholders who applaud your existence. Similarly, people who donate funds have a legitimate right to expect that they are funding that which they are interested in. The complexity comes from trying to align relevancy and practicing cultural competency with all of these varying interests. Yet, ultimately, if your museum is seeking to serve a growing audience of public as well as experts and scholars, then the interests of those in power cannot be the only voices worthy of being heard.

The Meaning of Diversity and Relevance

If mission relevance and cultural competency are inevitably intertwined, then it must be that we all engage in asking the right questions when we are seeking to recalibrate. There is no one answer to what constitutes being more diverse, and a lack of diversity is not the same as whether something is inequitable or in need of a more equitable platform or world. A few critical questions might include:

- What lack of diversity problem are we trying to solve?
- Are we having a race or different experience discussion such as age, gender, religion, or cultural traditions?
- Is the culturally competency question about eliminating racial discrimination and/or bias, or are we simply talking about increasing competence in order to make room for different ideas and experiences?
- Are there human, community, or structural system barriers that need to be changed?

A science museum dedicated to environmental exploration would experience great pain trying to accommodate a wealthy board member that is not open to the possibility of climate change. Seize upon that lone board member's point of view as an opportunity to find new ways to hear and engage different perspectives. Keeping the museum's mission in mind, utilize the board member's funding to create a forum for scientific debates about climate change and its impact or lack thereof on the environment. This response allows the museum to not only engage in its mission but to deepen the ways in which it shares scientific theories and ideas that the public should witness.

Relevance, like perfection, is in the eye of the beholder. It is the very nature of what keeps us from being monolithic. When we examine what was relevant in the past, we have to be open to looking through the lens of the past and be willing to judge whether that lens was wide enough to see all of the aspects, circumstances, and conditions of the past. Whose standard of relevance was being employed when your museum's purpose was founded? If by today's standard the purpose is still relevant but the standard of judging that relevance is too narrow, so will be your audience, your staff, your board, and your donors. As you assess the relevance of your mission, other critical questions might include:

- Are you utilizing a "diversity" of voices to provide you with feedback?
- Are you looking for diversity deeper than racial/ethnic origin?
- Have you considered demographic diversity such as education, income levels, geographic location, availability of resources within the respondent's community, etc.?
- Are you recognizing how economic differences impact capacity for free time for museums, to participate in art training or historic exploration, to study nature, to engage in creative thinking, scientific study, and conservation, etc.?
- What is the demographic environment in which your museum resides, and how is your relevance related to that environment?
- Is your museum the only one in town, and thus do you bear a greater responsibility for inclusiveness?
- Are there many museums or cultural institutional offerings in your area, and could your mission interpretation be expanded simply through greater partnerships and collaborations with other institutions?

These too can be complex intertwined issues, and there is no guarantee that straightening one domino might not cause others to be unstable. Don't shy away from the complexity. Just as was required during the civil rights movement of the 1960s, create strategies for building upon the change you are seeking and readiness for the consequences of your advocacy. Just also be conscious to avoid creating solutions to increase diversity that create new problems of disregard or exclusion. For example, we all agree that collection expansion and diversity are good, but don't create an unintended new category of exclusion and inequity through efforts to acquire new work or artifacts. As new steps are incorporated to advance inclusion, it is paramount to think long term and be circumspect. Every decision made in the past had consequences, and every decision made in the future will have impact. It is a moment to be willing to look at decisions and their impact from all sides and perspectives.

Active Institutional Reflection

Just as we question the relevancy of our own humanity in the universe, we should routinely examine the relevance of the missions and institutions we create and how we authentically engage with others. Questioning promotes exploration, allows for new self-awareness, and prevents stagnation. As humanity evolves, no society or institution can sustain itself long term being culturally monolithic or exclusionary in its practices or policies. Being curious and open to inclusion forges pathways for evolution, not extinction. The psychological act of embedding assessment and questioning into our personal and institutional DNA creates a foundation for a natural evolution of mission relevance that is inseparably steeped in increasing cultural competence and awareness. Such a foundation is intellectually stimulating, and thus far more likely to be sustainable as a means of promoting constructive sharing and co-existence. Critical questions might include:

- Is there anything about the interpretation of our museum's purpose/mission that is exclusionary, whether intentional or de facto by practice?
- Is the lens by which we are assessing mission relevance wide enough to encompass a contemporary audience?
- Are we operationally flexible enough to encompass broader definitions of "expertise"?

There must be all types of eyes and ears brought into the daily *unconscious* act of asking, "How is what we do relevant?" Avoid having only one person as the interpreter story or arbiter or monitor of relevance. Interpretation by academic experts is invaluable, but no more important than capturing the "first voicers" who actually lived the experience being presented. As a matter of course, consider that nearly everyone in your institution can be a source for providing feedback and judging relevance. The audiences that come through your doors, and even those who do not, can also be determiners of relevance and sources for interpretation expansion.

Change is inevitable, whether by choice or by external forces. Active reflection not only goes to the issue of relevance but can serve as a tool for measuring your institution's cultural competence. Active reflection should not be interpreted as a demand for tolerance or political correctness, but rather as a call for accommodating additional ideas, cultures, and even circumstances, so that the widest range of perspectives can be accommodated.

Individual museum growth is important, but so too must there be room created within the broader museum field for additional ventures and institutions. Just as existing institutions are expected to accommodate voices, the museum field must also allow for additional ventures and new museum definitions to come into existence. At the same time, entities coming into existence must do so respectful of the past while open to a wide range of interpretations and approaches to their missions and subject matters either from the start or with an expectation of evolution over time.

Changing Mindsets

Fulfilling a long-term institutional mission that is compatible with growing expectations *and* demands for unequivocal diversity, access, inclusion, and equity requires literal and psychological changes in mindset, behavior, and policy. To define mission relevance today requires not only having to change the internal hearts, minds, and policies of the experts who operate and/or wealthy museum founders and donors, but also the outside stakeholders who speak on your museum's behalf. It can feel like an overwhelming task, but just like building a healthy diet, it is achievable one step at a time.

First, it is critical to not only value the elements of cultural competence but to accept that first there must be an acknowledgment of what's missing: a lack of diversity and access, exclusion and/or inequity, and the origins of these conditions and where they exist in the organization. Too often, companies, governments, and organizations set out to establish policy and take actions to implement institutional diversity and equity standards before ever understanding what is meant by these terms. "What" is not "equitable" about our organization, in its mission, in its way of operating, in what is presented, in who we reach out to, and what voices are not being heard? Every doctor will tell you that except in an emergency the ailment has to be analyzed and understood before embarking upon a cure.

Second, be ready to test for and root out both implicit and hidden biases. Too often, the assumption is that "diversity" can be achieved by simply increasing the numbers, trying one thing different from what has been done in the past. This certainly can be a way to start. Take a chance on at least one thing that goes beyond what we have done in the past and we will begin to explore what it means to be more diverse, to have more inclusion for new voices, and to offer greater and more welcoming opportunities for engagement. But remember that "diversity" is not a numbers game. It is not a noun. Engaging diversity has to become a state of mind, as natural as brushing your teeth each night and being aware when you have failed to do so.

Third, recognize systemic and institutionalized wrongs and follow-up by developing a positive commitment toward achieving expanded diversity, access, inclusion, and equity. Using the terms of cultural competence is not enough. It requires managing our biases, both personal and institutional. Evolving into cultural competency is a state of mind and literal action. It is about having the willingness to be proactive in building understanding between people, to be respectful and open to different cultural perspectives, to strengthen cultural security, and to work toward equality in opportunity. It is not forced integration or tolerance, and it should not stifle your own aesthetic interests. It is about adopting an inclusive state of mind and being willing to recognize the potential for the negatives of the past to reoccur if there is not consistent vigilance to guard against it.

The Power of Inclusion

Accounting for changing demographics and demands for equity, social, or cultural justice should not be an either/or situation. Widening the circle allows for more inclusion because it brings about a diversity of voices, ideas, and experiences that can feed into the implementation of mission. Real sustainable change requires understanding that the voices and ideas of others are a critical part of having a broader vision of the world and mutual recognition of their respective experiences. If we are to truly move toward a world of greater cross-cultural understanding, expansion should not be driven simply by changing demographics or latest trends. After all, neighborhood gentrification can be as destructive to some as it is empowering for others. The most constructive path is for getting to know, recognizing, and accommodating the experiences of others and vice versa.

Within mission, museums should embark upon expanding collections, exhibitions, programs, staffing, trustees, and audience engagement because it is the only way to avoid intentional and de facto protectionism, segregation, bias, racist, sexist, educational, and/or classist policies. Ask the why questions and allow for the answers to be articulated even if it is difficult to hear or difficult to fund. Ultimately, this is the only way to be able to identify the systems that perpetuate oppression and change the parameters of what is socially tolerable. Without this understanding, we get comfortable with short-term solutions (i.e., sell some of the existing collection to replace it with works by people of color), and the underlying problems never get solved. Instead, another group/perspective gets excluded, and a new compounding problem is created.

Rather than just thinking about determining the relevance of your mission based on numbers or replacing one interpretation with another, build instead an institutional capacity for cultural competency. Breathe this value into your institution's mission and existence. Think just as much about what and why something is missing as you do about what should be added. To best inform what should be added, determine first whose voice should be a part of making the expansion decisions. As you adjust, be prepared to share, follow, and not always lead. This too will shift the balance of power and privilege to a more shared, inclusive model.

If our museums are to survive, they must also be willing to be even more connected locally—in real time and in the place where they reside. The audiences of today expect us to care about them. One-off solutions (i.e., annual exhibitions, special programs) have value and can make a difference, but we all want more than short-term impact. They look to see themselves in your purpose—in the way you interpret your mission—otherwise they may come in once out of curiosity and never come back if they don't think that you think that they are relevant to your interpretation of mission or that you sincerely want them as part of your audience.

Summary

Today's fight for "civil rights," for "liberty" and "justice," and to be treated as "equal" gets much more complex with each passing generation. How do you respect that which came before you while making room for the histories and visions still to be told? It is harder than just tearing down the physical signs of who can use which bathroom or eat at the lunch counter. The impediments can be more subtle, as we all carry bias in some way. The go-forward issue is how do we exert that bias or lack of experience in our personal and institutional lives. The values being fought for require digging deep and under the surface. It is a nuanced, detailed exploration that will always require periodic reassessment and adjustment to accommodate expanding customs and ideas. To do anything less is to fall once more into a position of rationalizing the status quo and risking fights and battles for position versus an existence of shared human accommodation and compromise.

Cultural evolution used to happen over generations, but now we see and expect change to occur in our own lifetime. Our world has come to have very little patience for the time it takes for evolution to take root. New ideas appear and are put in place, and past customs and standards are often changed in real time with nominal assessment or tactical testing. Meanwhile, many existing traditions, beliefs, missions, and systemic practices are operating like immovable objects exploding and pushing back against the evolution of rapid change in a single lifetime. This is how existing power, privilege, ideas, customs, and interpretations are cultivated, but eventually history has shown us that unless there is a way for all to participate and to feel valued, a civilization, a movement, and even a museum cannot be sustained.

Though long overdue, the good news is that every day, more and more museums and institutions are learning to actively acknowledge and detail the cultural experiences and contributions of *all* of our citizens. Corrective and sustainable solutions must be put in place to rectify the negative impact of centuries of past and current conditions of social and institutionalized biases and inequities that range from missions to funders, educators to experts, and staffs to boards. Sustainable solutions will grow out of shared engagement, a shift in mindset and institutional position, and multi-layered interpretations and opportunities for discourse and discovery among and with our diverse communities and publics.

In the end, enlarging the circle to allow for additional and fuller interpretations of collections, programs, and exhibits will keep your mission updated and relevant, giving you the ability to engage with and respond to additional audiences and changing demographics, as well as new trends, ideas, and systems of delivery. Seek evolutionary rather than forced change, adopt new mindsets, and accept that this is an ongoing effort. Taken together, these steps will make the partnership between mission implementation and cultural competency relevant, sustainable, and constructively permanent.

You are not just a bystander in a system that you have inherited . . . you must be active in its forward evolution or accept being an enabling beneficiary of past suppression. —Charmaine Jefferson

Charmaine Jefferson is principal of Kélan Resources, a nationwide consulting business specializing in integrating art, education, public policy, and cultural competency into the DNA of live programs, exhibitions, workshops, nonprofit management, collaborations, and resource development. She has extensive experience in museum missions, expanding relevancy and providing cultural competency training for nonprofits. Most recently, Jefferson completed eleven years as executive director of the state's California African American Museum in Los Angeles, and executive vice president of its nonprofit partner, Friends, the Foundation of the California African American Museum. Some of Jefferson's prior professional positions include executive director at the Dance Theatre of Harlem, where her combined six-year tenure included the capital expansion of the organization's headquarters and school and the company's historic Soviet Union and "Dancing Through Barriers" South

Africa tour. As a champion of linking art, culture, politics, education, community development, and administration, she completed a six-year mayoral-appointed role as deputy and acting commissioner of New York City's Department of Cultural Affairs. In the private sector, she has served on corporate boards, was vice president of business affairs for dePasse Entertainment, and director of show development and entertainment business services for Disney Entertainment Productions, leading creative development for the Disneyland Resort and opening of Disney's California Adventure.

Jefferson's 2018 volunteer services include mayoral appointee and president of Los Angeles' Cultural Affairs Commission; trustee of the California Institute of the Arts, where she also serves as co-chair of the college's academic and special projects committee; and on the finance, governance, and executive committees. She also co-chairs PBS SoCal's African American Community Council, is a member of the Community Advisory Board for the Los Angeles Chamber Orchestra, and is an inaugural and second-term member of the Cultural Equity and Inclusion Initiative Advisory Committee for the Los Angeles County's Cultural Affairs Commission. Jefferson's past volunteer services have also included gubernatorial appointee to the California Arts Council, co-mentor for former Deputy Mayor Austin Beutner's Los Angeles "City Fellows" program, respective service on the Board of Directors of Arts for LA and Jacob's Pillow Dance Festival in the Berkshires, as an ex officio trustee for the Metropolitan Museum of Art, and as co-chair of the Harlem Empowerment Zone.

NOTES

1. Gail Anderson, ed., *Museum Mission Statements: Building A Distinct Identity* (Washington, DC: American Association of Museums, Technical Information Service, 1998).

2. Joan Baldwin, "Museums and Investing in Social Responsibility." *Leadership Matters Thoughts On 21st Century Museum Leadership by Anne Ackerson and Joan Baldwin* (blog). November 6, 2017. Accessed November 6, 2018. https://leadershipmatters1213.wordpress.com/category/museums-are-not-neutral/.

3. "Museums Change Lives: The MA's Vision for the Impact of Museums." Museums Association. 2013. Accessed November 6, 2018. https://www.museumsassociation.org/download?id=1001738.

4. "Facing Change Insights from the American Alliance of Museums' Diversity, Equity, Accessibility, and Inclusion Working Group." American Alliance of Museums. 2018. Accessed November 6, 2018. https://www.aam-us.org/wp-content/uploads/2018/04/AAM-DEAI-Working-Group-Full-Report-2018.pdf.

5. Jonathan Knott, "Mission Critical." *Museums Journal* (May 2018): 27–31. Accessed November 6, 2018. https://www.museumsassociation.org/museums-journal.

3

Qualities of a Relevant Mission

A well-crafted, relevant mission reflects a museum with an intentional purpose making a difference in contemporary times. Just creating an eloquently worded mission is meaningless if the greater intent isn't to clarify the reason a museum exists and how its greater work will affect the future and the people it works with and serves. The words in a mission should flow out of fundamental beliefs, convictions, and a commitment to make a difference and contribute to the greater good. The twenty-first century museum must broaden, be inclusive, and reflect respectful engagement with the public.

Clarity about a twenty-first-century mission evolves from deep conversations—not just private, internal discussions, but external explorations and connections with a diverse public and stakeholders to position the museum as a key player in the community. Examining mission requires taking the time to understand the scope and impact of contemporary issues and the realities of local communities. This external work leads, in turn, to institutional assessment that involves honest reflection and open discussion, a review of current assumptions, and the ability to name and commit to the museum's goals and areas for change over time.

Understanding the change that influences a museum's mission requires naming and owning the beliefs and behaviors that have informed museum practices over time. The level of discourse will be different in every institution, depending in part on institutional history and in part on the conviction of leadership. Enlightened leadership will be dedicated to guiding an open, inclusive dialogue that engages many voices—beyond those who have traditionally been welcome—and helping the museum shape new ways of being and thus a different mission. This process is not a one-time effort, but should become an essential, ongoing component of institutional vitality and relevance. Leadership sets the tone, and leadership is key to ensuring commitment over the long term to achieve the mission and ensure that the museum embodies, reflects, and conveys the mission in its work.

At its most basic, a mission statement is a key component of the strategic framework that will guide, influence, and position a museum for meaningful work on behalf of a diverse public. A mission should be revisited and reaffirmed annually and, when necessary, it should be adjusted to stay vibrant, connected, and relevant in a changing world.

While a mission statement may seem simple enough in concept, it requires a multi-layered process to define the nature of what the museum aims to achieve, supported by guiding principles in service to the greater good. Trustees, the director, staff, and all who work in and for a museum must understand their role in advancing this mission. Ultimately, audiences and the public should be aware of the mission and understand how it involves them, engages them, and affects them.

In brief, the qualities of a twenty-first-century relevant mission statement draws its relevance from the underlying concepts that inform the mission, the impact of the statement itself, and the role it plays as a management tool and institutional compass.

A mission statement should:
- State clearly why the museum exists, how it makes a difference, what its impact on the future is, and who the museum is for, about, and with.
- Convey how the museum is relevant in contemporary times.
- Be brief—not more than eight words, if possible.
- Use action verbs and simple language that avoids industry jargon.
- Be supported with clear definitions of the words used in the mission, no matter how familiar, to enhance clarity of meaning for all stakeholders, internal and external.
- Be complemented by a clear vision statement, core values, and operating principles, along with other elements to make up a complete strategic framework.

As a management tool, a mission statement should:
- Be informed by agreed upon concepts, direction, and philosophy of the museum's role.
- Guide the internal decision-making process, and thus every decision made.
- Define internal operations to ensure they support the mission.
- Inform all activities the museum undertakes.
- Be understood and embraced by everyone, whether trustee, executive, staff member, or volunteer.
- Inform strategies that define the range of public engagement, collection focus, audience participation, visitor services, and other programs, activities, and services of the museum.

The mission must convey why a museum exists, how it makes a difference, and how it affects the future. It should not be a description of the museum or a list of activities the museum does.

"The Anywhere Museum collects, interprets, and exhibits the history of Anywhere" is not a mission statement. It is a description of the activities a museum undertakes, not a strategic mission. This misunderstanding of a mission statement's purpose has been a longstanding problem. How do you measure what your institution did at the end of the year with a mission that just lists activities? Did we collect? Did we interpret? Did we mount exhibits? Likely, the answer is yes to all, but to what end? Missions that list activities fail to convey why the museum exists and what greater impact it wishes to have on the people it serves, its community, and beyond. Such a mission statement is not a management tool, and it does not convey the leadership role that every museum has the potential to achieve.

A meaningful mission is the compass for the organization and should be inspiration for all that the museum does. It should be galvanizing for internal stakeholders and relevant to the many communities, visitors, and people beyond the museum's walls. Thus, selected words matter and telegraph intentional messages. Sometimes they can convey unintentional messages. This can be mitigated by including broad participation in the development of the mission. Broad participation comes from external interviews and review of drafts by selected external stakeholders for feedback. It cannot be stressed enough how important inclusion is for the process. By including external stakeholders, the museum is acting in a way that is more transparent, and through conversations and engagement with current and potential audiences, the museum is building relationships. In the end, the communication loop between museum and the public is a two-way, ongoing exchange of ideas, hopes, stories, and connections on all levels, and with the mission itself.

The mission should be short, clear, and easy to remember.

A mission statement can be as brief as eight words.[1] This level of brevity in museum mission statements is rare, but it is attainable, and it should be the goal. Creating a short and concise mission means culling, reviewing, and achieving laser-beam clarity about why the museum exists and what it is aiming to accomplish. It takes conviction and courage to stand with a short mission. It takes time to refine the words, and it should take time. Experience reveals that the gestation period for a stellar mission is about six to eight months, including periodic discussions, reviews, and refinements. The other advantage of a short mission is that it will be easily remembered and recitable, and it will be easily understood internally by trustees, staff, and volunteers, and externally by the public and constituents.

Monterey Bay Aquarium, Monterey, California
The mission of the nonprofit Monterey Bay Aquarium is to inspire conservation of the ocean.

This mission is short and clearly conveys the aquarium's long-term intent for its work and its message to the public. Its mission reaches far beyond its walls, and its impact is critically needed in a world of endangered oceans. Despite the brevity and inspirational nature of this mission, it is not necessary nor preferable to say "the mission of the nonprofit." By eliminating those introductory words, the punch of the mission improves and leads to the removal of "is to," strengthening the inspirational nature of this mission.

The mission should convey how the museum makes a difference and impacts the future.

A future-oriented mission requires thinking about the museum's global contribution, and thus inspires thinking about the institution as a vital player in its community and the greater world.

National Underground Railroad Freedom Center, Cincinnati, Ohio
We reveal stories of freedom's heroes, from the era of the Underground Railroad to contemporary times, challenging and inspiring everyone to take courageous steps for freedom today.

While this mission is grounded in the work of extraordinary, courageous individuals during the era of the Underground Railroad, that courage is translated into a greater platform upon which to encourage efforts to keep freedom a right and fundamental part of human life. The mission declares the museum's why, its impact, and how it makes a difference.

One noteworthy way the National Underground Railroad Freedom Center does this is through a Rapid Response Committee, which identifies a contemporary issue—such as immigration, equity, human rights, or racial injustices, and makes a public statement about the museum's position on the issue. The committee represents an ongoing commitment to be responsive to what is happening around us and speaking up about the values and rights the museum stands for.

Minneapolis Science Museum, Minneapolis, Minnesota
Turn on the science: Inspire learning. Inform policy. Improve lives.

This mission is relayed in an unconventional format and delivers complex ideas simply and clearly. It implies a sequence of activities that result in informed policy and improved lives. The why is conveyed. The mission is short, concise, inspirational, memorable, and easily understood. By using a refreshingly different construction for a mission statement, it breaks away from labored statements that are long, cumbersome, and ineffective.

Use action verbs and simple language, avoiding industry jargon.

One frequent error is to use vague phrases such as "is dedicated to" or "is about." This vocabulary should be avoided at all costs because it weakens the impact of the mission statement. It does not convey conviction; it conveys hesitancy. It suggests that someday the museum will have the conviction to do the courageous work and implies that it hasn't really committed to its path or ambition. One wonders when the museum will make up its mind. Remove those words and insert a powerful action verb. If you are dedicated to a purpose, name it and state it with confidence. A strong verb also emboldens the mission and thus the people it touches. It conveys liveliness, vibrancy, and a sense that something is happening.

> ***Sonoma Valley Museum of Art***, Sonoma, California
> Building community around art.

This mission is short, uses a strong verb, and conveys a desired result and outcome. It has been instrumental in changing the work of the institution and providing clear direction.

> ***State Historical Society of Iowa***, Des Moines, Iowa
> We empower Iowa to build and sustain culturally vibrant communities by connecting Iowans to the people, places, and points of pride that define our state.

While not the shortest mission statement, it unveils a sequence of ideas that are very much about the people and future of Iowa, and it is place-specific. The use of "we" in the mission statement shows broad ownership and reflects a commitment to the citizens of Iowa.

Select words that are clear and widely understood.

Mission statements written only by internal stakeholders risk sounding exclusionary, known and understood only by those in the know, and they will not be successful in conveying the role and mission of the museum to external stakeholders and potential constituents. Test versions of the mission with external stakeholders, or better yet, make these people a part of the mission development process. Are you implying that the museum is the entity with all the knowledge, or are you conveying a learning environment where all participate and learn together? Think about verbs, prepositions, and wording. The power of a well-crafted mission is its core usefulness as a management tool and public communication vehicle.

Define the terms used in a mission.

Words in a mission must be carefully considered so they reflect a deep understanding of what the museum is trying to achieve. The words should emerge after the intense conversations have occurred or the revision will amount to an exercise in semantics. Revising a mission must spring from self-reflection and a purpose that is enlightened, inclusive, appropriate, and feasible for the institution.

Define the words used in the mission, no matter how familiar, to enhance clarity of meaning for all who will use the mission statement as a management tool for guiding the work of the museum. Words such as "community" require a definition. Is it the town? The broader regional community? A specific community? Or is it the amalgam of communities the museum serves? Words in the current vernacular like "empower" or "leverage" require a definition as well to clarify what these behaviors look like and how they will permeate the work and attitude of the institution. To be clear, create a definitions document that accompanies the mission. See di Rosa Tool in chapter 8.

It has been demonstrated that each time an institution is forced to define a word, a deeper conversation emerges and different perspectives are revealed. Expressing the meaning of mission words provides an opportunity to build agreement and alignment of purpose in the mission and its scope.

THE MISSION AND ITS PLACE IN AN INSTITUTIONAL STRATEGIC FRAMEWORK

A strategic framework is made up of mission, vision, values, operating principles, and impact statements along with other elements that together form a core management tool that provides the compass for all a museum undertakes, represents, and does on behalf of the public.

- *Mission* captures why your museum exists, how it makes a difference in the world, and how it impacts the future. It also identifies who the museum is for. A mission statement should be short, inspiring, and guide the work of the institution internally while conveying to the public its purpose and role. The mission informs and drives the work of the museum every day, year-round. See examples in chapters 5 and 6.
- *Vision* describes the long-term impact and achievements that the museum aims to accomplish in relation to the environment in which it operates. The vision can be qualitative and should *not* restate the essence conveyed in the mission. The vision is an aspirational target set in the future—often ten years or more ahead. See examples in chapter 6.
- *Values* are the core beliefs that guide the behaviors and commitments that are embraced and upheld year-round by trustees, directors, staff, and volunteers. A museum's values should permeate and be evident in all that it undertakes. See examples in chapter 6.
- *Guiding principles* state agreed-upon ways of operating at all levels of a museum. They typically cover a range of topics such as audience engagement, board participation, financial principles, and diversity and inclusion. An example of a core principle is "to operate in the black," and another might be "diversity and inclusion permeates all we do and is evident in leadership, public engagement, collections, and interpretive strategies." Guiding principles are often not articulated yet are critical for a unified approach to operating the museum.
- *Impact statements* frame aspirational results that help clarify the larger external impact and are integral to the mission. A few institutions are creating social impact statements or audience impact statements for example. See the Impact Tool in chapter 8. See the perspective of the Wild Center for impact statements and the Oakland Museum of California for their evolving social impact statements in chapter 6.
- *Organizational culture* defines the expectations and tenets of the way trustees, directors, staff, and volunteers interact and work together. Culture is often inspired by values statements, and it influences institution-wide behaviors like decision-making criteria and processes, inclusive practices, ways of operating, and the nature of communication.
- *Outcome measurements* are a mix of quantifiable and qualitative statements that provide a measuring stick for assessing progress over time. They are typically a part of a strategic plan and reviewed annually. A baseline is established so the results can be measured each year to ascertain progress. It also requires that the tools for information gathering are identified and established in support of each outcome measurement and that information gathering occurs year-round. An example is, "Every Board member fulfills their responsibilities, and contributes to a vibrant and inclusive governing body." Sometimes the outcome measurement is "All aspects of museums operations advance meaningful public engagement." In both examples, information gathering would inform and track the improvements made.

Every museum must decide on the strategic framework that best informs its policies and practices. But a crisp mission is the heart of every framework and influences all of the other elements, so clarifying mission is the springboard for the refinement of what, how, and who is engaged in advancing the work of the museum on behalf of the public. Each museum will select the right mix of elements for their strategic framework. See chapter 7 on development of a mission statement.

EXAMPLES OF MISSIONS AND STRATEGIC FRAMEWORK ELEMENTS

Strategic framework elements should complement one another and together strengthen clarity about institutional position. Often the meaning and purpose of the components are confused, or the vision is a slightly reworded mission, or values are mixed with guiding principles and so on. It takes time to refine and think through how each of these elements will inform and support the institution.

Vision Statement

The following examples pair the mission with the vision revealing the why (the mission) and the aspirations to achieve in the future (the vision). The most impactful vision statements reflect an achievement in the greater community and world beyond the museum itself.

Eastern State Penitentiary Historic Site, Philadelphia, Pennsylvania
Mission Statement

Eastern State Penitentiary Historic Site interprets the legacy of American criminal justice reform, from the nation's founding through to the present day, within the long-abandoned cell blocks of the nation's most historic prison.

Vision Statement

Eastern State Penitentiary's innovative presentation, interpretation, and public programs will move visitors to engage in dialogue and deepen the national conversation about criminal justice.

The mission captures a deep purpose tied to the complex history of the criminal justice system with the long-term vision being about bringing the conversation into the public discourse about incarceration reform.

Svendborg Museum (Danish Welfare Museum), Svendborg, Denmark
Mission Statement

The Danish Welfare Museum strives to be an important cultural institution that addresses contemporary social issues, engages in and qualifies debates about the welfare state. We have created a dynamic museum through a close collaboration with people who have spent part of their lives in institutions and/or have experienced social vulnerability, exclusion, severe personal downturns or stigmatization.

Vision Statement

The Danish Welfare Museum aims to be the historical consciousness of the social welfare system and contribute to the cohesion of society.

While this mission is long, it does convey a complex idea that is rarely addressed in a museum setting. The vision aims to raise awareness around social welfare and the obligations of a nation and people to care and impact action. The aim is beyond the walls of the museum but it is central to what the museum represents.

President Lincoln's Cottage, Washington, DC
Mission Statement

Reveal the true Lincoln and continue the fight for freedom.

Vision Statement

Plant the seeds of Lincoln's brave ideas around the world so that all people, everywhere, can be free.

This crisp and clear mission conveys several complex ideas in a singular statement. It is focused on action and an ongoing commitment to advance the cause of freedom. The vision is the bookend that places the museum's work in a global context with an aspirational goal.

War Childhood Museum, Logavina, Sarajevo, Bosnia, and Herzegovina
Mission Statement

The mission of the War Childhood Museum is to continuously and in accordance to the highest standards document and digitize materials related to growing up in the war, and to present the archived materials throughout various media channels in order to educate a broad audience about this experience.

Vision Statement

The vision of the War Childhood Museum is to help individuals overcome past traumatic experiences and prevent traumatization of others, and at the same time advance mutual understanding at the collective level in order to enhance personal and social development.

This mission declares the museum's role with supporting descriptions. This approach is sometimes necessary for a governmental museum or a museum whose work departs from traditional topics and aims to convey difficult messages. The vision focuses clearly on supporting the victims of war and inspiring actions beyond the walls of the museum that change attitudes, affect individual health, and prevent such trauma in the future.

Values Statement

Carefully crafted values have an enduring quality, are inextricably linked to the mission and vision, and inform organizational culture.

The National WWII Museum, New Orleans, Louisiana
Mission Statement

The National WWII Museum tells the story of the American experience in *the war that changed the world*—why it was fought, how it was won, and what it means today—so that all generations will understand the price of freedom and be inspired by what they learn.

Values Statement

Commitment to the defense of freedom, courage, optimism, determination, sacrifice, teamwork, generosity, volunteerism.

This mission places the institution in a greater context—not just historical—bringing its purpose and role into contemporary life while honoring those who gave their lives for the freedom of others. The values cover a range of powerful words carefully selected to not only support the mission but to embrace the nature of the museum's ongoing work.

San Diego Museum of Man, San Diego, CA
Mission Statement

Inspiring human connections by exploring the human experience.

Vision Statement

To be San Diego's dynamic place to go to learn from each other, reflect on our place in the world, and build a better community.

Values Statement

At all times, we strive to be:

- **Adventurous** We try new things, push boundaries, and are fearless.
- **Passionate** We love what we do and share our enthusiasm with others.
- **Engaging** We inspire our visitors to actively participate in the museum and we have fun doing it.
- **Disciplined** We strategically evaluate everything we do for alignment with our mission, vision, and values.
- **Open** We create an inclusive environment and welcome respectful discourse.
- **Accountable** We all share equal responsibility for SDMoM's success.

The mission, vision, and values of the San Diego Museum of Man complement one another and inform what the museum does. The mission is a dramatic reframing of the work of an anthropology museum into a contemporary dialogue with the world about the core of what it means to be human. The vision statement discusses the museum's long-term hope of contributing to a stronger community in San Diego, and the values include six concepts with an explanation of each to ensure that they are understood both internally and externally.

NOTE

1. Kevin Starr, "The Eight-Word Mission Statement." *Stanford Social Innovation Review.* https://ssir.org/articles/entry/the_eight_word_mission_statement.

4

Mission Alignment Framework

The Mission Alignment Framework is a visual representation of museums in the evolving realities of our time, with the central portion representing any museum in relation to the external environment, and with the relevant twenty-first-century mission at the center supported by the four alignment areas. The Framework is designed to be a vehicle to trigger conversations, spur institutional assessments, and assist with the process of clarifying and defining a relevant twenty-first-century mission for a museum. At the end of the day, every museum chooses its reality and place in the world, whether tacitly or boldly with intention.

SKETCH OF FRAMEWORK AND CORE COMPONENTS

The Framework places every museum within the dynamic confluence of *Contemporary Issues and Realities* and the *Local and Community Context*. Acknowledging, assessing, and naming those external realities is central to beginning the process of defining a relevant position and mission for each museum. Each museum will assess contemporary issues and realities, as well as the local and community context, and choose those that it is particularly well suited to address along with acknowledging those external factors that all museums must respond to in order to remain relevant. Some of the ubiquitous issues impacting all museums include embracing inclusive, nondiscriminatory practices; understanding enduring racial injustices; enacting environmentally sound principles; and incorporating technology responsibly as a communication and management tool. A responsive, engaged institutional mindset emanates a commitment to look outward at changing external realities as part of an ongoing relevancy practice and learning culture.

In addition to the greater external issues, every museum has a responsibility to understand the unique issues of the community where the museum exists. This may touch on shifts in local demographics, changes in the economic vitality of a town or city, the community dynamic, and the health of local schools, for example. Thus the greater contemporary issues and realities are assessed alongside the specific context evident in a local community. The confluence and intersection of those issues reveal the avenues and opportunities for a museum to become a contributor to community vitality, to be part of the solution, and to become a player in supporting the well-being of the city or town where the museum resides.

Thus, understanding external realities has a dual impact: one is to build responsible, ethical internal practices, and the other is to identify the contemporary issues or trends where a particular museum is well suited to contribute to and make a difference for the people it serves and engages with through its public engagement work.

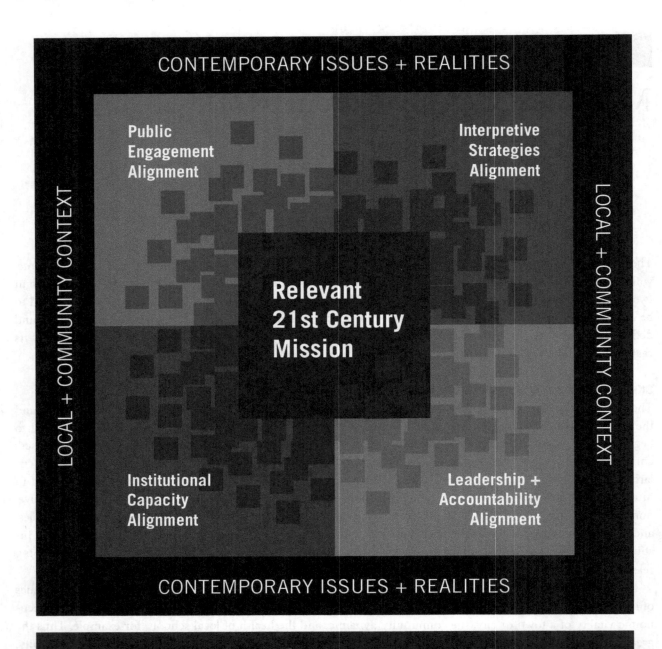

CONTEMPORARY ISSUES + REALITIES

LOCAL + COMMUNITY CONTEXT

Public
Engagement
Alignment

Interpretive
Strategies
Alignment

Relevant
21st Century
Mission

LOCAL + COMMUNITY CONTEXT

Institutional
Capacity
Alignment

Leadership +
Accountability
Alignment

CONTEMPORARY ISSUES + REALITIES

Mission Alignment Framework

At the center of the Framework is the ***relevant twenty-first-century mission***. The relevant mission reflects and is responsive to the world around the museum, and defines the specific role that aligns the museum for highest impact. This relevant mission and role should be appropriate to and best suited to the unique characteristics and qualities of a particular museum given its location and place in its community and region. Testing the ability, conviction, capacity, and approach to advance that relevant mission is in turn informed by the four alignment areas in each museum.

Four areas of alignment reflect museum operations and thus influence a museum's ability to live their mission. Through an assessment process, each alignment area reveals a museum's current priorities, strengths, and vulnerabilities, and thus as the mission is revised, points to aspects of museum operations for further work. Each alignment area informs institutional impact and the relevancy the museum seeks to achieve. Together, the four alignment areas influence each other, are interlinked, and evolve in response to external realities over time. One alignment area cannot change without impacting the other three areas. The four alignment areas must be in sync to properly support *a relevant twenty-first-century mission.*

Public engagement alignment defines the audiences, public, and communities (current and potential) relative to a specific museum, and the correlating understanding of how and in what ways the public influences and engages with the museum. It is the role of the museum as contributor to the community well-being in response to the complexities of local issues. It is the range of ways diverse voices and representation are embraced relative to perspectives, communities, histories, and cultural and individual identities. It is about determining relevance and inclusion of diverse people and perspectives in response to contemporary issues. It is about a willingness to dismantle old assumptions and rebuild new ways of being and engage the public. It is about museums being integrated into a multi-faceted network of people, communities, and entities where thoughtful work with and for the public contributes to a more just and equitable world for the greater good. It is about the people, the public, the communities, and the audiences that engage and participate with the institution, and how the museum learns from and with this broad engagement. It is about reaching out to currently underserved communities to invite, serve, and include them. It is about placing public engagement at the center of museum operations and defining it and how it permeates all the museum does.

Interpretive strategies alignment encompasses content and the range of onsite, online, and offsite methods that comprise the ways museums engage with the public. Interpretive strategies represent interpretive and visitor experience philosophies, public engagement activities, and the focus and representation in the collections. The amalgam of public offerings spans programs, exhibitions, social media, interactives, research libraries, digital access, websites, open storage for collections, labs, plus public amenities such as cafes and stores. Content covers the range of ideas, collections and tangible evidence, innovations, voices, and issues that comprise and inform the vehicles and strategies for sharing authority and co-creating experiences with the public. Content itself is as diverse as Native American stories, climate change, racism, artistic creations, the fight for freedom, cultural identities, the wonders of science, and the honoring of war heroes.

Collections, owned and borrowed, are the tangible expression and evidence of the priorities and interpretation of the stories the museum chooses. Collections help tell stories and support the mission and should be broad in representation for balanced inclusion to reveal the full story. Collections reflect values, voices, representation, and perspectives. Collections reveal choices, a lens, and biases. Collections can assist in telling the fuller and more complete panoply of stories of the past and today to create greater relevancy and reflection of multiple realities, cultures, histories, and voices.

One example is The Legacy Museum, a part of the Equal Justice Initiative, in Montgomery, Alabama, which lays bare stories of enslavement, lynchings, and present-day racial practices revealing histories and stories not understood or given the urgent attention required. Laws like the Native American Graves Protection + Repatriation Act of 1990 is one example of Native peoples and museums coming together to negotiate extremely different cultural values and beliefs and the complexities of ownership rights and privilege.[1] Museums today are under scrutiny to address long-embedded colonizing practices with the goal of becoming inclusive, collaborative, and balanced.[2] Zoos are emphasizing species protection to contribute awareness with the public. Botanical gardens are not just identifying plant species but looking at the relationship of plants to humans for the future of the planet.[3] (See Richard V. Piacentini's perspective in chapter 5.)

Institutional capacity alignment focuses on the distinct infrastructure and institutional competencies of each museum. The capacity of an institution reveals the depth of commitment and the proper alignment necessary to ensure the successful implementation of the mission. Institutional capacity includes fiscal health and stability, operational infrastructure, policies and procedures, institutional planning and priorities, technology and social media, the physical plant and grounds, public spaces and behind-the-scenes areas, and staffing parameters and structure. Each aspect of capacity dissected and assessed reveals levels of competency, strengths, gaps, and institution-wide understanding of what it takes to operate a museum regardless of size and focus. It also reveals what is needed to deliver on the promise of a mission. As museum missions evolve, the structure of museums will shift to be more agile and reflective of the practices and beliefs needed to operate a vibrant, inclusive, and reinvented museum in the twenty-first century. It is about recognizing that achieving relevance in a museum, and thus its mission, requires determining the right operations, the right infrastructure, the right staffing, and the necessary resources to deliver the right outcomes.

Leadership + accountability alignment emphasizes the critical role of boards, directors, and staff to envision a viable future by ensuring a relevant museum, the health of the leadership culture and work environment, and the strategic thinking needed to actualize the mission in order to be effective externally and internally. Further, this includes leadership styles as well as the collaborative nature of the work. Twenty-first-century leadership requires diversity of representation; relevant background and skills on the board, staff, and volunteer corps; a healthy, self-aware organizational culture; and the ability to understand the steps for undertaking transformational change that will take place over time. At its core, this alignment area requires the courage of leaders to assess capabilities, biases, and to define the ways to strengthen the leadership model. Leadership permeates the organization, touching on the power of staff to bring their expertise and perspective to the table for a vibrant internal culture. Accountability manifests both internally and externally. Museums have and will be called upon to explain decisions, institutional choices, and actions by internal stakeholders and the public. At the end of the day, the power to lead, change, and reposition museums for their greatest impact rests on the shoulders of the institution's leadership (see chapters 1 and 2).

FRAMEWORK AS A TOOL FOR AN ASSESSMENT PROCESS

The Mission Alignment Framework provides an option for supporting an institutional assessment to gain a perspective on museum vitality and inherent potential relative to the external landscape and relevancy in contemporary times. There is no one-size-fits-all assessment process, formula, or result. There is no singular strategy to find the right way to heighten relevance. Rather, this assessment process provides a moment to see opportunities to determine the right fit and position for a museum given all the factors that define its location, fiscal health, history and focus, level of visionary leadership, clarity of interpretive strategies and collections, approaches for public engagement, and so on. It is a moment to question, explore, and find a path forward that positions each museum for the greatest relevance and impact on behalf of the public. Consider what additional questions would be of value for your particular museum. Hone these questions to make them as helpful to your assessment process as possible.

After completion of an assessment, answer these questions to link the assessment to the Mission Alignment Framework:

- What does this assessment reveal? What change(s) will be needed moving forward?
- What work is the museum already undertaking that sets the stage for greater impact?
- How well does the museum respond to contemporary issues and realities?
- What changes are needed to advance the museum toward greater relevancy and thus a more relevant mission statement and museum?
- What is revealed in the four areas of alignment? Strengths? Areas to improve to better support a revised mission?

External Assessment: Contemporary Issues and Realities, and Local and Community Context

Gain a complete picture of contemporary issues + and realities. Conduct research and amass a list to work from for conversations with external leaders.

- Name the contemporary issues and realities relevant to your organization.
- Identify those areas critical to respond to (if not already doing so), and name those areas where you may be well suited to be part of the solution.
- Tap into the blogs, literature, and publications produced by the Center for the Future of Museums, a part of American Alliance of Museums, especially noting *Museum 2040* and prior years of *TrendsWatch 2014, 2015, 2016, 2017.*
- Look outside museum literature to expand perspectives and sources of information.

Clarify local and community context. Gather information through conversations with leaders and representative voices in your community and complement those connections with research and building relationships that are sustained over time, such as:

- Current local demographic and population relating to all types of diversity (age, ethnic background, cultural identities, types of communities, etc.)
- Social issues and community health overall (this could include racial tensions, growing homeless population, at-risk youth, poverty, income disparities, etc.)
- Economic vitality of your immediate community and regional setting (growth in local development, high cost of living, limited access to affordable housing, dependency on tourism, etc.)

- Political environment with local or regional government (government priorities, tax base and laws, etc.)
- Local business profile (types of business, dominatation by one or two significant employers, etc.)

Determine which issues your museum can address through its public engagement work and institutional commitment, and identify how the current internal capacity will need to be strengthened to support this work. Consider how the internal structure either hinders or supports innovative and inclusive practices.

Consider the range of contemporary issues, **such as:**

- Diversity, equity, accessibility, and inclusion. This is a dominant social issue in the national discourse. Addressing and advancing change and institutional achievement for equitable practices is essential to the future of museums.
- Climate change touches every institution. No museum can ignore diminishing environmental resources or the importance of managing an institution's carbon footprint. Green sustainable practices that contribute to better operative tenets for a museum's ability and responsibility to take action to protect the environment and planet.
- Technology and its many permutations has rippled through society, evident in a plethora of new modes of communication, new media platforms, business practices, public relations, and more. This area requires a shift in practices especially key for staying connected to contemporary audiences and for effective internal management practices. to name two areas. Digital platforms and social media are powerful tools that have changed the way people connect, engage, and respond to issues and one another.
- Global interconnectedness is a constant reality due in large part to immediate access to information about any topic, any place, any government, or any area in the world through technology, and the realization that decisions made in one moment in a specific location ultimately ripple into other economies, other nations, the natural environment, political relations, social realities, and cultural identities. An economic downturn on the other side of the globe or in our own backyard, as in 2008, can create a tsunami of financial strains and uncertainty.

Each of these areas, to name just a few, are changing at a brisk clip. Every day more literature, blogs, and data are shared about the changing reality in which people and museums exist. This points to the importance of making time to keep external changes and realities a part of the internal culture of a museum, and key elements to fold into decisions and considerations of what and how a museum remains connected and relevant.

Consider local and community context such as location-specific realities and correlating issues, declining or increasing populations in the local community, influx of new businesses and growth, economic decline, strain between tourism goals and local traditions, community tensions, etc.

- The realities and issues of a town, region, or locale may reveal many opportunities for listening and engaging with different communities beyond existing audiences, gaining a perspective on the challenges facings an adjacent neighborhood, or coming to better understand the vulnerability of a local economy. It is about realizing how a museum can participate in strengthening, improving, and adding to the vitality of the community through a genuine desire to be part of the solution and resilience of the place where a museum resides.
- A local area or region can reveal unique tensions between communities, distinct artists communities, the power of a strong congregation, or the challenges of the transgender community. Identity, belonging, and civil rights issues are prevalent challenges in many communities. Intersectionality opens the dynamic complexities of individuals who desire to be recognized for all facets of their identity that go beyond a singular conformity.

Institutional Assessment: The Four Alignment Areas

Consider the questions for each alignment area. Each of the four alignment areas have suggested questions to stimulate conversation about operative assumptions and current realities within a museum. There is no one solution to being relevant, but there are many avenues into the conversation of exploring what is possible, what is right, and what each museum will undertake. See examples and references throughout the book that highlight some of the thinking, work, and exploration that is occurring at the institutional level, the association level, and within the broader museum community.

Public Engagement Alignment

Understanding current and potential participation

- What are the demographics in the region? What demographic shifts are occurring?
- Who participates in the museum currently? What is the profile of users and participants?
- Does the profile of users reflect the communities and diversity in neighboring areas? The greater region? If not, what are the barriers to greater participation?
- How is public participation defined and executed?
- How are decisions made for what is offered? For and with whom?
- Are evaluation strategies (pre-testing, formative evaluation, visitor intercept interviews, for example) implemented to collect ongoing feedback to inform your understanding of the effectiveness of offerings as they align with meeting the needs of audiences? How is the information used?
- How are current research, market, and audience studies incorporated into decisions and the development of public offerings?
- Is there agreement across departments about the value in advancing the museum's mission in service to its public? How is that manifested?
- In what ways are different communities and groups engaged with the museum in conversations and collaborative efforts to build meaningful participation and engagement over time? What level of trust has been established with different communities?
- What type of training is provided to support the range of practices working with the public, diverse communities, and other organizations?
- How are local needs and realities incorporated into decisions about the range of diverse public engagement the museum will offer?

Role of museum in supporting community well-being

- How is the museum viewed within the community-at-large? If not, why not? Diverse communities? Is the museum viewed as an ally and contributor to community health and well-being? If not, why not?
- How does the museum envision its role within the community where it is located?
- Describe how the museum understands the dynamic realities of its community. How does the museum understand the community's vibrant assets and resources?
- What relationships and level of engagement does the museum have with local communities, political leaders, educators, and businesses to address needs?
- When challenging issues arise in the local community or a specific group, is the museum asked to be at the table to address and help resolve those issues? How agile is the museum in collaborating with communities to address critical current realities?
- How might the museum be a stronger contributor to the vitality of its community?

Interpretive Strategies Alignment

Content
- What is the content focus of the museum?
- How is it defined? How does it relate to the changing environment and contemporary communities?
- What strategies are used to achieve balance and inclusion of diverse voices, perspectives, and cultures?
- How is interpretation defined? How is the philosophy about content defined?
- How is the intersection of content, audiences, engagement, visitor experiences, and interpretation defined? What strategies are used to achieve balance and inclusion?
- How does the content definition influence public offerings, collection priorities, and use of collections? How does the content emphasis of the museum reflect contemporary issues and realities? Incorporate relevant local and community context?

Methods of serving the public
- What is the menu of public offerings? Onsite? Offsite? Online?
- How are decisions made for what is offered? Who is involved in that decision making? How is public participation envisioned and executed?
- Are evaluation strategies (pre-testing, formative, summative strategies, for example) implemented to collect ongoing feedback to inform an understanding of the effectiveness of museum offerings?
- What understanding of diverse communities and needs are understood? Are different communities and groups engaged in conversations and collaborative efforts to build meaningful engagement?
- How are local community realities incorporated into public offerings?
- How does every staff person understand and integrate public engagement in their work?
- What systems are in place for staff to learn and adapt their practices to support the institutional commitment to public engagement?

Collection framework
- What are the current collection strengths? Areas or gaps to be addressed?
- How have collections been built? Who decides? What rubric is used to strategize for the future?
- Do collections reflect contemporary realities? Diverse communities and broad representation?
- How are communities engaged in helping to build collections with greater relevancy and broad representation?
- What voices are accessed to interpret and understand collections?

Institutional Capacity Alignment

Financial sustainability
- How robust and diversified are the various streams of revenue coming into the institution, including earned revenue, contributed income, endowment interest, etc.?
- Based on the latest budget, where are the greatest areas of financial emphasis placed? How does your budget reflect institutional priorities and commitments?
- If a city, county, or state organization or a university museum, what percent comes from the parent organization and how stable is that funding? How does the leadership of the parent institution view the museum and its vitality relative to the health of a city or university?
- Are any sources of income threatened? Have any areas been declining?

- How strong are financial checks and balances relative to institutional goals and protecting museum fiscal resources?
- Is there a reserve fund set aside for emergencies? An endowment fund with clear management policies?
- How rigorous and extensive are current financial policies? How well are they followed?
- What ethical guidelines inform who and how contributions are accepted, managed, and invested?

Physical space and use of technology
- What is the balance of public space versus behind-the-scenes spaces?
- How does the physical plant and location of the museum support or limit what the museum is aiming to do?
- What is the overall condition of the physical plant? Grounds?
- Are resources set aside for ongoing capital improvements and maintenance?
- How up-to-date are the technology systems supporting the institution? Staff capacity to use digital tools effectively?
- How does maintenance, security, and upkeep ensure public safety? A space for engagement?
- How well does the physical space reflect a welcoming and easily navigable path through the public areas (e.g., way-finding, multilingual signage, etc.)?

Systems, policies, and procedures
- Do the systems, policies, and procedures reflect up-to-date standards? Do they reflect and embrace diversity and equity?
- Are staff and board familiar with key policies concerning human resources, finance, public engagement, marketing, etc.? Do they uphold these policies in their respective areas of responsibility?

Leadership and Accountability Alignment

Roles, responsibilities, and nonprofit leadership expectations
- How are the distinctions among board, directors, and staff responsibilities made clear?
- What is the evidence that the board, directors, and staff understand their role in advancing the mission and representing the institution in the community?

Board leadership and accountability
- How effective is the board acting responsibly on behalf of the institution and the public?
- How diverse is the board? What strategies are in place to recruit, support, and diversify the board?
- Describe how the board culture supports and welcomes diverse representation, perspectives, and engagement.

Executive/board leadership partnership
- Is the current board and executive leadership the right leadership to lead change moving forward?
- Describe the health and trust evident in the executive/board partnership? What areas are strong? Underdeveloped?

Leadership style and capacity
- Does the organization's leadership (at all levels) have the capacity to implement purposeful change in a rapidly shifting operating environment? Describe.
- Does the leadership embrace and encourage collaborative ways of working? What is the evidence of this?

Organizational culture

- How healthy and inclusive is the organizational structure? At the board level? Executive level? Staff level? Volunteer level?
- What structure, support, and training is in place to aid the board, the staff, and volunteers in the successful achievement of their responsibilities? The mission? Support of diversity, inclusion, and cultural competency?
- How is the vitality of the organizational structure assessed? Monitored?

Staff structure

- How well aligned is the staff structure to achieve the mission? Is it a silo structure or an integrated model?
- What level of representation is there on staff including ethnic and racial diversity, age, diverse expertise?
- What is the pay level and support for staff? How does it measure up to other nonprofit standards and the cost of living?

Volunteer corps

- Is the staff supported by a trained, diverse, and competent volunteer corps?
- What is the training and process for keeping volunteers abreast of the mission and future of the museum?
- What opportunities can be tapped and expanded in support of the mission and community engagement?

DIVERSITY AND INCLUSION: A CASE FOR HOLISITIC CHANGE

Diversity and inclusion is one of the most dominant issues of contemporary times. Following are some questions to consider about diversity and inclusion and their impact on achieving a relevant museum for the broadest public. The reader is encouraged to reference Charmaine Jefferson's essay in chapter 2. In short, achieving diversity and inclusion is fundamentally a holistic issue that permeates and impacts everything the museum does, how it orients its work, how it envisions its role, and how it operates. This issue is highlighted here as an example of how an external issue plays out throughout the museum if embraced in totality, with clarity, and intention.

Extent of Conversation about Diversity and Inclusion

- To what extent and frequency does your institution currently engage in conversations about diversity and inclusion?
- How has your museum defined diversity and inclusion? Diversity is broad and complex, including but not limited to, background, age, ability, ethnicity and race, socio-economic level, and so on. How diverse and inclusive is your museum?
- Why has your institution determined that diversity, equity, accessibility, and inclusion matter? What plans have been outlined to address improving diversity, equity, accessibility, and inclusion?

Internal Representation

- How diverse is the representation on the board, staff, and in the volunteer corps?
- What recruiting, hiring, and appointment practices support or hinder an inclusive practice?
- What level of onboarding occurs to welcome and include new board and staff members? What efforts are employed to retain and care for staff and volunteers?
- What strategies are in place to handle, educate, and mediate when conflict or diverse opinions arise?
- How does the board and staff understand their role and biases, and the impact of those beliefs and behaviors on an inclusive culture?

External Representation

- What level of understanding, research, and conversations does the museum undertake to understand and ensure balanced and inclusive feedback from the local community and its visitors, including understanding the centuries-long, deep history of racism in our country and in your community?
- What is the profile of current museum participants?
- How does the museum prepare the board, staff, and volunteers to uphold their role in creating an inclusive, welcoming, and learning environment?
- What policies and approaches are in place to attract and engage diverse audiences?
- What ongoing relationships and partnerships support a diverse and inclusive museum?

Institutional Approach to Inclusion

- What is the institutional strategy to achieve diversity in audience participation, inclusive operations, representation, etc.?
- How does the museum's approach and philosophy about inclusion support or hinder decisions, and impact?
- Does the current organizational culture accept and create an environment supportive of inclusion and diversity?
- What training and internal conversations have been put in place to support and advance the institution's position?
- What is the willingness and commitment to tackle this deep level of change among the staff? Among the board?

Inclusion throughout Museum Activities and Actions

- How is inclusion manifest throughout the museum?
- What is the balance and approach to interpretation such that a broad cross-section of voices, stories, content are reflected in the museum? How are exhibitions, programs, events, social media envisioned keeping in mind diverse audiences and community?
- How do collections reflect the broader population? If they do not, what efforts are being made to fill gaps and realign the collections to better reflect contemporary realities, broad representation, and communities?
- Who interprets? Who has the authority to tell a story, share their voice, or define their reality?

NOTES

1. Dan L. Monroe and Walter Echo-Hawk, "Deft Deliberations (1991)." In *Reinventing the Museum: The Evolving Conversation on the Paradigm Shift* (Lanham, MD: AltaMira Press, 2012), 72–77.

2. Wendy Ng, "Decolonize and Indigenize: A Reflective Dialogue." *Medium.*

3. Emlyn Koster, "The Relevant Museum: A Reflection on Sustainability." In *Reinventing the Museum: The Evolving Conversation on the Paradigm Shift* (Lanham, MD: AltaMira Press, 2012), 202–11.

5

Twenty Perspectives from Museum Leaders

INTRODUCTION

The twenty perspectives written by museum leaders featured in this chapter illustrate the level of commitment, courage, and innovation happening in museums in North America. The story of each institution reveals the specific challenges and reframing that has taken place to create a relevant museum in the twenty-first century. Each perspective is an example of the principles and characteristics of a twenty-first-century mission. Each individual contributor is to be celebrated for their honesty, candor, and courage to share the story of their museum.

Selection Process

These perspectives were selected based on a goal that collectively, the perspectives would capture a range of institutional types and sizes, diverse contemporary realities, and a leadership approach that might spark or encourage change for a trustee or museum leader reading this book. Not one perspective approached the process of honing mission and defining a relevant role in the same way. Further, these examples reveal the range of strategies for revitalization work specific to the institution and its unique position and resources.

These distinct perspectives spotlight:

- Evidence of leadership undertaking the reshaping of the mission and work of their institution in order to define a relevant role, and a commitment to reinvent their museum responding to the diverse issues in the world today;
- Diverse geographic locations reflecting the importance of place on mission with an eye to cover examples in North America. Some are urban while others are rural or in medium-sized cities;
- A range of museums varying in size budget from small to large; and,
- The storyline for each museum covers a considerable span of issues, from changing focus to avoid imminent closure, or a conviction to tackle decolonization on an institution-wide level, or a desire to incorporate cutting-edge research to inform the work of the institution, or new thinking and new ways of framing institutional work to speak to the changing landscape of environmental issues and cultural impact.

Museums highlighted in the perspectives convey the level of conviction needed to undertake institutional transformation, the value of community and public participation, and the knowledge that remaining relevant is an ongoing process.

The Perspectives

- *Abbe Museum*, located in Bar Harbor, Maine, is dedicated to the culture and traditions of the Wabanaki people, and has been evolving from a traditional museum model into a museum that embraces decolonization in all of its work.

- *Anchorage Museum*, located in Anchorage, Alaska, reinvented its traditional, discipline-focused approach into a multi-layered center for dialogue about Alaska and the circumpolar North addressing the confluence of issues threatening the Arctic while connecting Alaska to the global stage of climate change.
- *Bay Area Discovery Museum*, located in Sausalito, California, is integrating cutting-edge research to inform their work with children, families, and educators.
- *Burke Museum of Natural History and Culture*, located on the University of Washington campus in Seattle, Washington, is in the midst of reinventing its core ideology beyond science and research to embrace issues of inclusion, healing, and celebration while highlighting the intersection of collections and cultural stories.
- *The Contemporary Jewish Museum*, located in San Francisco, California, is a noncollecting museum dedicated to highlighting Jewish contributions in the arts tied to contemporary issues facing society.
- *The Arquives*, formerly the Canadian Gay and Lesbian Archives, located in Toronto, Canada, works toward a better understanding of issues of identity, acceptance of the broader LBGTQ community, celebrating diverse identities, and highlighting individual achievements.
- *Eastern State Penitentiary Historic Site*, located in Philadelphia, Pennsylvania, uses the site to highlight the history of incarceration and the social justice issues surrounding imprisonment in today's society.
- *Kaʻala Farm*, located on the coast of Oʻahu, Hawaiʻi, is a cultural site that brings together ancestral Hawaiian beliefs, contemporary issues of land and water, and cultural survival for the future of native Hawaiian ways of being.
- *Minneapolis Institute of Art*, located in Minneapolis, Minnesota, has mounted an effort to deconstruct and rebuild the institutional framework, organizational culture, and public engagement model to shift from a dominant, Caucasian bias to reframe the work through the lens of diverse communities.
- *National Civil Rights Museum*, located in Memphis, Tennessee, honors the legacy of Martin Luther King Jr. and connects his vision to contemporary issues of equity, freedom, and inclusion.
- *National Underground Railroad Freedom Center*, located in Cincinnati, Ohio, champions the heroes of the Underground Railroad and focuses on freedom and contemporary social justice issues.
- *Nevada Museum of Art*, located in Reno, Nevada, created a model that merges the dynamic elements of the environment with the concept of the West and art to challenge assumptions of perspective, climate and environmental fragility, and artists.
- *North Carolina Museum of Natural Sciences*, located in Raleigh, North Carolina, is committed to building a more sustainable planet through innovative programming, research, and public engagement.
- *Oakland Museum of California*, located in Oakland, California, models an innovative public engagement ideologue, and a commitment to achieve social impact as the test of measuring success and making a difference.
- *Phipps Conservatory and Botanical Gardens*, located in Pittsburgh, Pennsylvania, embraces environmental sustainability in all it does, from buildings, programming, and leadership, as it advances a better understanding of the inextricable connection of the plant kingdom and human interaction.
- *President Lincoln's Cottage*, located in Washington, DC, celebrates Lincoln's vision for equality with contemporary programs embracing issues of freedom.
- *San Diego Museum of Man*, located in San Diego, California, has reframed a traditional anthropology museum with encyclopedic collections to a museum that looks at what it means to be human in contemporary society, as the institution embraces a decolonization approach.
- *Santa Cruz Museum of Art and History*, located in Santa Cruz, California, reinvented itself to engage with the community in new ways and shift the museum into a central gathering place in the cultural life of Santa Cruz.
- *Tamástslikt Cultural Institute*, located in Pendleton, Oregon, is a tribal museum dedicated to the Umatilla people that ties ancestral beliefs, values, and culture to daily life and tribal identity.
- *The Wild Center*, in the Adirondacks, New York, uses the natural setting of its site to inspire environmental awareness and action both in the Adirondacks and in the world.

ABBE MUSEUM

Bar Harbor, Maine

Written by Cinnamon Catlin-Legutko, President/Chief Executive Officer

By 2009, in the midst of the Great Recession, the Abbe Museum had weathered multiple leadership changes following the opening of a new facility in 2001. Coupled with complicated financial decisions, the museum was on the brink of financial failure. Their relationships with tribal community members were dissolving. The Board of Trustees made one final move and hired a search firm to find a new president/chief executive officer (CEO). The first project on my hefty "to do" list was to finish a strategic plan and clarify the museum's mission and vision.

With no resources and unbridled ambition, I set about interviewing staff, trustees, and community stakeholders to learn about their hopes for the organization and the commitments they were willing to make. The plan was to be produced in-house.

After three months of conversations, the Abbe's strategic objectives became clearer, but language for the mission and vision statements were elusive. The staff began revising both statements and then sent them back to the Board for consideration and possible approval. To the team, the existing mission statement lacked inspiration and a "so what" factor.

> The mission of the Abbe Museum is to promote the understanding and appreciation of Maine's Native American culture, history, and archaeology. The Museum's collections, exhibitions, and programs focus on the Native American traditions in Maine and explore the broader Native American experience, past and present.

The staff studied various styles and worked through several activities. When they hit a dead end, they decided to take a break. Fiscal concerns aside, the staff recognized that if they couldn't agree on a clear educational purpose, they should probably shut the doors. This changed when the Abbe's director of development shared an article she read in the November 2009 issue of *Fast Company*, titled "Wordplay: Why Most Mission Statements are Dumb and How to Write One that Isn't." The article revisited Jim Collins and Jim Porras's Big Hairy Audacious Goal (BHAG) concept from *Built to Last* (1994), especially the example of Microsoft's BHAG, "A computer on every desk in every home, all running Microsoft software." A BHAG is "clear and compelling and serves as a unifying focal point of the effort, often creating immense team spirit. It has a clear finish line, so the organization can know when it has achieved the goal. . . . A BHAG should not be a sure bet . . . but the organization must believe we can do it anyway."

They also looked to Harold and Susan Skramstad's mission statement model, which suggests that a statement should include action, outcome, and value (AOV), and be short enough to fit on a business card. But sometimes models like this, even though they're inspirational, do not reflect an organization's life cycle. If you imagine an organization as a nearly immortal human, moving from birth to death, and sometimes back again, a prime museum is an adult. The Abbe was an organization perceived as being in adulthood, but it was actually hovering on the precipice of death. It needed a reboot, a rebirth. Empowered by these two models, the staff drafted a mission statement that was approved by the Board of Trustees. Ultimately, the mission statement, which is still used today, was a combination of a BHAG and an AOV statement.

> The Abbe Museum inspires new learning about the Wabanaki Nations with every visit.

The mission statement identifies three important concepts. New learning signifies that the museum prioritizes experiential education and acknowledges that misinformation about Native people is pervasive. When museumgoers learn, it is often new information that broadens their perspectives on Native history—present and future.

Second, we wanted to properly acknowledge the sovereignty of Wabanaki people by using the term Nations, which often goes unacknowledged by non-Native people in Maine. With this distinction, we moved away from the phrase "Maine's Native American culture" which is harmful language—Maine does not possess Native people. They are sovereign nations. Finally, the statement specifies "every visit," which means that wherever you encounter our work—in the museum, in the classroom, during community events—we will be consistent in our mission.

The Abbe's customer service commitment was then articulated in the vision statement. The existing vision statement failed to motivate staff and board performance. Only one paragraph of the original three is provided here.

> Representing the Native American people of Maine and the Maritimes—with emphasis on the Wabanaki, or "People of the Dawn"—is the foundation, focus, and future of the Abbe Museum. Through its professional staff, the Abbe is a leader in collections management, education, and preservation of material culture through archaeological fieldwork, research, and collaboration with other institutions.

The staff intended to craft a vision statement to guide and inspire the future Abbe Museum. The goal was to build a museum that focused on learners and make sure that our planning, programming, and service resulted in memorable and positive experiences.

> Each person who connects with the Abbe Museum will be treated to an outstanding experience.

From these new statements, the staff and Board charted a new strategic path for the Abbe Museum, focused on visitor experience, financial stability, and developing museum best practices while addressing neglected projects (e.g., developing a year-round program calendar, clarifying staff roles and duties, addressing the failing climate control system, and more). The plan was reworked until it navigated numerous financial rapids with great success, setting up the organization for the museum's next strategic planning process. The new plan envisioned a bigger future than they could have ever imagined in 2009.

While addressing organizational needs and financial concerns were the focus of the previous plan, deepening the Abbe's relationships with tribal communities was certainly a concern. A Native Advisory Council formed in 2012 to build new relationships, including collaborations with Wabanaki historians, culture keepers, and artists. The future of the Abbe relied on prioritizing tribal relationships. Success was contingent on uniting the Board and staff in their commitment and approach.

In late 2012, we began to "plan for the next plan," when the Abbe Museum Board of Trustees established a Decolonization Initiative and Task Force. The initiative was an outgrowth of the 2012 Board Annual Retreat, facilitated by Jamie Bissonette Lewey.[1] During this retreat, trustees and staff tackled the complex topics around museum practices and how many indigenous people are emotionally and spiritually harmed by traditional museum practices. An outcome of the retreat was a commitment from trustees and staff to better understand Wabanaki culture, history, and values; examine the Abbe's museum practices at every level to see whether they reflect those values; and take steps toward practices that embody this commitment. This is the essence of the initiative.[2]

The task force's initial convening considered the scope of its work and identified key concepts that underpin board and staff discussions. They identified sectors of museum operations that must be considered in the decolonization process: collections, operations, governance, strategic planning, exhibits, advocacy, programming, and events. Our organizational and strategic plans need to ask the overarching question, what can and should our museum do that is a service to Wabanaki people? Decolonization means, at a minimum, sharing governance structures and authority for the documentation and interpretation of Native culture.

We find the scholarly work of Amy Lonetree, Ho-Chunk, especially useful in helping us understand what museum decolonization means. From her academic writings, the task force identified three practices to guide board and staff:

- Decolonizing practices at the Abbe are collaborative with tribal communities. This means that when an idea for a project or initiative is first conceived, we have a conversation with Native advisors and make sure it's an activity that we have the right to share or pursue. We ask permission; we don't get halfway down the planning timeline and then check with Native advisors about how we're doing and if we're getting it right. Native collaboration needs to be at the beginning and threaded throughout the life of the project.
- The second characteristic of decolonizing museum practices is to privilege Native perspective and voice. The vast writings on the human experience are, with little exception, written by white academics and observers. When we begin to prioritize the accounts and observations of indigenous scholars and informants, the story broadens, expands, shifts, and brings clearer and nonoppressed perspectives of Native history and culture. There is room to consider academic writing and research in this practice, but when there is conflict, both points of view may be presented, as long as the non-indigenous research is not exposing sensitive information or causing harm to communities of people and their ancestors.
- Decolonizing museum practice includes taking the full measure of history, which ensures truth-telling and the inclusion of difficult stories. Histories of Wabanaki people connect to today's challenges. Issues of water quality, hunting and fishing rights, and mascots are connected to the past and the present. When we present this full history, we have a better opportunity to identify harmful statements and practices.

After approximately two years of research and learning, our decolonizing practices emerged. The museum looked ahead to strategic planning and engaged an outside museum planner who studied our initiative and other academic writings on decolonization. She was equally committed to guiding us through difficult conversations and facilitating large groups of stakeholders with often disparate views of what the Abbe should be. A year after three Board retreats and a Native Advisory Council convening for strategic planning, the Board approved the new plan in 2015.

The strategic plan makes a clear commitment to decolonization. Initially, the Board and staff thought decolonization would be a "spoke" of the plan, but it became evident that decolonization is our vision—the lens we look through to make decisions and set priorities. The vision statement needed a revision.

> The Abbe Museum will reflect and realize the values of decolonization in all of its practices, working with the Wabanaki Nations to share their stories, history, and culture with a broader audience.

We reviewed the mission statement several times and found that it still described our purpose and our passion. It remains unchanged, while our operations and resources are aligning with the Abbe's new vision.

> The Abbe Museum inspires new learning about the Wabanaki Nations with every visit.

The Abbe is committed to developing decolonizing museum practice that is informed by Wabanaki people and enforced by policies, managed by protocols, and overseen by inclusive governance structures. We will have structures in place that maintain this commitment to decolonization, regardless of the players involved—meaning the staff, trustees, and advisors. Our mission and vision statements guide us toward realistic activities and impacts.

The Board and staff continue to invest in learning. Each year we offer racial bias training for all seasonal staff, new staff, and trustees. The museum staff are trained in facilitated dialogue methodology developed by the International Coalition for the Sites of Conscience, which helps us engage in difficult conversations. And, at nearly every Board meeting, we invite guest speakers to teach us about new research or to consider a new decolonizing strategy. Most recently Amy Lonetree visited the museum to share her observations and expertise. To follow our work, visit our strategic plan and blog at abbemuseum.wordpress.com.

ABBE MUSEUM

Year Founded: 1928

Location: Bar Harbor, Maine

Mission Statement: To inspire new learning about the Wabanaki Nations with every visit.

Vision Statement: The Abbe Museum will reflect and realize the values of decolonization in all of its practices, working with the Wabanaki Nations to share their stories, history, and culture with a broader audience.

Distinct Characteristics: Institution-wide commitment to decolonization with ongoing input and feedback from an active Native Advisory Council and Wabanaki advisors and committees. Archaeology collection and ethnographic materials from the seventeenth through twentieth centuries, and major basket collection. In total, the collection represents ten thousand years of Native American culture and history in present-day Maine, New England, and the Maritimes.

Governance: Private, nonprofit 501(c)(3)

Budget: $1 million

Staff: Seven full-time, and ten to twelve seasonal guest services staff

Adoption Date of Mission and Vision: 2015

ANCHORAGE MUSEUM

Anchorage, Alaska

Written by Julie Decker, Museum Director and Chief Executive Officer

In 2014, the Anchorage Museum was four years out from a major expansion and had been through decades of major transitions. Founded in 1968, with one main gallery and a borrowed collection, the museum grew quickly along with its city—progress spawned by oil and opportunistic development. Each subsequent decade brought change to the museum, expanding in the 1970s, doubling in size in the 1980s, then moving from a city agency to a private nonprofit and doubling in size again within the first ten years of the twenty-first century. The museum began as a history and art museum and expanded its mission over the decades along with its building, adding science, culture, and a major partnership with the Smithsonian Institution. The museum, in some ways, was living with an identity crisis in 2014, at the same time the city was facing an identity crisis of its own. Anchorage is a young, urban town, still defining and creating a narrative that moves away from a colonized one that ignores the long arc of Indigenous continuity and considering the identity that will guide it toward its future.

The museum was a strong community institution in 2014, but it was struggling to balance the idea and economics of the blockbuster-exhibition model with the idea of a local museum housing large, chronological, permanent exhibitions that offered overviews and introductions to indigenous culture and romantic landscape paintings along with a general-science hands-on "discovery center." The museum's mission of art, history, and science was unspecific rather than place-based, and the idea of local seemed defined by simply serving a local audience. The architecture of the building outside and in also felt confused rather than cohesive—the brick façade of the 1980s addition butted against a modernist, contemporary, and transparent glass addition designed by the architect David Chipperfield, which sought to face the museum, literally and figuratively, toward the environment, the downtown, and the public. Inside, visitors would go from 1980s exhibits with dioramas, to a slick Arctic Studies Center featuring Smithsonian-loaned objects or to a colorful and loud interactive science-center space.

I was just taking the helm as director/CEO of the Anchorage Museum as 2014 began, after serving for two years as its chief curator. Anchorage is my hometown. Anchorage is also the gateway to America's Arctic and home to some of the most ethnically diverse schools and neighborhoods in the United States. The climate in Alaska is changing at twice the rate of other regions in the world, and Anchorage is facing economic transformations as the state weans off of oil revenues as the primary source of revenue. In this context, I saw an opportunity to address "local" in a much more relevant, empowered, and consistent way at the museum, to bind the museum and all of its spaces and program with one powerful narrative, to connect the museum nationally and internationally, and to entrench equity and innovation into the solutions we crafted. The museum needed a plan to thrive through demographic, environmental, and economic change, but also needed to embrace a new kind of risk-taking. Museums have long reflected the importance of creativity by giving artists, thinkers, and change-makers visibility through programs and exhibitions. Today, museums must learn to apply to their own institutions what they have celebrated in others: creativity, innovation, critical thinking, and risk-taking.

But change is not always easy, internally or externally, so I embarked on an effort in 2014 to create a new strategic plan for the museum, to take it forward, and to work with staff and stakeholders to examine the moment and the future. The plan was part of an effort to build an internal architecture for the museum by re-envisioning "permanent" spaces and programs, to examine the aspirational potential of a multidisciplinary museum and a museum of Alaska. The past narrative had often been about importing the "everywhere else" and seeing Anchorage as a disadvantaged location, far away from other urban centers. The new strategic plan centered around the recognition that our location in the world was not a deficit but our greatest advantage and greatest distinction.

Our opportunity was to turn the stereotypes of the North on their side and build authentic narratives around the people and environment of our region. Instead of important ideas, it was an imperative to host relevant conversations around climate change, colonization, and social change, and work with people from Alaska and around the world to imagine futures.

The future for the museum, with the strategic plan, became about finding innovative ways to be closely connected to both local and global communities. Our articulated target was not visitation, but participation and relevance—a new engagement that reached beyond bricks and mortar, into local community, and out to the broader narratives that impact our world.

Anchorage is at the epicenter of environmental and economic transformation. Building the city's capacity to thrive depends upon equitably engaging all community residents, whether indigenous or immigrant, engineers or artists, to identify feasible pathways toward a safe, secure future. Within this compelling environment, the museum has a key role to play in convening people and curating conversations that are not based in traditional disciplines, but are cross-sector and people-centered. We also moved from static exhibitions to creating invitations to participate in immersive experiences that only we could provide. We designed and built our own exhibitions and focused on what we might export rather than on what we would import. We used our infrastructure to empower voices, offer multiple perspectives, and generate ideas.

Along with the strategic plan, the museum updated its mission and values statements. Instead of a generalized statement, we worked toward an intentional and purposeful definition of the institution that would drive us to tell one overarching story and to build cohesion around everything that came under it. The mission statement became: The Anchorage Museum connects people, expands perspectives, and encourages dialogue about the North and its distinct environment.

The museum now serves its mission by organizing and presenting programs and exhibitions in Anchorage, as well as by traveling exhibitions and programs throughout the globe. The museum endeavors to serve the widest possible audience and to provide a cultural center where all of Alaska's cultures feel welcome. We present and host more than one thousand programs and events each year, offering a wide spectrum of culturally diverse programming. It is one of the larger museum facilities on the West Coast of the United States and presents and curates twelve to twenty vital and relevant exhibitions each year. The Anchorage Museum plays an active role in developing relationships and creating connection in the whole Arctic region (including the United States, Iceland, Greenland, Russia, Finland, Sweden, Norway, and Canada). It is the museum's ambition to build new networks among nations, institutions, and individuals. In particular, the museum's role in recognizing and promoting Pan-Inuit and global indigenous culture and perspective is groundbreaking. The multi-disciplinary approach and support for artistic social and cultural research is inspired by a vision of being a content producer rather than only a content collector. Now, just a few years since adopting the plan, the Anchorage Museum is now recognized in the United States and abroad as an important, relevant voice in the ongoing debate on the futures of the Arctic and the connections of the Arctic to the globe.

Today we collect and create the record of our times and specialize in new, contemporary, and community-based curatorial and programmatic thinking and practice. Indigenous curators and community curators work with underserved and newcomer populations. The museum is a leader in working with new media technologies to explore ideas around art and the environment, and has an expanded design department that includes a licensed architect and landscape architect in order to realize large-scale public, outdoor, and global community projects that go far beyond traditional museum design and into community development, design thinking, and community consultation. The museum has a curatorial staff that spans the disciplines of art, science, history, design, and culture, as well as a curator-at-large program that creates national and global connections. The museum's Polar Lab program brings artists from around the world to the international Arctic to engage in long-term, multi-year research projects in remote locations and extreme environments. A SEED Lab program brings design together with many sectors, including science, engineering, and agriculture to imagine future solutions for energy and equity.

The strategic plan was a critical catalyst for the organization. It broke down the barriers to collaboration between museum departments, aligned goals between staff and board, and communicated vision to funders, partners, and the public. It was a long and inclusive process with many conversations, necessitated by the major change in processes and vision—it was important to move forward collectively. Together, we seized the moment. Since the plan, we designed and constructed a new wing to bridge the functions and narratives of the building and its architecture, and began a process to align all of the museum's spaces, plans, visions, and programs. It was an opportunity to be visionary in not just the overall plan, but in our collections plan, our architecture, our community outreach, and in the experiences we create for visitors. To remove ourselves from insular thinking, we reached outside the institution to focus on community collaborations, engaged with the city in conversations about identity and futures, connected to Arctic research, and established international programs.

At the heart, we embraced risk, innovation, and creativity, and it is in that space, the space where we had to reach far beyond that known and expected, that we actually found safety and sustainability. The museum became a place that mattered to many. Museums of the twenty-first century have to be nimble, agile, and responsive institutions. Only by breaking down our own histories and expectations and reinventing our own ways of doing can we plan for what's ahead. By recognizing that the future is about change, so must we change, too.

ANCHORAGE MUSEUM

Year Founded: 1968

Location: Anchorage, Alaska

Mission Statement: The Anchorage Museum connects people, expands perspectives, and encourages global dialogue about the North and its distinct environment.

Vision Statement: The Anchorage Museum is recognized as a leading center for scholarship, engagement, and investigation of Alaska and the North.

Distinct Characteristics: The museum facilitates dialogue about issues of the North in Alaska and across the Arctic Nations to trigger greater awareness and action. It integrates artists in the ongoing interpretation of the North and intersection of art, the environment, and cultural vitality. The collection includes more than twenty-six thousand objects, including historic and contemporary art of the North and historical and ethnographic pieces dating back to the Russian-American period, plus a strong collection of contemporary Alaska Native art. The Atwood Resource Center holds more than five hundred thousand historic photographs and twelve thousand books, journals, and maps.

Governance: Private nonprofit, 501 (c)(3)

Budget: $13 million

Staff: Sixty-nine full-time, eighteen part-time

Adoption Date of Mission and Vision: 2014

BAY AREA DISCOVERY MUSEUM
Sausalito, California
Written by Karyn Flynn, Chief Executive Officer

I did not understand the power of a mission statement until I stepped off the Board and became the CEO of the Bay Area Discovery Museum (BADM) seven years ago. Our mission statement is our North Star, it provides rigor in measuring investments of our time and resources, both human and financial, and perhaps most importantly, it communicates our promise to the community. It took BADM six years and two changes of mission statement to find the one that accurately represents our work.

The BADM is a multi-faceted children's museum that provides STEM-based, inquiry-driven experiences, both onsite and in the community, that develop creativity and conceptual thinking skills, critical components of problem solving that are too often missing from early childhood education.

All of our programs and exhibitions are backed by research provided by our research division, the Center for Childhood Creativity (CCC). The CCC, launched in 2011, is the missing link between academic research and adults' work with children ages zero to ten years.

Chapter 1: Status Quo is Not an Option

Prior to becoming CEO at BADM, I was a trustee for five years. I assumed my current role in September 2011. At that time, the museum was still recovering from the 2008 economic downturn. While visitation levels had not been severely impacted, the financial situation had been, and to weather the storm, severe cuts had been made to visitor-facing functions. This lack of investment in the onsite experience, coupled with a culture that had become increasingly inward-focused, had led to declining visitor experience scores, a general air of stagnation, and less engagement with the broader community. Clearly, continuing along the same path was not a viable plan.

One of my first actions as CEO was to create a new strategic plan for BADM. Ultimately, this would be the first of two strategic plans within a six-year period. This first plan was created with a two-year lifespan and focused on (1) optimizing organizational efficiency, (2) revitalizing the visitor experience, and (3) launching the CCC. The first two goals were operational in nature and necessary to create a strong foundation for future growth. The third initiative was about developing a big idea around which BADM's future would be built. It was about establishing the CCC, an onsite research center focused on creativity development in early childhood, with the goal of achieving national influence and supporting a bolder, bigger vision.

With the launch of the CCC and a desire to be a more robust community resource for early childhood education, the museum needed a new mission statement that signaled its new ambitions. The mission statement that existed in 2011, "to engage, delight and educate children through exploration of and connection with the local environment and the diverse communities that live here" was too general and did not reflect our evolving work in research.

Our new mission statement needed to communicate not only our shift to being more outwardly focused, but it also needed to be "big enough" to encompass both the museum and the CCC (we are the same 501(c)(3) and share one mission). We also wanted our new mission statement to introduce the institution's new focus on creativity. The first iteration of our new mission statement was "to ignite and advance creative thinking for all children." Reflecting back, the most successful aspects of this new mission statement were that people found it inspiring and it helped us begin to articulate an exciting new future for BADM. Institutionally, this mission statement worked well from 2013 through late 2016.

In 2013, with our new mission in hand and the first two-year strategic plan nearing its end, we engaged a consulting firm to form a new strategic plan. The focus of this plan was to: (1) expand the breadth and depth of engagement with visitors at the museum, (2) expand the breadth and depth of engagement with low income communities in the Bay Area, and (3) advocate for the importance of creativity development in young children through the CCC.

Chapter 2: Defining the Big Problem

As our work evolved over the next three years, I found myself struggling to clearly communicate our value proposition to the community—beyond being a fun place to visit. I knew the answer to this question was vital to our future, and in summer 2016 we engaged a consultant to guide the institution through a Theory of Change exercise. The rigor of this work helped the institution identify the big societal problem we were helping to solve, the larger ecosystem in which we work, our particular role, as well as the other players and potential partners within this environ. To fully understand our new mission, it is important to understand BADM's Theory of Change.

BADM Theory of Change

In the United States, most early childhood learning experiences do not optimize the creative, cognitive, physical, and social emotional capabilities of children. Research shows that early childhood is the most critical time for brain development, when neural pathways are formed that determine how an individual will learn and think throughout their life. Despite a seventeen-dollar return for every dollar invested in early childhood education, our society does not invest enough. As a result, parents and educators often lack the competencies, support, and resources they need to provide research-based, developmentally appropriate learning experiences.

Most early learning experiences do not engage children in deep conceptual and critical thinking or develop their innate curiosity and motivation for learning. Additionally, many children face challenges having their basic needs met, and their engagement can be hampered by physical limitations, social barriers, stressful situations in their home or community, and a lack of access. Underlying all of these conditions are policies and politics, social and economic inequities, and a broader national culture that defines and measures achievement in limited and outmoded terms. As a result, there is not enough emphasis on complex, conceptual thinking at an early age, and young children are not developing the curiosity, resilience, and problem-solving skills they need to approach life's challenges. The subsequent negative impacts reverberate through an individual's life trajectory as well as through society as a whole.

BADM's Specific Role Within this Ecosystem

The BADM transforms research into early learning experiences that inspire creative problem solving. We believe creative problem solving—the flexibility, persistence, and openness to generate and apply novel solutions to challenges—is a fundamental skill best learned in early childhood when brain development and innate curiosity are at their peak. We create environments that promote creative problem-solving through child-directed, hands-on, integrated STEM experiences, which are some of the best ways to teach this skill. In turn, creative problem solving enhances children's learning abilities across all subjects, including the increasingly important fields of STEM. Working across formal and informal learning environments, we serve the diverse learning needs within our immediate and broader community by providing rich experiences for children as well as resources for families and educators. Through our work, we are transforming the way children learn and contribute to the world and raising expectations for the role of early childhood in preparing children to navigate life's complexities.

New Vision and Mission Statements

With our Theory of Change complete, we needed to refine our vision and mission statements to reflect our new clarity of vision and purpose. A board task force was formed and in early 2017 the board voted to adopt the following statements:

- Mission: Our mission is to transform research into early learning experiences that inspire creative problem solving.
- Vision: It is our vision that all children will have early learning experiences that unlock their full potential.

Chapter 3: The Impact of Our Mission on Leadership, Communications, Staffing and Internal Processes, Culture and Values, Financials, and Board Engagement

It has required significant change to implement our new mission and vision. And as everyone knows, true change takes time and is hard for most people. These changes have had an impact on every part of the organization from its leadership, to branding and messaging, to staffing and internal processes, to finances, to our board recruitment, and to culture.

While all of these areas were significantly impacted, perhaps the most important in terms of long-term success was the impact on the museum's culture and values. I had inherited an institution that was risk-averse, was not visitor-focused, did not value its membership base, and was not collaborative. To get to where we wanted to go, we had to act and work differently. We needed to embrace change and risk, to move quickly and decisively without always having all the answers, to work collaboratively and not believe that anyone person had all the right answers. We also had to hold people accountable for results and hold everyone to the same level of expectations. For the first time, it was no longer enough to be passionate about the work or committed to the institution—you had to be able to bring the mission to life and move the museum forward.

Chapter 4: Our Successes and Challenges

Our new mission statement reflects our past challenges and successes as well as our path forward.

BADM today is an institution uniquely poised to bring research about how children learn best to the people who need it most: parents and educators. It is an institution exploring what it means to incorporate technology into high-quality learning experiences through the world's first Early Childhood Fab Lab and our mobile engineering lab (Try It Truck). It is a place where visitors are finding additional value in visiting the museum through participation in our science, maker, and Fab Lab programs as well as our STEM Superhero festival. It is a place working to shift societal perceptions of early childhood through position papers, published by the CCC, on topics such as how to develop creativity, reimagining school readiness and STEM in early childhood.

We have many achievements to celebrate and have successfully overcome many challenges; however, there are some challenges that we will always contend with:

- The ability to attract and retain high-quality staff.
- The high cost of living in the Bay Area.
- The ability to secure funding to support work that has no immediate, tangible return on investment but for which we know there is a very high return on investment in terms of the long-term success of our society.
- The management of a diverse community of stakeholders that all need to move forward at the same speed.

BAY AREA DISCOVERY MUSEUM

Year Founded: 1987

Location: Sausalito, California

Mission Statement: Our mission is to transform research into early learning experiences that inspire creative problem solving.

Vision Statement: It is our vision that all children will have early learning experiences that unlock their full potential.

Distinct Characteristics: Located on 7.5 acres within Golden Gate National Recreation Area, the museum offers experiential learning opportunities for children ages zero to ten years through immersive programming and engaging exhibits. Our educational focus is on developing creative problem solving utilizing the STEM disciplines. We are home of the world's first early childhood Fab Lab (digital makerspace), have a preschool onsite (The Discovery School), and recently launched a mobile experience (The Try It Truck) that serves schools, libraries, and partners out in the community. Our programs and exhibits are informed by our research division, the Center for Childhood Creativity.

Governance: Private, nonprofit 501(c)(3)

Budget: $7.6 million

Staff: Seventy full-time, thirty part-time

Adoption Date of Mission and Vision: 2017

BURKE MUSEUM OF NATURAL HISTORY AND CULTURE

Seattle, Washington

Written by Julie Stein, PhD, Executive Director

A splendid new Burke Museum has risen at the veritable front door of the University of Washington in Seattle. The "New Burke" represents a dramatic departure from the typical natural history museum model—where exhibits are on one side of the wall and collections and research are on the other. In the new museum, visitors will be invited to see and participate in ever-changing activities and daily discoveries. In addition to exhibit galleries, the New Burke includes views into twelve research labs and workrooms, five collections spaces, an artists' workshop, and learning spaces where visitors can engage in hands-on activities and participate in the work of the museum. In the New Burke, 60 percent of the museum will be accessible or visible to visitors, compared to just 30 percent today.

More than a decade of planning laid the foundation for this transformation. With the 2019 grand opening on the horizon, the museum needed a mission statement that reflected continued curatorial and scholarly excellence, and an increased dedication to transparency, public engagement, and community involvement—one that aligned the institution and set a bold direction for its future. Over a six-month period in 2017, the Burke's staff and stakeholders engaged in a collaborative effort to articulate the mission of the New Burke.

Such an enterprise can be challenging in the best of circumstances: how do you capture the deeply held beliefs of a diverse staff and reflect the concerns of a broad set of stakeholders in one sentence, or, following organizational development trends, just a handful of words?

Words are powerful. Their power resides in their ability to express and evoke great emotion. And in 2018—a time when personal concerns and sensitivities are driving powerful social movements such as Black Lives Matter, MeToo, and March for Our Lives—reaching consensus regarding the wording of a mission statement proved to be a challenging (and occasionally divisive) rhetorical exercise.

As real estate agents like to say regarding a home's asking price, its value is a function of "location, location, location." In 2018, the highly debated, carefully selected wording of a mission statement is a function of "context, context, context." What do a statement's words mean precisely at this time—as opposed to fifteen years ago (or fifteen years hence)?

To illustrate: For centuries, the word "discovery" has taken center stage to describe the accomplishments of the Western scientific method. The mysteries of the human genome have been *discovered*. The atomic structure of the atom has been *discovered*. The tectonic shifting of the Earth's continents has been *discovered*. Discover is also perhaps the most common word used by marketing teams for museums, including the Burke, which boasts the tagline: "Discover the Life Before You." Yet the use of the word discover also proves problematic, as some in the community have begun to question how Columbus "discovered" America when it was already widely inhabited, and by extension, how many "discoveries" have been attributed to Western scientists when they have already been known to earlier sophisticated scientific observers who did not hail from western Europe. Thus, words like discover and many others that might seem at first like a natural fit for the Burke's mission statement were rejected under closer scrutiny.

The newly minted 2017 statement of the Burke Museum's mission focuses on people—and to meeting their experiential and emotional needs; whereas the Museum's previous mission, written in 2003, centers on the Burke—what it does and why it invites the community through its doors.

2003 Burke Museum Mission Statement

    The Burke Museum creates a better understanding of the world and our place in it. The museum is responsible for Washington State collections of natural and cultural heritage and sharing the knowledge that makes them meaningful. The Burke welcomes a broad and diverse audience and provides a community gathering place that nurtures life-long learning and encourages respect, responsibility and reflection.

2017 Burke Museum Mission Statement

    The Burke Museum cares for and shares natural and cultural collections so all people can learn, be inspired, generate knowledge, feel joy, and heal.

Incisive reading of the new Burke mission statement reveals the inclusion of two words that rarely appear in museum mission statements: heal and joy. Why were these words and their associated meaning included in today's expression of the Burke's mission? The debate that occurred among the museum's various stakeholders before these human feelings were incorporated into the mission was considerable and difficult.

The sense that the museum should be a place for healing stems from the strongly held feelings—expressed by both the museum's indigenous stakeholders and some staff—that a visit to a museum that holds appropriated cultural heritage is a painful experience. The knowledge that many cultural objects in museums were taken from their rightful owners is a difficult reality to accept. Yet the Burke's efforts to repatriate and create access to many of these objects have fostered strong partnerships between the museum and the Native American and Pacific communities whose cultures are represented in the collections. A mutual understanding that the Burke functions as a respectful steward of these artifacts—preserving and protecting them—enables the region's indigenous peoples to come to a central place, celebrate their culture, and share it with their non-indigenous neighbors. Still, the acute pain of history persists and requires acknowledgment that there is yet the need for considerable healing to take place in order to ameliorate the cultural wounds of the past.

And then, in a response to the call for healing, the concept of joy as a competing emotion for the Burke's seminal experience arose in the minds of other stakeholders. Was it not joyful to see thousands of excited school children experiencing the wonders of the natural world, perhaps for the very first time? Was it not joyful to see Washingtonians of all ages marvel at the art and artistry of the state's indigenous peoples as they developed a deeper appreciation for the cultural heritage of the first people to inhabit our corner of the world?

As one group passionately expressed its need to include a call for healing in the museum's mission and another emphasized the importance of joy, others questioned the efficacy of including any such human-centric emotions at a place they believed should be devoted primarily to scientific research and the creation of new knowledge. The exercise of the scientific method seeks to promote observation, experimentation, and replication of results, and many scientists felt strongly that these emotions diminished the seriousness of their scholarship.

How then do feelings and science co-exist in a museum? Should the Burke's mission statement be a place to air such human emotions? And if so, how best to reconcile such conflicting emotions between those stakeholders who expressed their pain and need for healing and those who felt profound joy whenever they entered the Burke's space?

And thus one can see that, in order to shape the current iteration of the Burke's mission, much passionate, sometimes heated discussion was needed. From these discussions came nuanced understanding of people devoted to fulfilling the many roles of the Burke Museum in the community, and from that understanding came tolerance and appreciation.

Thus, what may have started as an exercise to pare down and modernize the Burke Museum's statement of mission as it moves into its spectacular new space instead evolved into an exercise in deep self-reflection, understanding of the other, and ultra-careful wordsmithing.

The end product acknowledges:

- The Burke's primary mission to protect, preserve, and share its remarkable collections;
- The extraordinary work of the Burke's many science-based divisions and the drive of its curators, collections managers, and visiting scholars to generate new knowledge;
- The historic sorrow of those in the community who honor their ancestors and their culture, and who are triggered by the involuntary appropriation of their cultural heritage; and,
- The sheer exhilaration derived from visiting and working in such a dynamic place as the Burke, which is real and should be celebrated.

Further, it sets aspirational goals for the museum's impact. These goals—that people can learn, be inspired, generate knowledge, feel joy, and heal—are not exhaustive, and the museum will not achieve them every day. But the Burke can and should strive for them, both in its own work and in its interactions with the community.

BURKE MUSEUM OF NATURAL HISTORY AND CULTURE

Year Founded: 1885

Location: Seattle, Washington

Mission Statement: The Burke Museum cares for and shares natural and cultural collections so all people can learn, be inspired, generate knowledge, feel joy, and heal.

Distinct Characteristics: Opening in 2019, the Burke's new, 113,000-square-foot facility will turn the museum "inside-out," breaking down traditional barriers by integrating exhibits with see-through research labs and visible collections storage, thus inviting visitors to be part of a working research museum.

Governance: Administered by the University of Washington College of the Arts and Sciences; supported by the 501(c)(3) Burke Museum Association.

Budget: $12.5 million

Staff: Eighty-nine full-time, sixty part-time

Adoption Date of Mission: 2017

THE CONTEMPORARY JEWISH MUSEUM

San Francisco, California

Written by Lori Starr, Executive Director

Considering the Contemporary Jewish Museum

As a Jewish museum that focuses on changing exhibitions with no permanent collection, the Contemporary Jewish Museum (CJM) is a *kunsthalle*—ever-changing, adventurous, and experimental. Founded in 1984 by local community leaders, it was housed in the Jewish Federation building on Steuart Street in San Francisco and was called the Jewish Community Museum. Contemporary art was the primary focus, and the museum presented important exhibitions such as *The Jewish Identity Project: New American Photography* and *Too Jewish: Challenging Traditional Identities*, both originated by The Jewish Museum, New York. In the late 1990s the museum was offered a chance to take over what was then a de-commissioned former PG&E power substation on Jesse Square as part of the Redevelopment Agency's effort to create the Yerba Buena Community Benefit District, which would be home to the Yerba Buena Center for the Arts, the Children's Discovery Museum, Museum of the African Diaspora, Yerba Buena Gardens and the MLK Memorial, San Francisco Museum of Modern Art, and envisioned someday, a Mexican museum.

The museum hired Polish-Jewish architect Daniel Libeskind, the son of Holocaust survivors, to re-envision the former power station, which has historic designation thanks to its Beaux Arts facade of 1907 designed by Willis Polk after the great earthquake. The Board renamed the museum as the Contemporary Jewish Museum prior to its opening to the public in June 2008. It forged its mission statement, which reads:

The CJM makes the diversity of the Jewish experience relevant for a twenty-first century audience. We accomplish this through innovative exhibitions and programs that educate, challenge, and inspire.

Libeskind was asked to design a museum that would respect the industrial past of the power station while at the same time express optimism around the Jewish future. And thus the building itself proclaims on its roofline in Hebrew: Chai or Life. Other architectural elements evoke Jewish concepts. The thirty-six-window Yud references the numerology of eighteen, which in Jewish mysticism also means "life" only in the Yud, twice as much. The thirty-six windows also refer to the thirty-six "righteous ones" of the Hebrew Bible—only these many are needed to save the world. And perhaps the most spellbinding architectural element of all is Libeskind's Pardes Wall in the lobby. The wall tilts forward toward the historic brick interior—the new meeting up with the old. In Hebrew, Pardes means, in its most simple form, "orchard." With its fluorescent lights that spell out the word, the Pardes Wall beckons the visitor, saying "the fruit of learning lies beyond."

It is with this language rooted in Jewish teaching that the CJM thrives as a changing exhibitions and programmatic space, a place of convening and celebration, and an iconic landmark amid this now bustling neighborhood, which in 2019 will see the vast expansion of the Moscone Convention Center, along with the Transbay Terminal and Salesforce Tower. Thousands more will crowd these streets and encounter the CJM. In anticipation, the CJM has embarked on a new phase in its evolution.

For the first five years in its new facility, the museum experimented primarily with the presentation of traveling exhibitions such as *Houdini, Curious George, Maira Kalman*, and *Kehinde Wiley: World Stage Israel*, and developed an ambitious school and family program and one of the only paid teen internships in any U.S. museum.

In 2014, the CJM created its first strategic business plan and sharpened its exhibition and program philosophy. More emphasis would be placed on originating exhibitions, publishing about them, and touring them. Programming would live on the Jewish spectrum and in Jewish "time." Some exhibitions would be deep on the Jewish spectrum; others not so much but inspired by Jewish ideas. Examples of the former began to roll out in original exhibitions such as *Designing Home: Jews and Mid-Century Modernism, Arthur Szyk and the Art of the Haggadah,* and *Archie Rand: The 613.* These were deep on the Jewish spectrum. In contrast, other original exhibitions would ask big questions. *Night Begins the Day: Rethinking Time, Space, and Beauty* queried "what is this earth and what is humanity's place in it?" *N.E.A.T: New Experiments in Art and Technology* revisited a legendary exhibition of the 1970s; this time, though, it asked the question "What is it about the Bay Area that has inspired so many artists to create work based in digitization and mechanized forms?" And to complement these original exhibitions with their digital and print publications, the CJM brought to the Bay Area exhibitions that would not have come here otherwise. *Stanley Kubrick: The Exhibition* is one such example. While this major traveling show has appeared in museums around the world, the CJM was the first and only Jewish museum to present it. It provided an opportunity to study Kubrick as a Bronx-born Jew whose art was forged via his life experiences of the 1930s and 1940s and the dawn of the digital age. The Kubrick exhibition provided the springboard for the CJM to engage with Jewish theologians and film historians in an altogether unique way—to interpret his work through a Jewish prism. In this respect, the CJM began to see itself as an originator of new Jewish scholarship and a cultural innovator.

The museum continued to experiment with original exhibitions while exploring Jewish cultural figures, such as Amy Winehouse, Bill Graham the legendary rock promoter, San Francisco native Rube Goldberg, and New Yorker cartoonist Roz Chast, through traveling exhibitions from other museums. Simultaneously, new work from contemporary artists were commissioned for exhibitions such as *Jewish Folktales Retold: Artist as Maggid* and thematic exhibitions of selected artists' works such as *From Generation to Generation: Inherited Memory and Contemporary Art.* This latter example illustrates what the CJM has come to do best: engage with a topic of exploration such as the role of trauma and its impact on the lives of artists who have not experienced it first-hand but instead have "inherited" this trauma through their families. At the heart of this show were works by Jewish artists who had inherited the trauma of the Holocaust, and it branched out to present artists of other heritages who also had experienced inherited trauma—of the Vietnam War, of the Armenian Genocide, or simply the fantasy of planetary trauma as in Mike Kelley's Kandor.

The success of these exhibitions depended upon the way in which they were conceptualized—not by the curatorial team in a vacuum but in dialogue with the museum's educators, programmers, marketing team, and specialists in access and inclusion. This holistic approach, driven by an institutional culture that places the highest value on dialogue, debate, and collective creativity, serves the CJM well. Since the 2016 election, the staff has intensified its commitment to multiple perspectives, propelling us further as an activist museum that originates content to advance civil dialogue. Our access programs include people of all abilities, and we are only one of two museums in California who have a full-time access coordinator. In this spirit, the museum is now developing two exhibitions of tremendous relevance to Jews and non-Jews alike. We are looking at two Jewish female figures of the Hebrew bible to inspire two exhibitions. Queen Esther of the Purim Story reveals herself as a Jew to her husband the king and in doing so, saves her people. Inspired by this "revealing of self," the museum is presenting an original exhibition, *Show Me as I Want to be Seen,* the first exhibition by a Jewish museum on the topic of gender, gender representation, queer, and other nonbinary identities. The other exhibition, *Femme(inist) Fatale* is centered on the character of Salome, the Jewess temptress who fascinated artists of the late nineteenth and early twentieth century. Public programs will allow for unpacking of this topic in light of the #MeToo movement. In this way, the CJM forges new territory as a museum of constant change and hybridity that mirrors the complexity of contemporary life in dialogue with Jewish historical narratives.

The museum could not have embarked on this trajectory without benefiting from the Jewish intellectual capital of the Bay Area in particular. In consultation with Jewish philosophers, historians, and theologians, the CJM is creating a new kind of synergy that explores where Jewish ideas meet up with art and where art meets up with Jewish ideas. In 2016, the museum inaugurated its "incubator" space—the Helen Diller Institute. Within its *Beit Midrash* (house of learning), the CJM is able to host visiting scholars who engage in exhibition development and educate staff and volunteers. Here we also teach a museum studies class and a museums and social justice class, and host a multitude of community organizations. The institute situates the curatorial, education, and creative services team in close proximity with areas for prototyping activities for the expanding school and family audience, and visiting scholar space. This gift has proven transformative in helping the CJM to become not only an activist museum elucidating topics of the time, but also a research institution that can keep asking, "What is the Jewish museum of the future?"

THE CONTEMPORARY JEWISH MUSEUM

Year Founded: 1984

Location: San Francisco, California

Mission Statement: The Contemporary Jewish Museum makes the diversity of the Jewish experience relevant for a twenty-first century audience. We accomplish this through innovative exhibitions and programs that educate, challenge, and inspire.

Distinct Characteristics: Since its founding in 1984, the CJM, a noncollection institution, has distinguished itself as a welcoming place where visitors can connect with one another through dialogue and shared experiences with the arts. Through our exhibitions, publications, public programs, and visitor-centric educational experiences, the CJM interprets exhibition themes through a Jewish lens and engages with a wide and diverse audience, over half of whom do not identify as Jewish.

Governance: Private, nonprofit 501(c)(3)

Budget: $8.15 million

Staff: Forty-three full-time, sixty-five part-time

Adoption Date of Mission: 2008

THE ARQUIVES (FORMALLY THE CANADIAN LESBIAN AND GAY ARCHIVES)
Toronto, Ontario, Canada
Written by Raegan Swanson, Executive Director

What do you do when your organization's mandate no longer aligns with its name? This question has occupied the minds of the Canadian Lesbian and Gay Archives' (CLGA) staff and volunteers for the past few years. Since 1993—when our name was last changed—the LGBTQ2+ initialism has evolved and grown. Despite growing understandings of a larger, varied, intersecting, and—somewhat ironically, terminologically speaking—heterogeneous queer and trans community, however, the name of our institution remained the same.

The CLGA was established in 1973 by *The Body Politic*—one of Canada's most influential LGBT magazines, in print from 1971 to 1987—editorial collective. *The Body Politic* and the Archives became separate entities in the first years of the Archives' operation. The organization was named the Canadian Gay Liberation Movement Archives, and then became the Canadian Gay Archives in 1975; its descriptive title read: "For lesbians and gay men," as it was noted by some that the name gave the impression that women were not represented in the collection. The Canadian Gay Archives incorporated in 1980, received charitable status in 1981, and adopted its current name in 1993. The CLGA volunteer team has always been at the heart of our organization and, in 2017, over 160 volunteers gave 13,000 hours assisting with collections, communications, fundraising, community engagement, and administrative work. The CLGA now has three staff members, including an executive director, community outreach coordinator, and an administrative assistant.[3]

To understand where the CLGA is today, we must review the history of our organization and mandates. In 1975, a statement of purpose was created for the Canadian Gay Archives: "A conspiracy of silence has robbed gay men and lesbians of their history. A sense of continuity which derives from the knowledge of a heritage is essential for the building of self-confidence in a community. It is a necessary tool in the struggle for social change." To fight this silence, the Canadian Gay Archives would be responsible for:

> The collection, preservation, and arrangement of information and materials in any medium by and about gay people, with emphasis on Canada; and the encouragement of and assistance in the use of this material, as well as assistance in the search for new sources.

In 1995, the CLGA worked to review and update the mandate that had been in place for twenty years. In 1997, the new mandate was introduced:

> The Canadian Lesbian and Gay Archives was established to aid in the recovery and preservation of our histories. Its mandate is to acquire, preserve, organize and give public access to information and materials in any medium, by and about lesbians and gays, primarily produced in or concerning Canada. To support this function the Archives also maintains major non-archival collections including a research library, international subject files, and international collection of gay and lesbian periodicals.

At our Annual General Meeting on May 29, 2017, a CLGA volunteer made a motion to set the name change process into action. The hope was to select a new name for the organization that would better suit its mandate. In 2016 and 2017, the CLGA went through a strategic planning process in which we reviewed our mandate and vision, and updated it to better reflect our reality and equitable aspirations. Today, our mandate is to:

- Acquire, preserve, organize, and give public access to information and materials in any medium, by and about LGBTQ2+ people, primarily produced in or concerning Canada; and,
- Maintain a research library, international research files, and an international collection of LGBTQ2+ periodicals.

Assisted by the recently updated mandate, the Name Change Steering Committee worked with consultants to select a name.

This update in particular was necessary, especially the inclusion of the number "2" to represent 2-Spirit Indigenous Communities in Canada. Although the CLGA had some small collections related to 2-Spirit community members, their communities were—and continue to be—woefully underrepresented in our collection. In addition to adding the "2" to our mandate, the CLGA has adopted and begun using a traditional land acknowledgment. This acknowledgment is now as important as our mandate and vision, and holds the CLGA accountable to respect the traditional lands on which we operate.

> The Canadian Lesbian and Gay Archives is located on the traditional lands of the Mississaugas of the New Credit First Nation, the Haudenosaunee, the Anishnaabe and the Huron-Wendat. Today, Toronto is still the home to many Indigenous people from across Turtle Island and we are grateful to have the opportunity to work on this land. The CLGA strives to gather the stories of the unheard and silenced voices of the 2SLGBTQ+ first peoples of this land. We acknowledge that some stories have already been lost, and we aim to ensure that those that remain and those that are to come are preserved for the future.

On May 7, 2018, the CLGA announced that our new name would be The Arquives, with a descriptor reading "Canada's LGBTQ2+ Archive." The name change process was an arduous affair. The Steering Committee, comprised of four volunteers and one staff member, guided the consultants during the nine-month process. The CLGA wanted the name to align with the vision and values of the organization, as well as our mandate. We were also conscious of avoiding terminology that might become obsolete, given that the initialism "LGBTQ2+" changes regularly. As such, we wanted the legal name to be a set word or phrase that could flexibly accommodate changes in LGBTQ2+ communities and the possibility of a changing mandate.

The CLGA is routinely asked by the public and LGBTQ2+ communities to provide tours, history lessons, and gallery space for queer artists. In the coming years, we hope to be able to meet the demand of the public by finding a new building that will allow us to become a functioning museum and exhibition space in addition to our traditional archival collecting, description, and reference services. As we have thousands of artifacts and ephemera in our collection already, this seems like a natural next step in the evolution of our name and mandate. In the future, our descriptor could read something like: "Canada's LGBTQ2+ Archive, Library, and Museum." With a set name, the descriptor can align with our mandate and respond to societal changes. The final element is our tagline and our slogan, which we chose not to change as it still reflects our mandate: "Keeping our stories alive!"

The Steering Committee and Board of Directors understood that not everyone would agree with the chosen name, no matter which was chosen. The CLGA means different things to different people; however, the chosen name would have to gather meaning through the actions and programming of the CLGA and its volunteers. Changing the name gave us an opportunity to show LGBTQ2+ communities that we are actively trying to make our space and collections more inclusive. Trans, bisexual, queer, and 2-spirit folks are no longer left out of the name, which is often prospective visitors', volunteers', and donors' first point of engagement with our organization. We have consciously paired our name change with new community outreach programming—specifically, hiring individuals from underrepresented communities to help us engage with the material that we have and work with us to build a collection that better represents LGBTQ2+ communities in Canada.

Reviewing the past mandates of the CLGA is an important action that reminds us of our journey. The mandate has grown more inclusive and has changed to better fit the communities we work to represent. The silence of LGBTQ2+ histories, which was so prevalent when the organization was formed, has changed as well: Some of that history is no longer silenced, with the records of various experiences being housed at the CLGA. We also acknowledge that our collection is not as representative as it should be, with those who live within the intersections and margins of our communities still facing silence and persecution. The name of our organization, its mandate, its vision, its tagline, and the land acknowledgment will be used collectively to introduce the Arquives to our next generation of volunteers, donors, and researchers; to safeguard and keep alive LGBTQ2+ histories in Canada; and to end the silence for those who have been and those who continue to be oppressed.

THE ARQUIVES

Year Founded: 1973

Location: Toronto, Ontario

Vision Statement: The Canadian Lesbian and Gay Archives aspires to be a significant resource and catalyst for those who strive for a future world where lesbian, gay, bisexual, and trans people are accepted, valued, and celebrated.

Mandate: The Canadian Lesbian and Gay Archives was established to aid in the recovery and preservation of our histories. Its mandate is to:

- Acquire, preserve, organize, and give public access to information and materials in any medium, by and about LGBTQ2+ people, primarily produced in or concerning Canada;
- Maintain a research library, international research files, and an international collection of LGBTQ2+ periodicals.

Distinct Characteristics: Largest independent LGBTQ2+ archives in the world.

Governance: Working Board of Directors

Budget: 450,000 CND

Staff: Three full-time

Adoption Date of Vision: 2017

EASTERN STATE PENITENTIARY HISTORIC SITE
Philadelphia, Pennsylvania
Written by Sean Kelley, Senior Vice President

We didn't set out to write a new mission statement. We liked our mission statement, clumsy and wordy as it was.

It was 2016, and we had been evolving quickly. As we set to writing a new strategic plan, our mission statement seemed to be serving its purpose just fine. We didn't realize how much we had outgrown it.

We had opened Eastern State Penitentiary to the public in 1994 in a state of true ruin. In the year of the opening, the abandoned prison had no running water, no climate control anywhere on the property, and virtually no electricity. A single telephone line ran behind a donated wooden desk, and the first time it rang it seemed like a minor miracle. We required every visitor to wear a hard hat and sign a waiver stating that risks—including death—were inherent to entering the building. We were open 110 days that first year with just over 10,000 visitors.

We eventually wrote a standard "kitchen sink" mission statement, listing historic preservation first, providing public access to the building second, telling the stories of men and women who lived and worked in the building third, and, finally, "creating a neutral public forum where issues of contemporary corrections can be addressed." The mission felt largely aspirational.

That "neutral public forum" proved to be the real challenge, although it wouldn't become completely unworkable for many years.

Over time, we raised more than sixteen million dollars in capital funding, addressing the most critical historic preservation and life-safety issues. We added visitor amenities. We expanded our hours to 361 days a year. Our annual historic site audience grew to more than a quarter of a million visitors, with an additional one hundred thousand visitors attending a Halloween fundraiser that provided the bulk of the organization's operating revenue. We researched forgotten stories and complex historical narratives, produced an audio tour, and developed a guided tour program rooted in dialogue. The first three elements of our mission required many years of focused work, of course, and will never be "complete." But these elements didn't trigger institutional soul-searching.

To address the fourth element, the neutral public forum on contemporary issues, we partnered with artists. Beginning nearly at the start of public tours, in 1995, we commissioned site-specific art installations to encourage reflection on the history and contemporary legacy of Eastern State Penitentiary. To date there have been nearly one hundred artist installations on the site.

Artist Virgil Marti created a memorial for Oscar Wilde, whose 1895 conviction for homosexuality and incarceration in a prison modeled after Eastern State Penitentiary outraged our visitors a century later and triggered inevitable comparisons to current policy debates. Nick Cassway's *Portraits of Inmates in the Death Row Population Sentenced as Juveniles* (2005) reflected on capital punishment. William Cromar's *GTMO* (2006) engaged our visitors in discussions about the rule of law and role of the courts in detention and incarceration, using the U.S. facility at Guantanamo Bay as a reference point. Michelle Handelman's *Beware the Lily Law* (2009) illuminated the plight of transgender individuals in the U.S. prison system today. Jesse Krimes' *Apokaluptein16389067:II* presented a thirty-nine-panel mural the artist created on smuggled bedsheets during his incarceration in federal prison.

But we, as an institution, were virtually silent on anything that happened after the last man was transferred out of Eastern State Penitentiary in 1971. We didn't address the war on drugs. We didn't discuss mandatory minimum sentences. We didn't draw our visitors' attention to the United States' truly historic expansion of its prison population, creating the highest rate of incarceration in the world by far. We didn't illustrate that the shameful racial disparity in the prison population throughout Eastern State Penitentiary's history was actually growing *worse* in recent decades, in an era that many Americans were now beginning to call "mass incarceration."

Indeed, even as issues of criminal justice increasingly became seen as the civil rights issue of our times, our exhibits and tour content remained squarely trained on events at least forty years in the past. We were, after all, a neutral public forum.

Things changed quickly. Creating an interpretive plan in 2010—our first—forced us to look more critically at our choices. How much did we know about our visitors' take on "neutrality," anyway? We finally began to ask them. We rewrote the conclusion of our audio tour, now addressing the changes to laws and enforcement that drove the massive growth of the prison population since 1970, and the fact that the United States alone has chosen this strategy.

In 2014 we built *The Big Graph*, a massive infographic sculpture that illustrates these patterns, and added the racial breakdown of the prison population over time. We feared that the statistics on the graph regarding race and the U.S. prison population could be used by some visitors to reinforce ugly and hateful stereotypes. We chose, therefore, to use the word "crisis" when discussing the racial disparities in our justice system on signage and in the main audio tour script that accompanies the graph.

What Should Our Nation Do to Address This Crisis?

We developed two "nonnegotiables" to support our frontline staff when interpreting prisons today—one, that the U.S. overincarcerates its citizens, with no justifiable public safety results, and two, that the racial disparities in our system are unnatural and an indication of injustice.

Were we still a neutral public forum? Not all of our interpretive staff felt so. Although most embraced the new direction, two out of twelve eventually left. To our surprise and relief, however, in summative evaluation, the vast majority of visitors reported that the graph, even with its word "crisis," felt "neutral."

But things got more complex. As we built a companion exhibit to the graph, the goal of neutrality became un-workable. The new exhibit, with its intentionally balanced-sounding title *Prisons Today: Questions in the Age of Mass Incarceration*, forced us to be honest about what our board and staff had come to see as a basic truth: there are too many Americans in prison. The exhibit was going to illustrate the very weak link between rates of incarceration and violent crime rates. It was going to highlight states such as New York, New Jersey, California, and Texas that were already lowering their prison populations and their violent crime rates, simultaneously. And the exhibit was going to illustrate how a refusal to look beyond emotion, to evidence, had doomed a generation of lawmakers to making very poor decisions for public policy.

Were we really going to say, "on the one hand . . . but on the other" about the war on drugs and mandatory minimum sentences? Increasingly, that felt patronizing. An honest look at our programming over the previous twenty years led to the uncomfortable conclusion that in most cases our version of "neutrality" had taken the form of silence.

At a critical, but unanimous, meeting of the Board of Directors in December of 2016, we decided to drop the pretense, on this one specific point, of neutrality. The exhibit would open with the statement, "Mass Incarceration Isn't Working."

We were evolving in other ways too. We began to quietly hire formerly incarcerated individuals to put a human face on mass incarceration policies. Our new guides can describe their personal experiences to visitors when the subject comes up. Preparing for that program brought many of us into prisons to seek input. One advisor, a reentry specialist who had himself been incarcerated in state prison, joined our Board of Directors.

Our nation incarcerates 2.2 million people, and yet there is no national prison museum. By the fall of 2016, already a year into writing a new strategic plan, and with our mass incarceration exhibit garnering attention from policy makers and museum professionals, we realized that we were the closest thing our nation has.

In 2015, a committee of Board and staff members, the Strategic Planning Committee, selected an outside contractor to assist us in writing a new strategic plan. It became clear almost immediately that our mission statement was out of date. Once we really looked at it, it was clear the contractor was right. We were already pursuing a far more ambitious vision than our current mission outlined. And the word "neutral" jumped off the page.

The committee started with a strategic vision statement. This twelve-page document went through multiple overhauls during the course of a year, with extensive input from frontline staff, administrative staff, Board members, colleagues from partner organizations, and other stakeholders. This document eventually served as the framework for a new, single-sentence mission statement, a single-sentence vision statement, and a ten-point statement of organizational values.

Civil rights attorney and founder of the Legacy Museum Bryan Stevenson says of social justice work, "Proximity is important." Our network of advisors, including formerly and currently incarcerated people, policy experts, lawmakers, victim advocates, and reentry professionals, and our time spent visiting prisons and community advocacy organizations, have inspired the growth that has led to our new mission and vision.

Neither a social service agency nor an advocacy organization, we find now that we are the stewards of a unique platform to reach an audience that is largely disengaged from deep conversations about criminal justice, race, poverty, and our ever-evolving prison system.

We welcome this challenge.

EASTERN STATE PENITENTIARY

Year Founded: 1999

Location: Philadelphia, Pennsylvania

Mission Statement: Eastern State Penitentiary Historic Site interprets the legacy of American criminal justice reform, from the nation's founding through to the present day, within the long-abandoned cell blocks of the nation's most historic prison.

Vision Statement: Eastern State Penitentiary's innovative preservation, interpretation, and public programs will move visitors to engage in dialogue and deepen the national conversation about criminal justice.

Distinct Characteristics: This historic prison museum incorporates contemporary perspectives on criminal justice into all aspects of its exhibits and public programming. While remaining nonpartisan, the Eastern State leadership team has moved decisively away from claims of "neutrality." Programs include an award-winning exhibit on mass incarceration and a team of formerly incarcerated tour guides to help humanize conversations about criminal justice today. The site is maintained as a "stabilized ruin" and experienced 400 percent attendance growth between 2007 and 2017.

Governance: 501(c)(3) corporation managing property owned by the City of Philadelphia

Budget: $10.6 Million

Staff: Fifty-five full-time, forty part-time

Adoption Date of Mission, Vision, and Values: 2017

KAʻALA FARM

Waiʻanae Valley, Hawaiʻi

Written by Kay Fukuda with Eric Enos, Executive Director

A Place of Refuge and Healing

Many Native Hawaiians from the Waiʻanae side see the cultural landscape of the Upper Waiʻanae Valley as a modern-day puʻuhonua, a way to link to the past, stabilize their lives, and direct their future. Kaʻala Farm perpetuates this philosophy with programs that promote healing through connection with the land, interaction between people of different generations, and centering oneself around a collective purpose.

People find their calling at Kaʻala Farm. Restoring the loʻi is like putting meat back on the "bones" of the stone terraces that were once cultivated by Native Hawaiians. Kaʻala Farm provides a space for Native Hawaiians and other groups to come together and discuss common challenges and ways forward. It is a place where traditional values and practices are integrated into education, food, and health-based initiatives.

In June 2012, a fire that began in Lualualei spread into the back of Waiʻanae Kai Valley and consumed the waterlines, the Hale Naʻauao, and edges of the edible forest of Kaʻala Farm. With the help of community, the waterlines have been restored, the Hale rebuilt, and the edible forest expanded to include ʻohana gardens.

Many disasters, whether natural or manmade, can strike quickly, like fires and storms, or they can grow and make communities unwell. Symptoms like obesity, poor health, increased school drop-out rates, homelessness, joblessness, domestic violence, etc., can be seen and felt in the community. These traumas are often passed down to the youth, who become the next victims of what can become a cycle. We saw a pressing need to address the root causes of poor health and well-being, and to help families develop wellness and the skills to rebuild community. Communities need to be safe and healthy places to raise families; that should be everyone's birthright. The rebuilding of Kaʻala was more than the creation of structures and garden; it was the beginning of rebuilding of community with a sense of place and cultural wellness.

We realized that in order for communities to be healthy, the land needs to be healthy. There needed to be Ua Mau Ke Ea O Ka Aina I Ka Pono (Justice for the ʻAina). We created a manifesto to bring back ola (life) to our ʻaina (land) and reconnect our ʻohana nui (extended family) to growing and eating healthy traditional food.

- We believe water rights are our kuleana to value, manage, and share.
- We believe land has its own rights that need to be honored. By giving rights to the land, we give rights to us all. Healthy land grows healthy people.
- We believe food justice guarantees access to affordable healthy food for all of Hawaii's people. Healthy food is more than a commodity; it is a basic right.
- We believe economic justice creates opportunities so that each person has enough resources to have a dignified, productive, and creative life.
- We believe educational justice is the passing of knowledge that recognizes the experience and dignity of learners and their culture, and balances the competition for life's resources and rewards.
- We believe kalo and other traditional food brings people together and supports the relationship of ohana with appreciation for our ʻaumakua (ancestors).
- Kalo for Justice—kalo is linked to water rights under the constitution for traditional and customary uses; streams have rights to water, kalo has rights to water, then people have rights to water.

With this manifesto and as stewards of a land asset in Upper Waiʻanae Valley, Kaʻala Farm recognized the tremendous potential for community involvement and positive outcomes flowing from shared resources. First, Kaʻala

Farm provides access to the land and technical support to separately staffed partner organizations whose missions align with Ka'ala Farm's, and, second, weaves together the resources in the Wai'anae Valley.

We envisioned Ka'ala Farm as the "University of Ka'ala," where people engage in teaching, learning, research, and practice. This new model facilitated the participation of many groups and organizations for lo'i restoration, planting, growing, and cultural/educational activities at Ka'ala Farm.

We also realized that this vision was beyond the physical boundaries of Ka'ala Farm. Ka'ala Farm was only one resource, and there were many community resources in Wai'anae.

It is a special place. We understood that with all these resources, the Wai'anae Valley has the potential to be a place of rebirth and renewal. There was a need to weave together these abundant resources.

We asked:

- What are the steps that need to be taken to move the Wai'anae Coast from a poverty mentality to one of wellness?
- How do we build and act on what we have learned?
- How do we activate the community?
- How do we create community stewards?

There was a need for a paradigm shift. To shift away from segmented, short-term programs to more holistic programs that are multi-dimensional and target the community at different level.

One way was to walk in each other's footsteps, to understand other perspectives and viewpoints. From there find ways to create piko where 'ohana live, work, and play on the 'aina, to create healthy keiki, communities, and futures.

We wanted to find out what was going on in the community. It was decided to conduct a series of huaka'i (travel to sites with a defined purpose) within the Wai'anae Moku. The purpose of these huaka'i was to provide opportunities for Wai'anae organizations, agencies, schools, businesses, families, and youth to experience the coastal areas, streams, forests, and mountains of the Moku, and to learn about the history and culture of these lands. The theme of these huaka'i was "Follow the Water"—to find and restore community and natural resource abundance. Five very successful huaka'i have been conducted and have provided an opportunity for community members and others to fully experience the challenges and successes on the Wai'anae Coast. They have looked at community resources (natural, people, programs) and seen what is out there, shared insights, and discussed ideas.

As a result, old partnerships have been re-energized and new partnerships are developing between academics, government agencies, Native Hawaiian trusts, and a variety of community-based organizations. Ka'ala Farm has seen increased interest, activity, and people on the land. This has increased the amount of community engagements and networking by Ka'ala leadership personnel. This dynamic process has solidified the leadership role of Ka'ala Farm on the Wai'anae Coast.

These activities have had a two-fold effect on Ka'ala staff: the expansion of programs and groups at Ka'ala Farm, and increased community networking. The expansion of programs has required more management oversight, evaluation of various groups' requests for access to the land, and establishment of protocols for continued involvement. Increased community networking has taken away staff time from directly working in the field. However, this has provided opportunities for diversification of funding streams and leveraging of additional resources.

We realize that this is a long process with much to learn and much to share. However, things are moving in the right direction. We are weaving ideas and elements together to create a basket of abundance. There is still much to do. Coming together in the spirit of lokahi (harmony and unity) is the next step. As the community looks forward and learns more, the sharing this new knowledge will move the community towards "Justice for the 'Aina" and, in turn, holistic wellness. This maybe a long journey, but there is much to be gained.

Mahalo nui loa and Aloha 'aina.

The History and Culture of the Upper Wa'anae Valley:

- Land, water, knowledge, skills, experience, relationships, partners, alliances.
- Natural Area Reserves on O'ahu. Within these areas one can find rare endemic plants and animals, many of which are on the edge of extinction.
- Abundant sunshine, expansive beaches, fresh water, and ample land are some of the Wai'anae Coast natural resources.
- The area is rich with cultural sites and knowledge.
- It is the birthplace of O'ahu. It is the birthplace of the god Maui.
- It has the largest population of Native Hawaiians in the world.
- There are many cultural practitioners, productive farms, and able fishermen.
- There is knowledge passed down from generation to generation.
- A relearning of Native knowledge is occurring.

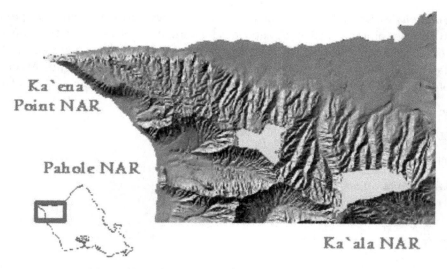

Ka'ena Point NAR

Pahole NAR

Ka'ala NAR

O'ahu Natural Area Reserves

Photo source: http://dlnr.hawaii.gov/eco

KA'ALA FARM

Year Founded: 1976

Location: Wai'anae Valley, Hawai'i

Mission Statement: The mission of Ka'ala Farm, Inc. is to reclaim and preserve the living culture of the Po'e Kahiko (people of old) in order to strengthen the kinship relationships between the 'aina (land, that which nourishes) and all forms of life necessary to sustain the balance of life on these venerable lands.

Values Statement: Ka'ala Farm, Inc.'s restorative work is embodied by the saying: "If you plan for a year, plant kalo. If you plan for ten years, plant koa. If you plan for a hundred years, teach the children aloha 'aina."

Distinct Characteristics: Ka'ala Farm provides a space for Native Hawaiians and other groups to come together and discuss common challenges and ways forward. It is a place where traditional values and practices are integrated into education, food, and health-based initiatives. Located on the Waianae Coast, Ka'ala Farm is situated between the ocean and the peaks of the Waianae Mountains. It has three natural area reserves, many cultural sites, and a dramatic coastline. It is the birthplace of O'ahu.

Governance: Private, nonprofit 501(c)(3)

Budget: $390,000

Staff: Six full-time, three part-time

Adoption Date of Mission and Values: 1983

MINNEAPOLIS INSTITUTE OF ART

Minneapolis, Minnesota

Written by Kaywin Feldman, Duncan and Nivin MacMillan Director and President,
with Karleen Gardner, Director of Learning Innovation

Changing the Museum for a Changing World

In 2006, the Minneapolis Institute of Art (Mia) opened a one hundred million dollar building expansion with the goal of putting more of the collection on view and thereby doubling attendance. In fact, the new building had absolutely no effect on visitor numbers; it was the wrong answer to the wrong question. The museum's challenge was not the percentage of art on view in the galleries; it was the lack of a compelling mission and dynamic strategic direction. The mission statement at the time identified the museum's purpose as "to be the leading art museum in the country." This statement did not describe a motivational mission with external impact, but instead reflected an internal need for validation and recognition—which is not a mission.

Almost simultaneously, the speed of societal, technological, demographic, and economic change began to increase at an astonishing speed. After the end of the Cold War, the U.S. Army War College developed the acronym VUCA to describe the new context in which the world operates, with four distinct challenges:

- Volatility
- Uncertainty
- Complexity
- Ambiguity

The business community quickly adopted VUCA as a clarion call for agile and aware leadership since leaders must remain bold but flexible in the midst of a volatile, uncertain, complex, and ambiguous world. Museums have to not only embrace change, but also anticipate it, constantly scanning the external environment and consumer trends in order to inform strategy and adapt tactics.

The days of primarily preserving and perpetuating an institution—"keep on keepin' on"—have passed and the status quo is actually the riskiest place to be. Museums must be adept at harvesting and understanding data and also analyzing contemporary trends. Armed with this information, they need to create agile strategic plans that are constantly examined and repeatedly challenged. The days of the ten-year "long-range plan" binders are over. At Mia, our strategic plans never have more than three strategic directions, which can all be explained on a single page. While we remain committed to the strategic directions, our tactics to get there change regularly, enabling us to remain agile and opportunistic.

A New Mission Statement

In 2008, Mia's Board adopted a new mission statement, empowering us to "enrich the community by collecting, preserving, and making accessible outstanding works of art from the world's diverse cultures." The community is rooted firmly in the center of our mission and remains the focus of Mia's work. As a 103-year-old encyclopedic art museum, collecting and preserving outstanding works from across the globe also remain core. Just as important is making our collection and content accessible to everyone, which we do through free admission and a visitor-centered approach in exhibitions, installations, and programs. Ultimately, it is Mia's vision to "inspire wonder through the power of art."

Dynamic New Approach, 2012–2016

With the understanding that the traditional museum model was no longer sustainable, the *Dynamic New Approach (DNA)* identified innovative ways for Mia to adapt. A significant part of the development of this plan included an analysis of current cultural, social, economic, technological, and political trends affecting museums and the market and rich discussions among staff and stakeholders.

In considering the current trends in philanthropy and membership, the museum recognized that a new financial model must incorporate additional ways to raise revenue and build loyalty, which would diversify Mia's financial structure and use data in decision making related to the market and participant behaviors. Changing consumer behavior demanded that we integrate a dynamic museum experience across all modes of interaction; museum consumers are no longer just visitors—they are active participants and influencers of content and brand. They may be participating onsite, offsite, or digitally. Limited leisure time also meant that visitors brought heightened expectations for engaging experiences offering meaning, relevance, and surprise.

The plan contained three key directions:

- Audience engagement maximizes new opportunities to attract and engage audiences through innovative programming, expanded partnerships, participatory activities, and greater online development.
- Globalization will enable Mia to "globalize the local and localize the global" through topical and responsive programming and collection development.
- Museum, Inc. adopts a twenty-first-century business model that focuses on the participant, diversifies revenue, and leverage opportunities presented by convergence and technology.

The ultimate goal of the DNA was to maximize the community's use of the museum, its collection and programs, and find new ways to attract and engage audiences in meaningful ways. Some highlights of the results of the DNA include the following:

- Clearly defined and enhanced our brand, which is now consistently represented across the organization and easily recognized by our public;
- Designed an entirely new lobby and entry experience;
- Created a new membership model which includes a free level, therefore eliminating financial barriers to participation;
- Began the process of implementing a new customer relationship management software platform to support data-driven management of Mia's visitors;
- Established a cross-functional collaborative team approach for exhibition development and interpretation, digital content initiatives, content strategy, and customer relationship management and loyalty program; and
- Developed new audience-centered, participatory, and experimental approaches and processes for our permanent collection.

Organizational Culture

"Culture eats strategy for breakfast."

—*Peter Drucker*

During the early phase of this plan, we recognized that we needed to enhance our capabilities and organizational culture to support this work. The alignment of strategy, capabilities, and culture are crucial for true organizational change.

We looked to the corporate world for models of culture plans and found inspiration in those of Netflix, Zappos, and Zingerman's. Using these examples, we engaged in rich discussions and formalized and articulated what we were already doing best and identified attributes that reflect the character and personality of our organization. We now embed our culture into museum practices, including new staff onboarding, job descriptions, hiring practices, staff recognition, and performance reviews.

Mia Culture Statement

The Mia is an audience-centered institution where everyone provides excellent service and cultivates honest and positive relationships. We value:

- Generosity
- Agility
- Emotional intelligence
- Positive energy
- Drives results

Mia culture determines our:

- Engagement with the museum, audience, and with one another
- Shared sense of happiness and satisfaction
- Performance toward our goals
- Mutual trust
- Sense of pride to be working at the Mia

Value Proposition: A new take on the classic art museum where family and friends can enjoy the triumphs of human creativity.

Simultaneously, the Mia team developed a value proposition to articulate what differentiates us among cultural attractions in the Twin Cities and to define our unique offerings for our desired audiences.

Mia 2021 (2016–2021)

Enjoying record attendance, support, and participation over the course of the DNA, Mia was in a position of strength and stability, which provided the ideal opportunity for Mia to take new risks and to innovate further. Our strategic plan *Mia 2021* builds on the significant achievements of the DNA while also taking advantage of new opportunities.

> The goal of Mia 2021 is to serve and strengthen the many communities that make up Mia's audiences and to deepen our relationships with those communities. This dynamic plan will train our focus outward to engage people in the art and history of world cultures past and present and will ensure Mia's long-term sustainability. —Kaywin Feldman, Nivin and Duncan MacMillan Director and President

Like the DNA, Mia also shaped this plan while examining the changing external environment in which the museum operates. Specific topics that shaped our thinking included the importance of diversity and inclusion, the rise of big data and enhanced understanding of consumer behavior, the dominance of mobile technology, greater competition for leisure time, the need to slow down and connect with humanity in a distracted world, changes in philanthropic giving and generational transfer of wealth, and the need for stronger sustainable financial models. Considering the critical trends listed here, Mia created a plan that focuses its work over the course of five years on enriching the community with the following three primary strategic directions:

- Fueling Curiosity harnesses Mia's art expertise, audience research, and the positive impact of storytelling in creating rich content that is compelling to our increasingly diverse community (online and onsite). Mia will share our collection stories across new mediums, encouraging our community to question and create relevant meanings.

- Engaging Communities positions the museum to better serve our audience by responding to the changing demographics of the city (external factors) to foster future relevance and sustainability as an institution (internal drivers).

- Deepening Relationships will sustain an audience committed to supporting our future. By recognizing individual interests and preferences—consistently and in all interactions—and offering opportunities for relevant personalized content and engagement, Mia will increase our value to our audiences and foster allegiance in current and future audiences.

Mia is in the second year of *Mia 2021*, and we are making incremental progress as we continue to build the foundations for much of this work. Admittedly, innovation and change are messy and challenging, especially when integrating and adopting models and practices from outside the museum world. Initiatives can take much longer than anticipated, and small failures are the norm, which we view as learning and growth opportunities. Mia continues to hire for new skill sets and expertise that did not exist previously. We celebrate short-term wins and keep our eyes on the future, knowing that we are working to change the museum for our changing world.

MINNEAPOLIS INSTITUTE OF ART

Year Founded: 1915

Location: Minneapolis, Minnesota

Mission Statement: The Minneapolis Institute of Art enriches the community by collecting, preserving, and making accessible outstanding works of art from the world's diverse cultures.

Vision Statement: Inspiring wonder through the power of art.

Distinct Characteristics: The museum aims to better serve its audiences by responding to the changing demographics of the city to foster future relevance and sustainability as an institution. Mia highlights the past to the present, enables global conversations, and offers a participatory setting for inspiration. Mia is home to more than ninety thousand significant works of art representing five thousand years of world history.

Governance: Private, nonprofit 501(c)(3)

Budget: $33 million

Staff: 179 full-time, 64 part-time

Adoption Date of Mission and Vision: 2014

NATIONAL CIVIL RIGHTS MUSEUM

Memphis, Tennessee

Written by Terri Lee Freeman, Executive Director

Your Mission is Your Reason for Being

When you hear our name, the National Civil Rights Museum, you immediately think of a mission for the museum. The straightforward thought is, likely, to protect, preserve, and educate about our nation's civil rights history. And to some extent you would be correct. But if we look at the role of museums in our society today, we have to think more broadly.

When I arrived at the museum in late 2014, I was deliberate in listening to the museum's many constituents—staff, Board members, donors, patrons. I devoured media that talked specifically about the museum or simply included it as a part of a bigger story. But I also listened closely to the news of the day, and it was chock-full of contemporary civil and human rights issues and, more troubling, violations. The mission statement of record for the museum was certainly reasonable:

> The National Civil Rights Museum at the Lorraine Motel, the assassination site of Martin Luther King Jr., chronicles key episodes of the American civil rights movement and the legacy of this movement to inspire participation in civil and human rights efforts globally, through our collections, exhibitions, and educational programs.

But it did not go far enough in defining how the museum would remain relevant, active, and sustainable into the future. With the goal of ensuring that the museum would continue to be relevant to young and old, local, national, and international audiences, and not simply be a "local attraction" (as described by one of the folks I met with during my listening tour!), we had to make sure our mission was action-oriented, engaging, and forward-thinking. So, approximately seven months after my hire, we, the staff and I, proposed the following mission to the Board.

> The National Civil Rights Museum chronicles key episodes of the American civil rights movement, examines today's global civil and human rights issues, provokes thoughtful debate and serves as a catalyst for positive social change.

We were certain this mission statement told the story of what the museum did and would do in the twenty-first century. And the Board agreed with one exception, they felt it was critical to include the descriptor of our location as an actual historic site. We accepted their concerns and modified the statement to read as follows:

> The National Civil Rights Museum located at the Lorraine Motel, the assassination site of Dr. Martin Luther King Jr., chronicles key episodes of the American civil rights movement, examines today's global civil and human rights issues, provokes thoughtful debate, and serves as a catalyst for positive social change.

This is the mission statement that informs and directs everything we do. We can break this statement down into separate phrases that describe our work and provide our visitors, donors, Board members, and staff with a clear understanding of what are reasonable activities, partnerships, and positions for the museum to engage in.

While we had significant conversation about including the first phrase about the museum's location and the tragic event that put us on the map, the fact remained that that tragic event was why we existed. As an authentic historic site, it was important for us to make sure that those visiting would recognize that history happened here. That said, it was also important that they recognized that history continues to be affected within the walls of the museum through our involvement and presentation of the issues that present themselves far too frequently as civil and human rights injustices. As an educational and cultural institution, we would do our constituents a disservice if we only talked about what happened during the late twentieth century and did not recognize the unfortunate similarities we see a half century after Dr. King's assassination.

As we updated our mission, we were intentional in identifying action verbs in defining our reason for being. We wanted the public to recognize us as a dynamic versus a passive institution. Our desire to examine today's global civil and human rights issues is to express our intent to look at all sides of issues that present themselves today in the area of civil and human rights. Our goal is not simply to present "a" perspective but to illuminate various perspectives on issues. We typically accomplish this through presentation and panel discussions. Similarly, we want to provoke thoughtful debate by encouraging our visitors, guests, and members to think about the information they see, hear, or experience. While the National Civil Rights Museum does not take any political positions, we do stand on the side of the principles of freedom and justice for all despite race, creed, color, and/or sexual orientation. We accept that people walk through our doors with a particular ideological perspective. It is not our place to change that perspective, but rather our duty to help people recognize that other perspectives exist. Finally, our mission speaks to our intent to serve as a catalyst for positive social change. It was important for us to ensure that our public recognized us as a service organization that works toward a greater good. Our role is not simply to plant information and educate, but also to inspire those who interact with us to action that will foster a more perfect union for everyone. Often this is done through the presentation of everyday, ordinary people who have gone on to do extraordinary things. This, in my estimation, is our highest calling. And we are constantly trying to measure the impact we have to inspire people to action.

It is this four-part mission that drives all of our activities. It helps us weed through the many opportunities that are presented on a daily basis and focus us on the things that are within our wheelhouse. We employ our mission as we acquire artifacts for our archives, select exhibitions for our temporary gallery, develop public programming, create collateral materials, determine appropriate speaker opportunities, and design educational training opportunities for educators, students, and adult learners.

And it is important to note that the mission keeps us focused on what grant opportunities are worth our effort. Raising money is incredibly time intensive. Our team must have a guidepost for how they approach soliciting funds. Importantly, the mission prevents us from going after limited funding that is not specifically mission-centric.

From my vantage point, as an executive operating in the nonprofit space for nearly three decades, there is no more important governing document (principle) than the mission statement. While an organizational vision statement is aspirational, the mission is operational. They work together: the former being the long-term North Star, and the latter being the daily touchstone. Nonprofit organizations must know where they are going, but they also need a clear roadmap to help them reach their destination.

NATIONAL CIVIL RIGHTS MUSEUM

Year Founded: 1991

Location: Memphis, Tennessee

Mission Statement: The National Civil Rights Museum, located at the Lorraine Motel, the assassination site of Dr. Martin Luther King Jr., chronicles key episodes of the American Civil Rights Movement, examines today's global civil and human rights issues, provokes thoughtful debate, and serves as a catalyst for positive change.

Distinct Characteristics: The museum is housed within the historic Lorraine Motel, the assassination site of Dr. Martin Luther King Jr., which has been preserved and staged to look as it did in 1968. Additionally, the museum includes the boarding house where James Earl Ray was alleged to have fired the fatal shot and the complete evidence collection as received by the Tennessee Bureau of Investigations. Our role is not simply to provide information and educate, but also to inspire those who interact with us to take action that will foster a more perfect union for everyone.

Governance: Private, nonprofit 501(c)(3)

Budget: $7.9 million

Staff: Thirty-eight full-time, three part-time

Adoption Date of Mission: 2015

NATIONAL UNDERGROUND RAILROAD FREEDOM CENTER

Cincinnati, Ohio

Written by Jamie Glavic, Assistant Vice President, Marketing and Communications, with Dion Brown, President and Chief Operating Officer

The National Underground Railroad Freedom Center is a museum of conscience, an education center, a convener of dialogue, and a beacon of light for inclusive freedom around the globe.

Our physical location in downtown Cincinnati is just a few steps from the banks of the Ohio River, the great natural barrier that separated the slave states of the South from the free states of the North. We tell the dramatic story of the enslaved crossing over that river on the journey to freedom, assisted by men and women of all backgrounds through a secret network of escape routes that came to be called the Underground Railroad.

Since opening in August 2004, the Freedom Center has filled a substantial void in our nation's cultural heritage. Rooted in the stories of the Underground Railroad, we illuminate the true meaning of freedom by presenting permanent and special exhibits that challenge our visitors, public programming that provokes dialogue and action, and educational resources that equip and inspire modern abolitionists. This distinctly American experience is the tie that connects us to the universal and ongoing struggle for freedom, past and present.

Our mission is to reveal stories of freedom's heroes, from the era of the Underground Railroad to contemporary times, challenging and inspiring everyone to take courageous steps for freedom today. Two keywords in our mission statement carry equal weight—*challenge* and *inspire*. In order to move forward as a people and achieve equity, we must come together and be active participants in complex dialogues that bare ourselves to productive discomfort—challenging ideals we may have thought to be true; exposing realities we may be unaware of due to privilege, geography, or circumstance; and understanding the biases that we all have.

The legacy of chattel slavery is woven into the fabric of American life—economically, politically, and socially. Slavery didn't end in 1865. Voting rights were not available to all Americans by 1920. The 1968 Civil Rights Act did not heal the racial divide of our nation. Progress is often misconstrued as resolution.

True progress is a radical and intentional act—one collective step at a time—requiring relentless evaluation of who is present, who is not, who is at the forefront, who should step back, and how to adjust to continue moving toward inclusion and equity. We believe in inclusive freedom—all people enjoying rights and privileges of equal number, equal quality, and equal kind.

This history—our collective history—is incredibly relevant. And we as an institution most certainly are not neutral. From its inception the Freedom Center has played a visible, proactive, and positive role on issues of local, regional, and national importance that involve intergroup strife and conflict. In times of increasing social division and public strife, we are vocal and present in taking positions on issues and offering a constructive path forward.

In October 2010, the Freedom Center opened the world's first permanent museum gallery dedicated to modern-day slavery and human trafficking, *Invisible: Slavery Today*. The exhibition explores the causes of modern-day slavery, the economic forces that have contributed to its growth, and the response of governments and the justice system. In 2014, we launched a new website in the fight against modern slavery, endslaverynow.org. This online resource illustrates the many ways individuals can get involved in the fight. From volunteer opportunities to resource sharing to curating an "action" library, this website was designed to assist you when you ask, "What can I do?"

In January 2017, we opened the Open Your Mind: Understanding Implicit Bias Learning Lab. Implicit bias is defined as the attitudes or stereotypes that affect our understanding, actions, and decisions in an unconscious manner. This groundbreaking museum education initiative was designed in partnership with the Kirwan Institute for the Study of Race and Ethnicity at The Ohio State University to assist the public in understanding and recognizing bias and other forms of discrimination, as well as to explore recent debates in the realm of implicit bias research. Admitting and identifying personal biases can be difficult. Nearly two decades of scientific research has persuasively demonstrated that each of us harbor implicit bias even if we seem to hold no explicit prejudice. Society is saturated with attitudes and stereotypes about social groups and people encompassing a range of intersectional identities and over time these feelings and beliefs can become more ingrained. The purpose of the learning lab is not to make people feel ashamed about their biases but to make them aware of unconscious behaviors that can be corrected with knowledge and training.

We are often asked how we navigate current events and issues without getting political. The reality is that our mission charges us to be political. There's a difference between being political and being partisan. Our foundation is the era of the Underground Railroad—a secretive movement that acted against the law of the land. Freedom's heroes in this struggle not only spoke out against injustice but actively participated in breaking the law to challenge societal norms and inspire true change.

Simply put, we care about people; therefore, we care about policies. This leads to being political.

For example, on June 26, 2015, we issued the following statement regarding the ruling of the Supreme Court of the United States in the landmark same-sex marriage civil rights case of *Obergefell v. Hodges*:

Today, history has been made. The ruling of the Supreme Court in Obergefell v. Hodges was made possible by works and the bravery of activists like Bayard Rustin, Harvey Milk, and Edith Windsor. We thank Jim Obergefell and the plaintiffs who testified and changed the course of history. Justice Kennedy's remarks affirm the fact that we all have the same legal right to marriage. At the National Underground Railroad Freedom Center, we believe in inclusive freedom—where we all have equal access to the same rights and agree with the words of President Barack Obama, that today, "we have made our Union a little more perfect."

In November 2016, we issued the following statement following the viral remarks of white supremacist Richard Spencer:

The National Underground Railroad Freedom Center tells stories about the past to educate and inform the present in order to prevent historical atrocities from recurring. This is our charge as a museum of conscience. We are the watchers and keepers of history.

We are appalled and alarmed at the recent hate speech of a white nationalist that has gone viral. Hatred is not an American value. We cannot be bystanders. We cannot "wait and see." We cannot wish this away.

Now is the time for all Americans to confront and stand up to hatred. We will not be silent. We join and support the United States Holocaust Memorial Museum in publicly denouncing racist ideologies and hate-filled rhetoric.

On August 12, 2017, we issued the following statement regarding the events unfolding in Charlottesville:

We believe in inclusive freedom—all people enjoying rights and privileges of equal number, quality, and kind. We stand with the oppressed communities of Charlottesville—and this nation—who are traumatized daily by white supremacy. We cannot and will not be silent or silenced. We condemn racism, hatred, ignorance, and violence.

On January 12, 2018, we issued the following statement in response to President Trump's comments on immigration:

As an organization devoted to exploring and understanding the legacy of slavery in order to ensure freedom for all, we at the National Underground Railroad Freedom Center are appalled by the offensive language reportedly used by the

President in reference to Haiti and African nations. This language is unacceptable and the attitude being articulated perpetuates white privilege and superiority—undermining people of color in our global community.

As an organization devoted to freedom, inclusion, and unity we denounce racist rhetoric. This is our charge as a museum of conscience, education center, and convener of dialogue. The language used by the President, followed by the lament about not attracting more northern European immigrants, is beyond alarming. The leaders at the National Underground Railroad Freedom Center call on the public to take a stand and share that this language is not reflective of the attitude of all American people. As our history dramatically demonstrates, the success of our nation is thanks to our diversity and as a result, the American dream cannot and should not be an impossible dream for immigrant communities of color.

None of these statements have had or would have a negative impact on our 501(c)(3) tax status. These statements are an extension of our mission, which is why our Board and staff instituted and support a rapid response policy. When an incident, local, regional, or national in scope, occurs that calls out for formal comment, the Board chair, president, or communications department can initiate a conference call to discuss whether the Freedom Center should issue a public statement.

If the group recommends the formulation of a response, they will outline the nature of the statement and assign a communications staff member to draft and distribute a statement. Alternately, the group can also recommend that a member of the National Advisory Board drafts a statement. This occurred on May 25, 2017, when National Advisory Council member David Blight was asked to draft a response to President Trump's mischaracterization of the supposed influence that President Andrew Jackson might have had on the start of the Civil War.

Racism, anti-Semitism, anti-Muslim, anti-LGBTQ, anti-immigrant, and misogynistic rhetoric does not exist in a vacuum. There has been a continuum of events that have led to the normalization of oppressive actions, behaviors, and beliefs. The Freedom Center is dedicated to changing the world by changing the way we view ourselves and one another so that, together, we can walk in the footsteps of Frederick Douglass, Dorothy Height, Nelson Mandela, Harriet Tubman, Elie Wiesel, and countless other everyday freedom heroes. Our mission requires it. Our society needs it.

NATIONAL UNDERGROUND RAILROAD FREEDOM CENTER

Year Founded: 1994

Location: Cincinnati, Ohio

Mission Statement: We reveal stories about freedom's heroes, from the era of the Underground Railroad to contemporary times, challenging and inspiring everyone to take courageous steps for freedom today.

Distinct Characteristics: The National Underground Railroad Freedom Center is a museum of conscience, an education center, a convener of dialogue, and a beacon of light for inclusive freedom around the globe. The Freedom Center has the world's first permanent museum gallery dedicated to modern-day slavery and human trafficking and implicit bias learning lab.

Governance: 501(c)(3)

Budget: $4.5 million

Staff: Twenty-one full-time, five part-time

Adoption Date of Mission: 1998

NORTH CAROLINA MUSEUM OF NATURAL SCIENCES
Raleigh, North Carolina
Written by Emlyn Koster, PhD, Director

In Pursuit of Relevance

In hindsight, the first mission of Apollo and introduction of the Anthropocene should have bracketed a period of profound introspection, reflection, and inspiration across the nature and science museums sector. There was a powerful opportunity to manifest the founding raison d'être of "the museum" from The Muses in Greek mythology. . . . As a matter of external accountability, it is urgent that the talk of societal needs, institutional directions, and conference declarations be matched by the holistic actions and impacts of major nature and science museums.[4]

Holistic Growth

Opened in North Carolina's capital, Raleigh, in 1879 with a mission to illustrate the natural history of the state, field naturalist and inaugural director of the State Museum of Natural History Herbert Hutchinson Brimley had a prescient outlook, "The building of a museum is a never-ending work. . . . A finished museum is a dead museum, and such a one must deteriorate and begin to lose usefulness from the time its growth stops." In 1986, the museum's name changed from Natural History to Natural Sciences and, seven years later, the institution was reassigned from the Department of Agriculture to the Department of Environment and Natural Resources with a mission to "interpret the natural world and relate this knowledge to the global environment." In 1998, the museum's growing collections and research activities were accommodated in a nearby satellite facility. Propelled by its vision of external meaningfulness and its favorable contexts of the state's fast-growing capital and vibrant Research Triangle region, the museum's sense of relevance intensified.

Four probing questions began to frame the museum's determination to be a topical resource. Asking "what do we know?" with a southeast U.S. lens, the first major expansion opened in 2000.[5] Then asking "how do we know?" with a global lens, a connected wing expansion opened in 2012 featuring imagery of the Earth's western hemisphere with an interior theater experience asking "what is happening now?" Meanwhile, the museum's thirty-eight-acre public Prairie Ridge Ecostation, presenting natural habitats and stewardship opportunities, opened in 2004. The institution's growing citizen science project menu—onsite, offsite, online, and outdoors—responded to the culminating question of "how can the public participate?" Overall, the museum's interpretative stance reflects North Carolina's instructive slice of the natural world.[6]

In hindsight, the museum took a bold risk in doubling the institution's size just twelve years after a major expansion and pioneering a new type of visitor experience for nature and science museums. The Nature Research Center wing was designed to demystify the process of science by juxtaposing researchers and visitors.[7] With onsite attendance doubling to one million, the museum became, and remains, North Carolina's most visited museum and Raleigh's top attraction. The cumulative impacts of the two-phase expansion were not only significant in museological, civic, and state terms: they also gave the whole institution an appetite for continued innovation. Adding to the museum's current campus is its first satellite branch serving one of the state's poorest counties.[8]

Operating Parameters

This museum has an atypical operating environment: (1) it is a hybrid of a natural history museum, science center, aquarium, zoo, children's museum, and nature interpretive center; (2) it has a comfortable continuity from the past into the present and future; and (3) its organization has the following mix of operational dimensions.

Resources

About 70 percent of the museum's annual $15.7 million operating budget is provided by a state appropriation. The rest is generated through joint research positions with the University of North Carolina System, corporate sponsors, private donors, grants, and earned revenue sources. The nonprofit Friends of the Museum administers grant accounts, revenues from events, food/retail operations and facility rentals, membership, and program earnings. Assisting almost 150 full-time staff is volunteerism exceeding 80,000 hours annually.

Free Admission

The advantages of no general admission charge include significantly reduced barriers to community-wide access and an ease of visit circumstances in terms of company, frequency, duration, and incremental learning. The challenges—which must be overcome—include potentially insufficient attention to market dynamics, competitive value, attendance data and visitor trends, benchmarking, and business savvy. Membership growth hinges more on the perceived value of the museum's purpose than on transactional benefits.

Blurring Boundaries

The state's new Department of Natural and Cultural Resources encompasses aquariums; parks; zoo; land and water stewardship; museums of art, history, and the natural sciences; historic sites; arts programs; a symphony; archives; libraries; and an African American heritage commission. This breadth stimulates the blurring of traditional silos across the arts-humanities-sciences spectrum: examples include pairing nature-inspired symphonies with images of nature and library assistance in distributing tree-mounted cameras for statewide wildlife surveys.

Networking and Collaboration

Intrinsic to the museum's culture is an atypical breadth of networking, often finding itself as the only such institution at gatherings such as E.O. Wilson Biodiversity Days, Jackson Hole Wildlife Film Festivals and Conservation Summits, World Wildlife Day at the United Nations in New York, and Conservation International. This mindset is also spurred by multi-faceted collaborations with universities, the Smithsonian Institution, National Environmental Education Foundation, and project networking in the research, education, and citizen science arenas.

Return on Investments

Whereas the private sector mainly sees itself in financially based cost-benefit terms, the nonprofit sector must also embrace social and environmental impact "bottom lines." This museum's focus on external relevance with its revenue portfolio recognizes that maximum advance of its mission hinges on envisioning, planning, operating, and communicating in return-on-investment terms.

Evolution of Mission

When the museum completed its two-phase expansion, its mission was:

To enhance the public's understanding and appreciation of the natural environment in ways that emphasize the biodiversity of North Carolina and southeastern United States and relate the region to the natural world as a whole and engage the public in scientific research that affects their daily lives.

The opening twenty-four-hour fanfare for the new wing on Earth Day 2012 attracted a crowd estimated at seventy thousand. Media and community reactions were very favorable.[9] Internally, there was euphoria and exhaustion as well as an eagerness to take stock of further opportunities.

What followed was a period of internal reorganization to merge research activities in both wings as one new section, followed by a series of institutional assessment, cultural, and planning developments. Raleigh's hosting of the 2014 conference of the Association of Science-Technology Centers, with more than seventeen hundred delegates from more than forty countries, was a timely rallying opportunity. First was an update of the museum's history in the *North Carolina Naturalist*, the quarterly magazine for stakeholders: the sequel to an article "The Evolution of a Dream" in a 2004 issue was a story in a 2014 issue titled "Profile of a Remarkable Resource," and this was reinforced by an external magazine story positioning the museum on a global stage.[10]

Next was an update of the museum's values involving a cross-functional task force of nominated staff with employment ranging from one year to three decades. It defined values as the service-driven ways that we think, act, and react with a three-tier structure:

Foundation = Integrity + Professionalism + Commitment
Approach = Inclusion + Collaboration + Innovation
Outcome = Engagement + Impact + Sustainability

Aligned with its long-established duality of research and education, the museum's tagline to accompany its new logo aptly became:

Celebrating Nature, Advancing Science.

Updating the museum's mission statement in 2014 was inspired by the American Alliance of Museums' metaphor of a beating heart and the declaration at a National Science Foundation–funded convening of natural history museums at the Smithsonian's National Museum of Natural History:

Humanity is embedded within nature and we are at a critical moment in the continuity of time. Our collections are the direct scientific evidence for evolution and the ecological interdependence of all living things. The human species is actively altering the Earth's natural processes and reducing its biodiversity. As the sentient cause of these impacts, we have the urgent responsibility to give voice to the Earth's immense story and to secure its sustainable future.[11]

Internally, it was emphasized that a mission statement must be authentic, uplifting, and distinctive. An incremental process involved several discussions of trends, potential words and phrases, then rankings of candidate statements. Opinion polls of staff, Friends of the Museum Board members, and Advisory Commission members resulted in a strong consensus to bring humans into the museum's mission picture for the first time in the institution's history:

To illuminate the interdependence of nature and humanity.

The concluding step—or so it was then thought—was a series of form-follows-function adjustments to strengthen the museum's organizational structure. During 2015 to 2017, several developments pointed the museum in a direction of needing to define not just the what but also the why and how dimensions of its proverbial beating heart. The main influence in 2016 was the American Alliance of Museums' decadal re-accreditation, which concluded:

The Museum has succeeded in regenerating itself . . . [it has] forthrightly evolved its interpretative philosophy and strategy to address bigger stories about humans as an inseparable element in the ecosystem of all life, and therefore to be concerned about matters of conservation and sustainability.

Additional influences, including town hall meetings about UN Sustainable Development Goals, emphasized the community's appetite for helpful steps; the Anthropocene emerged as a summary way to grasp human interference with natural systems; and a three-year Institute of Museum and Library Services grant evaluating the museum's research-public interface encouraged the engagement of schools and adults in critical thinking skills, citizen science projects, and career paths, in turn to realize how science connects with their lives and surrounding environments.

It became apparent that the museum's 2014 mission statement—to illuminate the interdependence of nature and humanity—potentially created wrong impressions of nature and humanity as separate dynamics; plus, a call to action was missing. Surveys found that only a third of visitors found this statement appealing. Internally, concerns also arose over what had become nebulous meanings of nature and humanity: instead, word clouds confirmed a preference for the natural world. Of five newly considered statements, this one emerged with a top ranking:

> To illuminate the natural world and inspire its conservation.

An unambiguous focus on two interrelated vital tasks—illuminating the natural world and inspiring its conservation—has accelerated the museum's thinking and acting in several more concertedly responsible ways. Examples include a redoubled emphasis on enhancing the total visitor experience; an internal Greener Future Committee to increase recycling and reduce waste in food service, retail, and facility management; a partnership with the National Environmental Education Foundation to, for example, collaborate on the development, dissemination, evaluation, and scaling of visitor engagement campaigns focused on activating pro-environmental behaviors; and an acceleration of efforts to narrow the gap between citizens and scientists, onsite and in the community, as the museum gears up to join the Raleigh Convention Center and other Research Triangle players in hosting the 2019 Citizen Science Association conference.

Reflections

For too long, metrics such as the size of collections and annual attendance have been inadequate proxies for a museum's value.[12] Popularity and meaningfulness are not necessarily correlated in a cause and effect way: museums drifting toward sensation or reliant on so-called blockbusters suffer the consequences, sooner or later. Museums failing to renew and add contemporary subject matter—which is especially important for nature and science museums—grow stale with a risk of declining attendance and perhaps even closure. Increasingly, the museum's performance metrics that really matter include content, audience, and profile variables. As a core driver of their accountability, museums focused on nature and science, in particular, should take all feasible steps to maximize their relevancy and sustainability with these interrelated performance equations:[13]

Relevancy   = Meaningfulness + Popularity
Sustainability = Relevancy + Renewal

It is vital in the twenty-first century that museums make themselves matter.[14] More than ever, surely the beating heart of our sector must strive to be in sync with the beating heart of the whole Earth and all its inhabitants.

> It is a matter of accountability whether . . . institutions opt to be part of the solution or part of the problem. . . . Successfully heading in this direction depends on three facets of institutional culture being in place. The first concerns mission and vision—is there a clear and firm commitment to be of value to the societal and environmental problems we face? The second concerns leadership—is there a preparedness and competence to be an activist? The third concerns strategy—is there a relentless pursuit to be more externally useful and to nurture new perspectives in funding stakeholders?[15]

To be indispensable school and public resources in the Anthropocene, nature and science museums must strive for external relevance with mission statements devised and used as their compass of intended scope and impact. The North Carolina Museum of Natural Sciences—now approaching its 140th anniversary—is concertedly on this course.[16]

Selected Bibliography

Bell, J., Chesebrough, D., Cryan, J., and Koster, E. "Museum-University Partnerships as a New Platform for Public Engagement with Scientific Research." *Journal of Museum Education*, 41, no. 4, (2016), 293–306.

Earnhardt, T. *Crossroads of the Natural World: Exploring North Carolina.* Chapel Hill: University of North Carolina Press, 2013.

Koster, E. "From Apollo into the Anthropocene: The Odyssey of Nature and Science Museums in an External Responsibility Context." In *Museums, Ethics and Cultural Heritage*, edited by B. Murphy, 228–41. New York: Routledge, 2016.

Koster, E. "The Anthropocene as Our Conscience." In *Designing for Empathy, Perspectives on the Museum Experience*, edited by E. Gokcigdem. Lanham, MD: Rowman and Littlefield, 2019.

Koster, E. "Evolution of Purpose in Science Museums and Science Centers." In *Hot Topics, Public Culture, Museums*, edited by Linda Kelly and Fiona Cameron. Newcastle-upon-Tyne: Cambridge Scholars Publishing, 2010.

Koster, E. "Broadening the Reflections on Science Center Attendance. Informal Learning Review." In *Reinventing the Museum: The Evolving Conversation on the Paradigm Shift*, edited by Gail Anderson. Lanham, MD: AltaMira Press, 2012.

Koster, E. "The Relevant Museum: A Reflection on Sustainability." In *Reinventing the Museum: The Evolving Conversation on the Paradigm Shift*, edited by Gail Anderson. Lanham, MD: AltaMira Press, 2012.

Koster, E., Dorfman, E., and Nyambe, T. "A Holistic Ethos for Nature-focused Museums in the Anthropocene." In *The Future of Natural History Museums*, edited by E. Dorfman, 29–48. New York: Routledge, 2018.

Koster, E., and Pendergraft, L. "Bringing the Mission to the Community: State Museum Opens a Satellite in an Underserved Rural Region." *Informal Learning Review*, 131, (2016), 11–15.

Koster, E., and Schubel, J. "Raising the Relevancy Bar for Aquariums and Science Centers." In *In Principle, In Practice*, edited by J. Falk, L. Dierking, and S. Foutz, 197–220. Lanham, MD: AltaMira Press, 2007.

Koster, E., Yalowitz, S., and Watson, B. "Natural History: Past, Present, Future." In *Informal Learning Review*, 113, (2012), 22–24.

Martin, M. *A Long Look at Nature: the North Carolina Museum of Natural Sciences.* Chapel Hill: University of North Carolina Press, 2001.

Roberts, L. "On a Global Stage: A Day in the Life of the N.C. Museum of Natural Sciences." In *Walter, Raleigh's Life & Soul*, October 2014.

Weil, S. *Making Museums Matter.* Washington, DC: Smithsonian Institution Press, 2002.

Weil, S. "From Being About Something to Being For Somebody: The Ongoing Transformation of the American Museum." *Daedalus*, 128, 3, (1999).

Weil, S. "Beyond Management: Making Museums Matter." *International Council of Museums, International Committee on Management Study Series*, 12, (2006), 4–8.

Williams, I. "36 Hours in Raleigh." *New York Times*, March 6, 2014.

NORTH CAROLINA MUSEUM OF NATURAL SCIENCES

Year Founded: 1879

Location: Raleigh, North Carolina

Mission Statement: To illuminate the natural world and inspire its conservation.

Vision Statement: A topical resource for the challenges and opportunities of the Anthropocene.

Values Statement:
   Foundation: integrity, professionalism, and commitment.
   Approach: inclusive, innovative, and collaborative.
   Outcomes: engagement, impact, and sustainability.

Distinct Characteristics: The North Carolina Museum of Natural Sciences encompasses a natural history and natural sciences museum with elements of an aquarium, zoo, science center, and children's museum. This museum asks four basic questions about the natural world: What do we know? How do we know? What's happening now? How can you participate? This framework is integrated into a suite of onsite, offsite, online, and outdoor experiences. Collection includes 4.1 million specimens in natural history and an extensive living collection. The campus comprises downtown headquarters, a nearby ecostation and collections/research facility, and a satellite branch 120 miles away in one of the state's poorest counties.

Governance: North Carolina Department of Natural and Cultural Resources

Budget: $15.7 million

Staff: 147 full-time, 40 part-time

Adoption Dates of Mission, Vision, Values: 2014–2018

NEVADA MUSEUM OF ART
Reno, Nevada
Written by David B. Walker, Chief Executive Officer

It is no coincidence that the Nevada Museum of Art has an interdisciplinary focus on the way humans creatively interact with their environments. Nevada is situated in North America's largest desert—the Great Basin. The state has seen atomic tests, military installations, and large-scale mining operations, but also experimental communities like Burning Man and some of the largest land-based artworks in the world. This extreme environment is also home to the Nevada Museum of Art in Reno. So it came as no surprise when artist and MacArthur Foundation Fellow Trevor Paglen approached the museum in 2015 to imagine the unimaginable: to send a satellite sculpture into orbit as an artistic gesture. The project is called *Orbital Reflector*. We are now preparing to embark upon an exploration of the most extreme environment of them all: outer space.

For those unfamiliar with the Nevada Museum of Art, and perhaps mystified by Paglen's *Orbital Reflector*, my essay attempts to elucidate the connections between our past, and ongoing mission to be "a museum of ideas."

Established in 1931 by Dr. James Church during the Great Depression, the Nevada Museum of Art is one of the oldest cultural institutions in Nevada. Dr. Church was a University of Nevada, Reno, humanities professor, a lover of art, and early climate scientist who established the first snow survey station in the world on nearby Mount Rose. The museum was not created by a founding collection, but rather a desire to engage community in ideas and conversation. From the very beginning "art + environment" has been central to our mission.

People gravitate to extreme environments like Nevada to experiment, test, and take risks. There are fewer rules here, and it's easier to realize the unthinkable. We see Nevada—its geography, cultures, and industries—as a place that informs what we do every day. Our building, for example, designed by architect Will Bruder, reflects our dramatic geography and took its cues from the Black Rock Range a few hours north of Reno. When it opened in 2003, architecture writers noted that the building's sculptural style underscores the institution's relationship to the surrounding environment.

More important, the new building was a return to our founder's idea that the Nevada Museum of Art would be Northern Nevada's living room. Art lovers and non-art lovers of all ages once again began to regularly gather to share in the exchange of ideas, attend educational and public programs, view a range of exhibitions, and enjoy social experiences in an inspired setting. Although some locals have compared the building's black, futuristic exterior to the "Star Wars" film character Darth Vader, the contemporary interior and comfortable scale lacks the all-too-common art museum pretense.

As Nevada has grown, so too has our Hispanic and Latinx population. Between 2000 and 2010, Nevada had the largest Hispanic population increase of any other state in the nation. It was important to us to include this growing population and celebrate its culture, so in 2013 we launched a six-year research and development initiative designed to advance a shared cultural understanding—in a sustained way. Early collaborations with the El Museo del Barrio in New York City proved valuable to our structuring of this model, and in only a few years we enjoyed successful results—and we are all richer for it. At the same time, we are applying this same approach to our work with Nevada's Native American communities.

In 2009, we established our unique Center for Art + Environment. This internationally recognized research center "dedicated to supporting the practice, study, and awareness of creative interactions between people and their environments" has come to define the museum's mission and hosts hundreds of visiting researchers, scholars, writers, and artists from around the world annually, as well as local students of all ages.

The center collects physical and digital archives from artists working on all seven continents. These include materials on Michael Heizer, Walter De Maria, Center for Land Use Interpretation (Wendover), Burning Man, Cape Farewell, Lita Albuquerque, Helen and Newton Harrison, Ugo Rondinone, Trevor Paglen, and many more. The steady growth of the center led by its director, William L. Fox, an author, art critic, and cultural geographer, has helped to give the museum an international identity and is a primary reason why nearly 20 percent of the museum's annual operating revenues come from sources outside of Nevada—a measure of validation of the role the center plays in the larger world.

The center, along with the entire museum staff, also organizes a popular triennial Art + Environment Conference. During each conference, major exhibitions are organized by the museum's curators that serve as thematic backdrops for the presentations. Speakers are wide-ranging and have included such luminaries as Maya Lin, Vito Acconci, Leo Villareal, Petah Coyne, Nicholas Galanin, Kianga Ford, Trevor Paglen, Patricia Johanson, Rem Koolhaas, and futurist/provocateur Bruce Sterling, who provides the highly anticipated summary at the conclusion of each gathering.

The conference attracts important attendees, presenters, and thought leaders from around the globe. They have become our "community" and eagerly gather to exchange bold ideas, new knowledge, and diverse creative practices. Our staff and trustees are continually charged by these significant gatherings and the important relationships they seed.

One such example—a partnership with the Long Now Foundation—explores the deep future. In 2016 we began working with conceptual artist and experimental philosopher Jonathon Keats, who proposes an alternative to the Gregorian calendar. *Centuries of the Bristlecone* will "bring the calendar back to life," according to Keats. Because the lifespan of a bristlecone pine can exceed five thousand years, it is the most long-lived of timekeepers, but also influenced annually by environmental conditions. Growth data from a grove of bristlecone pines on Mount Washington in eastern Nevada will be monitored and relayed by satellite to a computer that will calculate an exact date based on the tree's daily increase in girth. The computer will control a large mechanical calendar situated at the Nevada Museum of Art—for five thousand years! Keats, like many artists today, is increasingly interested in engaging a larger public outside the walls of a traditional museum or gallery.

Another example is Ugo Rondinone's *Seven Magic Mountains*—a monumental, site-specific artwork we produced in the desert just outside Las Vegas in collaboration with the Art Production Fund. This popular artwork by the renowned Swiss artist features seven, thirty-five-foot-high day-glo totems comprised of painted Nevada limestone boulders. It is no accident that the installation site is a short distance from Jean Dry Lake, where Michael Heizer and Jean Tinguely created pioneering land art works in the 1960s. And, just over the ridgeline, thousands of prehistoric petroglyphs are pecked into the rocks—ancient land art. Seven Magic Mountains continues to attract nearly one thousand visitors per day, and the museum is now working with the artist, Bureau of Land Management, Clark County, and our title sponsors to make it a permanent installation.

Within our institutional walls, organizing landmark exhibitions, publications, and documentaries that place Nevada within a larger context has been one hallmark of the curatorial department.

City of Dust: The Evolution of Burning Man explored, for the first time, the remarkable story of how the legendary Nevada gathering known as Burning Man evolved from humble counter cultural roots on San Francisco's Baker Beach into the world-famous desert convergence it is today. Never-before-seen photographs, artifacts, journals, sketches, and notebooks revealed how this temporary experimental desert city came to be—and how it continues to evolve. Most of the materials were drawn from the Center for Art + Environment Archive Collection, and we are thrilled that it was the scholarly centerpiece of a larger Burning Man art exhibition at the Smithsonian American Art Museum's Renwick Gallery in 2018.

Unsettled served as the primary backdrop exhibition for the 2017 Art + Environment Conference. The exhibition presented more than two hundred artworks by eighty artists living or working in a super-region defined by the museum as the "Greater West"—a geographic area stretching from Alaska to Patagonia, and from Australia to the American West. Ranging across thousands of miles, this super-region shares many similarities: vast expanses of open land, rich natural resources, diverse indigenous peoples, colonialism, and the ongoing conflicts that inevitably arise when these factors co-exist. A collaboration with iconic artist Ed Ruscha and the Anchorage Museum in Alaska and Palm Springs Art Museum in Southern California, *Unsettled* will travel to both museums.

The idea of the Greater West grew out of our historical Great Basin/Sierra Nevada permanent collection and our desire to grow this regional collection into a super-regional collection. This caught the attention of Miami-based art collectors Debra and Dennis Scholl, who recently announced they will gift the largest collection of Aboriginal Australian contemporary works of art in the United States (theirs) to the Metropolitan Museum of Art, The Patricia & Phillip Frost Art Museum, and Nevada Museum of Art. Bold and compelling ideas backed by original scholarship can be magnets in unexpected ways.

As the museum looks to the future, we are exploring what it means to be a state-wide cultural institution. We have engaged Pritzker Prize–winning architect and theorist Rem Koolhaas and his Office of Metropolitan Architecture to provide concept and design feasibility studies for significant museum expansion in Reno. He is asking us to consider the way Nevada is leading the global conversation around the intersections of data and culture. At the same time, we are working with a group of stakeholders and the City of Las Vegas to establish a Nevada Museum of Art in Symphony Park near downtown Las Vegas.

Big ideas unfold in the desert. What will continue to distinguish the Nevada Museum of Art is a commitment to interdisciplinary education, research, experimentation, collaboration, bold ideas, and risk. Achieving broader relevance and enlightened dialogue around what museums of the future can become is a worthy institutional endeavor—perhaps now more than ever.

NEVADA MUSEUM OF ART

Year Founded: 1931

Location: Reno, Nevada

Mission Statement: We are a museum of ideas. While building upon our founding collections and values, we strive to offer meaningful art and cultural experiences, and foster new knowledge in the visual arts by encouraging interdisciplinary investigation. The Nevada Museum of Art serves as an educational resource for everyone.

Distinct Characteristics: Thematic exhibitions, collections, and educational programming establish the museum as a leader in the field of art and environment, with a focus on examining the ways that people interact with natural, built, and virtual environments. This field of inquiry stems from the museum's geographic location in a region known for its diverse indigenous cultures; extreme desert environment; pioneering land art; rich natural resources; military, industrial, and nuclear history; and complex land and water issues.

Governance: Private, nonprofit 501(c)(3)

Budget: $7 million

Staff: Twenty-nine full-time, thirty-two part-time

Adoption Date of Mission: 2014

OAKLAND MUSEUM OF CALIFORNIA

Oakland, California

Written by Lori Fogarty, Director and Chief Executive Officer

Museum Evolution

Nonprofit orthodoxy states that organizations should always start with the mission, as if the mission is an immutable, sacred script—the Rosetta Stone that is the key to decoding our challenges, establishing our priorities—leading to all the right decisions. I would argue against this kind of originalist view of mission statements. In my experience, the value of a mission statement is realized when we review it as our organization evolves, when we test it to see if it does indeed help set priorities, shape programming, define success, and especially when it reinforces the core values and principles of our organizations.

I've done lots of strategic planning in my almost thirty years in cultural institutions and museums, both as a staff member and a board member, and reviewing and writing mission statements is always one of the most fraught parts of the process. Some stakeholders hold that the mission statement is inviolate, or they balk at the necessary time it takes to deconstruct a mission statement. Many argue that it is a waste of time to try to wordsmith by committee and suggest that the goals and priorities are most essential in strategic planning.

However, when board and staff do grapple with the big "Why?" and "So what?" of the organization, it can lead to amazing revelations. We had just such an experience at the Oakland Museum of California (OMCA) when we undertook strategic planning in 2012. This marked a period of significant change for OMCA. We had recently completed a major renovation of our landmark building and had reinvented ninety thousand square feet of collection galleries. We had also moved to independent governance and operation after more than four decades of serving as a department of the City of Oakland. These two enormous institutional transformations led to the restructuring of our staff, making us a "forty-year-old startup," as we said at the time. Indeed, it was a moment to look with truly fresh eyes on the future mission and vision of the museum.

Over what became a twelve-month process (I believe every organization starts with the hope of a six- to nine-month process for strategic planning—it always takes longer), we undertook three phases of planning: Discovery, Discernment, and Decision Making. As we approached the transition between Discovery (benchmarking other institutions, assembling staff and Board task forces on key topics, convening thought leaders) and Discernment (kicked off with a Board retreat to focus on the emerging goals), we had an epiphany.

We began to see that our vision to achieve greater relevance—both locally and statewide—was steering us to a much more future-thinking approach. Indeed, if we truly wanted to be a convener of conversations around the most urgent issues facing Oakland and California and to foster more engaged citizens and stewards, we could no longer see ourselves as being exclusively about history and heritage. I clearly remember our "Aha!" moment. After some real soul searching (and wordsmithing), our Board and staff leaders refocused the mission on the future and on activism.

> The mission of the Oakland Museum of California is to inspire all Californians to create a more vibrant future for themselves and their communities.

After approving this new mission, we developed the major pillars of our *2013 Strategic Plan: Inspiring California's Future*. The mission has served us well as we've examined implications for programming, audience development, community engagement, collection access, and financial sustainability. For example, we've been developing exhibitions such as *All Power to the People: Black Panthers at Fifty*, a project grounded in historic struggles for civil rights in Oakland that also looked at contemporary issues and called for continued urgent action for racial equity today. Similarly, we developed a Collections Plan that outlines the history and strengths of our collection, but also identifies areas for priority growth based on current trends throughout California. It clearly states that the purpose of our collection is to tell stories that foster community bonding, bridging, and self-knowledge.

We found, however, that rewriting new mission and vision statements and reaffirming our core values of community, innovation, excellence, and commitment wasn't quite enough to propel the institution toward the impact we envisioned. Two years after completing our strategic plan, we began to construct a "Theory of Change" based on our need to be even clearer about what we were striving to achieve as an organization. We were working on a number of major initiatives—audience development, community engagement, visitor-centered programming—but we were struggling to identify the "So what?" We also asked ourselves, "If we achieve our goals in these areas, how will the world around us be different?" "What change are we trying to effect in our community?"

So, in 2015, we began to add language and structure to our Theory of Change. We were able to more precisely identify our inputs, activities, outputs, and even outcomes. But—like many museums and cultural organizations—we still weren't quite able to tell the story about how the world would be different if we achieved our goals. And that is when we set out to develop our "Social Impact Framework."

To begin the process, OMCA staff looked to other fields, such as health and human services, to define social impact, because very few museums—at least in the United States—have yet to articulate or measure their public benefit beyond economic impact. We looked to our own research to determine how our local communities and visitors have expressed their needs and the benefits they derive from cultural experiences. We have had many discussions, with both the Board and staff, to deeply investigate how the work we do can authentically impact the city around us and—most importantly—the people who live here.

This process led to our developing a Social Impact Framework. As we consider this framework, we see our mission as our purpose, then extend that mission to identify the challenge or need we are striving to address in our community, articulating what impact we will make if we're successful in our work (our social impact), and determine how we will measure this impact through indicators.

After a two-year process culminating in spring 2018, we identified our most central and significant impact as social cohesion, or creating the space and context for greater connection, trust, and understanding between people and social groups. This impact addresses the challenge of social fragmentation, or the fallout from inequities within institutions, the state, and civic society resulting in a decline in social cohesion and increased social exclusion. Our current impact indicators are:

- Our visitors express a sense of welcome and belonging at OMCA.
- Our visitors recognize that their stories matter in museum exhibitions and programs.
- Our visitors express connection to their neighbors on the museum campus and at OMCA programs.
- Our visitors express their ideas and are open to the ideas of others.

We began to measure our social impact in 2018 with visitors and look forward to sharing our findings with the field in the near future. Of course, we understand that achieving this kind of impact will require OMCA to continue to transform itself. In addition to influencing programming and content decisions, we must ensure that its structures, policies, and procedures are inclusive and equitable. This impact will require close partnerships with community members, fellow nonprofits, community collaborators, and key institutions and leaders in the City of Oakland. We must also consider the long-term sustainability of these activities.

To highlight this last requirement, OMCA has identified our "goal posts"—the "North Stars" that must guide our work in the coming years. One goal post is the social impact described above. The second is the goal of financial sustainability, which we define as:

- Our income sources are well diversified between earned, contributed, public, and invested income.
- Our income sources are reliable and repeatable and not dependent on single sources of funding or blockbuster exhibitions.
- Our institution is well capitalized, with sufficient funds for cash and facility reserves as well as funds to fuel innovation.

While our journey continues, we will strive for honest self-reflection. We begin with our mission, but it is through evolution—questioning what we do, how we do it, and why—that our work will make a positive difference in the world. Our mission is not the end game but a point of departure.

OAKLAND MUSEUM OF CALIFORNIA

Year Founded: 1969

Location: Oakland, California

Mission Statement: To inspire all Californians to create a more vibrant future for themselves and their communities.

Vision: OMCA is the heart of a thriving community and a statewide leader.

Values: These values are fundamental to our institutional culture and guide our work together:

Excellence:

We are committed to excellence and working at the highest standards of integrity and professionalism.

Community:

We believe everyone should feel welcome and part of our community, both within the museum and with our visitors and neighbors.

Innovation:

We embrace innovation and calculated risk-taking to achieve our mission.

Commitment:

Our work at the museum demonstrates a sense of purpose and a shared accountability for the institution's success.

Distinct Characteristics: Created as a "museum of the people," the museum came together in the 1960s from three smaller museums dating back to the early twentieth century into a comprehensive resource on the art, history, and natural sciences with a focus on California. The collection comprises close to two million artifacts, objects, art works, and specimens. Over the past decade, OMCA has transformed its galleries, exhibition and program development processes, community engagement strategies, and organizational structure to place the visitor and the community at the center of its mission and vision. Museum programs and exhibitions are developed with active community input and collaboration and address urgent issues and relevant themes that resonate for Oakland, with broader statewide and national impact.

Governance: Private, nonprofit 501(c)(3)

Budget: $15.8 million

Staff: 101 full-time, 31 part-time

Adoption Date of Mission, Vision, and Values: 2013

PHIPPS CONSERVATORY AND BOTANICAL GARDENS
Pittsburgh, Pennsylvania
Written by Richard V. Piacentini, Executive Director

Redefining Mission, Vision, and Values at Phipps Conservatory and Botanical Gardens

In 1893, Henry Phipps donated a conservatory to the City of Pittsburgh as a place for people to enjoy the beauty of nature. It was run by the city's public works department until 1993, when the collapse of the steel economy in Pittsburgh made it impossible for the city to continue managing the organization. On the eve of its one hundredth year, Phipps Conservatory was transferred from public to private management. The Phipps Friends group incorporated as a 501(c)(3) organization and assumed responsibility for running the organization. Their initial mission statement was quite long by today's standards:

> The mission of Phipps Conservatory and Botanical Gardens is to promote awareness, enjoyment, and understanding of plants and their diverse interactions with mankind. Phipps Conservatory collects, maintains, and displays living plants for the appreciation and benefit of all persons in Western Pennsylvania and abroad. Phipps Conservatory fosters learning about plants through educational and recreational programs and promotes research on their cultivation and natural history while conserving the architectural heritage of its historic building. Phipps Conservatory fulfills its role as part of a larger botanical community advocating responsible stewardship for plants and the habitats they sustain worldwide.

Our mission has changed since then, and the following examples will show how our institution's buildings, operations, and programs evolved in tandem with the development of our mission, vision, and values.

Once under private management, we began work to improve visitor amenities and replace dilapidated facilities. In the late 1990s we created a master plan, and during this process we learned about a new program called Leadership in Energy and Environmental Design (LEED). We discovered that buildings are responsible for approximately 40 percent of the energy and water we use and pollution we produce. Because we care about the environment, we decided to pursue LEED certification for our new Welcome Center. When that building opened in 2005, it was the first LEED-certified visitor center in a public garden. We then went on to build the first LEED-certified greenhouses (Platinum EBOM), and a Tropical Forest Conservatory that is one of the most energy-efficient conservatories in the world.

The process of learning about LEED and what it was trying to achieve was inspiring, and we decided to apply similar principles to all our operations and programs. Our staff and trustees became passionate about sustainability. We also found ourselves thinking in systems, which is how nature works. It was at this moment that the Living Building Challenge was launched in November 2006 as the most rigorous green building standard in the world. It is based on systems and regenerative thinking, so it was only natural that we would embrace it. In January 2007, our board voted to approve pursuing the Living Building Challenge for our new education, research, and administration building, the Center for Sustainable Landscapes (CSL).

Later that summer, during a board retreat to develop a new strategic plan, the board decided to modify our mission statement. The statement became:

> The mission of Phipps Conservatory and Botanical Gardens is to inspire and educate all with the beauty and importance of plants; to advance sustainability and worldwide biodiversity through action and research; and to celebrate its historic glasshouse.

In 2012 it was further modified, to its current form:

> The mission of Phipps Conservatory and Botanical Gardens is to inspire and educate all with the beauty and importance of plants; to advance sustainability and promote human and environmental well-being through action and research; and to celebrate its historic glasshouse.

Addressing some of the most pressing human and environmental issues of our time was now part of our mission, and Phipps could approach this in a very unique way by connecting people, plants, health, and planet together. As our vision statement makes clear:

> Phipps is the place where people discover the beauty of humanity living in harmony with nature.

We would come back to this vision statement again and again as we worked to align our buildings, operations, and programs with it. In essence, it gave us the rationale to "walk the talk." No longer could cost be an excuse; the statement made clear that the inaction or minimal effort to be sustainable that we and others lived by could no longer be justified. We know what we must do to live in harmony with nature, and it is not technology that is holding us back—it is due to a lack of will. The powerful message was conveyed by our new values statement:

> Phipps is committed to promoting sustainability, environmental awareness, preservation and renewal; collaborating with and contributing to the community; creating and presenting beauty; and adhering to the highest quality and integrity.

As a cultural institution, we have the perfect venue to make this happen.

Milestones on the Road to Transformation

Four for Four: When we started the process to find a design team for the CSL, we were committed to achieving the Living Building Challenge and LEED Platinum certification, including these requirements in the request for proposals we sent out for design services. Just prior to signing a design contract, we learned about the new Sustainable SITES Pilot program, which is a LEED-like standard for landscapes. Because we are a botanical garden, and it is important to us to know that we are operating at the highest level of sustainable landscape construction, we decided to pursue this as well. During construction, we learned about the WELL Building Pilot program, which focuses on how buildings affect human health, and decided to pursue this too. When the building was completed in 2012, we went on to achieve the highest rating for all four certifications; the CSL is still the only building in the world to achieve this remarkable distinction.

Food that is Good for People and the Planet: When we started the design of our café in 2003, it was on track to be a typical museum café with food prepared offsite, featuring a lot of fast food and processed food items, a minimal kitchen, and a lot of disposable plastic. Our exposure to LEED made us ask deeper questions about the construction of our building and how our mission should shape our operations. One day during construction, I noticed a worker installing café floor tiles from a box labeled "Made in Turkey." I was surprised because I thought we were supposed to use local materials. When I made inquiries about it, I was told not to worry, for we had "already received the points for local materials." I was not happy with that answer; we were pursuing LEED because we thought it was the right thing to do, not to just get our points and then return to the old way. That was a major turning point for us. From that point on, we decided we would do whatever we thought was right, whether we got points or not, and we would carry this through to our operations and programs too. This was the beginning of developing a values statement for the organization that would help us make decisions. Before the café opened, we completely changed the way it would operate. We put in a stove and a hood, so food could be made fresh onsite. We decided to feature local and organic foods. By the end of the first year, we eliminated plastic disposable serveware and began composting all pre- and post-consumer waste. We pursued and achieved Green Restaurant Certification. In 2009, we also eliminated bottled water. In 2011, we started our own Let's Move Pittsburgh program, based on former First Lady Michelle Obama's national program. Because a lot of children visit Phipps, we felt it was hypocritical to say we care about children's health and then serve junk food and soda in our café—so we stopped selling them. We recognized that we would lose a lot of money not selling these high-profit items, but in the end we decided to go with our values. There are some things we just won't do for money.

From Pittsburgh to Paris: We are very concerned with climate change and the impact it is having on the planet. When we compare our actions to our values, it is clear that "adhering to the highest integrity" compels us to walk our talk. What message would we be sending to our constituents if we presented a strong case against climate change but operated no differently than any other corporation or organization? We are constantly looking at how we can improve. Two of our buildings are net-zero energy, another net-zero energy building is under construction, and a fourth is in design. Since 2005, 100 percent of our campus electricity has been produced onsite or purchased from renewable resources. Since 2010, we have offset all the carbon we produce to heat all of our buildings. In 2015, we decided to divest from fossil fuel investments and reinvest those funds in renewable energy. If we aspire to raise awareness about climate change, we cannot justify making money off of investments in fossil fuel companies. We were excited when the Paris Climate agreement was signed in 2015, and even though the United States has withdrawn, we are still committed; between 2005 and 2016 we reduced our CO_2 emissions by 56 percent per square meter of building, twice as much and twice as fast as the Paris agreement.

Our mission has evolved over the last 125 years, but in the end we are still true to the original purpose and essence of Phipps, which is to create a place for people to enjoy the beauty of nature. As we've expanded and reimagined the ways we can address that purpose, we have created one of the greenest museums on the planet, a place where every program, building, and action is a reflection of our mission, vision, and values.

PHIPPS CONSERVATORY AND BOTANICAL GARDEN

Year Founded: 1893

Location: Pittsburgh, Pennsylvania

Mission Statement: To inspire and educate all with the beauty and importance of plants; to advance sustainability and promote human and environmental well-being through action and research; and to celebrate its historic glasshouse.

Distinct Characteristics: Created as a place to connect people to the beauty of nature, Phipps today remains true to its original essence while evolving into a leader in sustainable buildings, programs, operations, and research. Welcoming nearly half a million guests each year, its campus includes the first LEED-certified visitor center in a public garden, the first LEED-certified greenhouse, a Tropical Forest Conservatory that eliminates the greenhouse effect, and the Center for Sustainable Landscapes, the world's only facility to meet Living Building Challenge, WELL Platinum, Four-Stars SITES, and LEED Platinum.

Governance: Private, nonprofit 501(c)(3)

Budget: $15.3 million

Staff: Eighty-two full-time, sixty part-time

Adoption Date of Mission: 2017

PRESIDENT LINCOLN'S COTTAGE

Washington, DC

Written by Erin Carlon Mast, Chief Executive Officer and Executive Director

When I became the executive director of President Lincoln's Cottage in 2010, my top priority was to chart the future of the organization. Our previous strategic plan had expired after our grand opening in 2008. While nothing was inherently broken, it was clear to me that the mission and vision created during the capital restoration project no longer adequately reflected—much less guided—the work of our team. While our mission hadn't evolved, our program did so continually and responsively in keeping with our founding mandate to provide a transformative experience.

The first mission statement created by our team in 2004 read: "We preserve and interpret President Lincoln's Cottage to engage the public in an exploration of Lincoln the leader and private man." It was a description of methods, not a path for the future. There was a disconnect between the mission and both the founding mandate and experience we were providing. We went through a rigorous strategic planning process from 2010 to 2012, resulting in a new vision and mission. At the time, we still had to prove our statements aligned with our then-parent organization, the National Trust for Historic Preservation. Preservation is of critical importance to the cottage, but it's a means to an end, not the end game.

In January 2016, we amicably separated from the National Trust and became an independent 501(c)(3). We eagerly embarked on a new strategic planning process. In May 2017, the President Lincoln's Cottage at the Soldiers' Home Board of Directors ratified our new vision: "Plant the seeds of Lincoln's brave ideas around the world so that all people, everywhere, can be free" and new mission: "Reveal the true Lincoln and continue the fight for freedom." In just a few words, our new mission demonstrated our commitment to truth-telling—the issue at the heart of Lincoln's political ideology—and the desire for far-reaching and long-term impact, inspired by Lincoln's own wish that the United States would serve as a beacon of hope for everyone around the world seeking to be free.

Our mission, vision, and tenets reflect what distinguishes the cottage. Located in a residential part of Washington, DC, it is the only place the public can readily visit that captures all sides of Lincoln during his presidency. While living at the cottage, Lincoln visited with wounded soldiers; engaged with self-emancipated men, women, and children; and developed the Emancipation Proclamation. The human cost of the Civil War surrounded him, undoubtedly impacted his thinking, and strengthened his resolve to challenge the status quo. We recognize that what Lincoln accomplished here was a midpoint—neither a beginning nor an end to our struggle for freedom. Lincoln had a clear end goal, and, like him, we see great value in remaining flexible in how we achieve our mission.

I'm often asked when the cottage pivoted, the assumption being that we made a dramatic change from a traditional historic house museum to one focused on innovative programming and current issues. The truth is that the dramatic pivot was the collective decision to restore the cottage in the first place. The capital project, which commenced in 2000, occurred parallel to the National Trust convening two mini-conferences at Kykuit to address the crisis of historic house sustainability. The conferences drafted recommendations for the field and concluded that if museums and historic sites wished to remain relevant and essential to contemporary society, something had to change. That gave us freedom to push the envelope as well as significant pressure to succeed.

Starting day one, the cottage was a new model of what a historic site could be. We never had a traditional "velvet rope," lecture-style, or first-person tour for the cottage, because the stories we wanted to share were not best supported by those approaches. We chose instead to create a "Museum of Ideas," that focused on the monumental decisions Lincoln made while living here and the many influences on his thinking. We did not throw out the guide-led tour, but changed the very nature of it, making it conversational and endlessly adaptable, so that it was truly responsive to the public. This approach demands significant ongoing investment into the tour, starting with supporting the people who lead them every day. It pays dividends, too. Everyone, including VIPs, donor prospects, and Board members, have taken the "standard" tour, and everyday guests on the tour have converted to donors. On one occasion, a visitor called post-experience to share that she and her husband often joke about mission statements, but they read ours, loved it, and felt it perfectly explained what we stood for so much that they became supporters. The tour is both an experiential expression of our mission and a wellspring of ideas for new programming and partnerships. Since the tour is offered 362 days a year, it offers a continual feedback loop, providing a diversity of perspectives on our mission, every single day.

In 2014, we realized that while we were founded as a "Museum of Ideas," that concept, too, needed to evolve just as our mission and vision had. It adequately explained what we were but not why we were doing it. We engaged a consultant in helping describe our organizational culture and archetype. Why is it that we do what we do and how we do it? The result was affirming that our democratic society and the world at large needed a "Home for Brave Ideas," that this place had served that role historically, and that we were committed to being that place today. Programs we hosted during the 2016 presidential election cycle, such as a unique collaboration with DC Improv, the interactive public art UNITY project, and an evening of reflection on November 9, 2016, exemplified this. And every year we host various organizations carrying out Lincoln's "unfinished work" such as Polaris and the Center for Inspired Teaching. They tell us that being here provides inspiration and space for transformative reflection.

Perhaps the highest profile example of how a revised mission transformed our possibilities is our Students Opposing Slavery (SOS) program. Through this program, we developed an international network of youth abolitionists. The cornerstone of the program is the SOS International Summit. The program has served over 150 students from over twenty countries, and was awarded a Presidential Medal in October 2016. People unfamiliar with the cottage who first learn of SOS are inclined to assume it is an outlier program, as it's not a typical program offering at a historic site. Yet SOS is far from a side project; it both sprang from and intersects with all we do. The genesis of SOS was a collaboration on an exhibit on modern slavery in the United States for the 150th anniversary of the Emancipation Proclamation. The idea for the exhibit itself came from staff research and conversations with the public on daily tours, including the mistaken yet prevalent notion that the Thirteenth Amendment ended slavery. The motivation for doing the exhibit was to explore the unbroken arc of history on forced labor in the United States, to provide knowledge and a call to action for our audiences. When we launched the exhibit and then the program, some colleagues expressed concern that were they to do the same kind of thing at their museum, they would be alienating visitors, donors, even Board members. We had no such concerns, in no small part because we had built the relationships, track record, and credibility with our stakeholders—including the visiting public.

Reshaping our mission and vision provided greater clarity around President Lincoln's Cottage's purpose. Articulating tenets for the organization created consensus around our philosophy and the inspiration for our values. The cottage sits on a federal campus, the Armed Forces Retirement Home, and is a National Historic Landmark and National Monument. Yet we're a nonprofit, the only national monument in the United States that doesn't receive federal operating support. Naturally there is initial confusion for prospective audiences—including donors—about our purpose and our needs. Our mission answers that for them, decisively, but it upends the historic site paradigm that they know. By focusing on our authenticity and what makes this place distinctive, we have been able to differentiate ourselves even among the crowded field of Lincoln sites and museums, most of which opened decades, if not a century, before us. Our mission has also drawn in new partners, donors, and Board members, who have enriched the organization beyond measure, making our big step to an independent nonprofit public charity possible.

Though we've had successes, scientifically measuring them has been a serious challenge. Our field often measures impact using outputs such as annual visitation, economic impact, and other factors that, while beneficial, really do not reflect our purpose. At President Lincoln's Cottage, we measure such outputs in addition to having a longstanding visitor survey designed to capture qualitative metrics, but we also recognized we needed an entirely new method to measure success. Since opening, visitors had been reporting that their experience at the cottage fundamentally affected them. For example, visitors have reported feeling their minds opened, being "substantially changed," and finding that they were reflecting on their experience at the cottage weeks, months, and even years later, even if they had no direct contact with the site itself in the interregnum. However, this was anecdotal—and beyond our capacity to systematically capture. To that end, we worked with an expert in architecture and neuroscience with ties to Johns Hopkins University and Catholic University of America to design and conduct an eighteen-month phenomenological study, which concluded in the fall of 2017. The study is the first phase of a planned neuroscientific study and found statistical results that we are indeed delivering on our mission.

Beyond programming, we make a point of living our mission and vision in all we do. How we operate and how we do history matters. For example, we launched a campaign for certified-slavery-free floor coverings for the cottage over a more historically accurate material made under potentially questionable labor conditions. This may seem like common sense, but in a field that prizes accuracy, it was actually a conscious departure from the normal criteria for preservation decision making. Everything from our human resources practices, to our museum store merchandising, to our contracts with vendors are viewed through the lens of our mission. Our values spring from our tenets. For example, in one year we focused on empathy and accountability, each of which was demonstrated in various stories that happened in this historic place. Historians are fond of imploring others to use history in decision making, and I believe strongly that we should practice what we preach. That begins with our mission and vision. Lincoln used this site to advance freedom—so should we.

PRESIDENT LINCOLN'S COTTAGE

Year Founded: 2008

Location: Washington, DC

Mission Statement: Reveal the true Lincoln and continue the fight for freedom.

Vision Statement: Plant the seeds of Lincoln's brave ideas around the world so that all people, everywhere, can be free.

Distinct Characteristics: President Lincoln's Cottage, the cradle of the Emancipation Proclamation, is located on the grounds of the Armed Forces Retirement Home. The cottage is known as a "Museum of Ideas" with a continuing period of significance, versus a traditional historic house. Our experiential programming leverages the power of what Lincoln and his contemporaries accomplished here, providing context and inspiration for contemporary challenges. The value Lincoln placed on liberty, justice, unity, and democracy guide our work.

Governance: Private, nonprofit 501(c)(3)

Budget: $1.7 million

Staff: Eleven full-time, seven part-time

Adoption Date of Mission and Vision: 2017

SAN DIEGO MUSEUM OF MAN

San Diego, California

Written by Micah Parzen, PhD, JD, Chief Executive Officer

Mission as Springboard

With sweat dripping down his brow on a hot summer day in August of 1967, Martin Luther King Jr. reminded the world, during his famous "Where do we go from here?" speech, that: "The arc of the moral universe is long, but it bends toward justice." At the San Diego Museum of Man (SDMoM)—a more than one hundred-year-old anthropology museum located in beautiful Balboa Park—we have embraced the idea that the arc of the moral universe not only bends toward justice, but it also bends toward love. It bends toward compassion. It bends toward a greater good. To be sure, that arc may not always bend in the ways we expect it to bend, and it may not always bend at the pace we so desperately want it to bend, but it does bend.

As a museum devoted to the study of what it means to be human in all of its manifestations, our institutional starting point at SDMoM is that each and every one of us, whether we realize it or not, is here on this earth to support the process of that bend. Each and every one of our institutions, whether we realize it or not, is here to support the process of that bend. And, whether we realize it or not, our entire industry exists to support the process of that bend. It is our collective why.

An ambitious new mission statement—"Inspiring human connections by exploring the human experience"— adopted in early 2012, following a year-long strategic planning process, served as the springboard for our ongoing efforts to do our part to support the bend. It represented a radical departure from the SDMoM of the past, which enjoyed a decades-long heyday as one of the great museums of the Southwest, but had lost its relevance—and so its way—by 2009. Finding itself in an unsustainable downward financial spiral, it was clear that SDMoM's traditional mission of "Collect, preserve, interpret, communicate," which celebrated inclusion on the surface, but unwittingly reinforced the deeply embedded colonial context out of which the museum emerged and within which it long existed, had run its course.

Over time, our commitment to live up to the promise of our newly adopted mission and become "San Diego's dynamic place to go to learn from each other, reflect on our place in the world, and build a better community" (our vision) led us to a series of realizations about our relationship to the bend. We realized, for example, that we support the bend every day through our work in the museum, in the classroom, and in the community. When a visitor enters our doors and leaves unexpectedly changed in some fundamental way, we are part of that bend. When a little girl has a moment of inspiration that—whether she knows it or not—will change the path of her life forever, we are part of that bend. And when two friends engaging in a public program share a bellyful of laughter that can't help but make us smile, we are part of that bend.

We also realized that we support the bend when we are courageous as an institution. When the U.S. Supreme Court announced its historic decision legalizing gay marriage, for example, we flew an enormous rainbow flag from the iconic California Tower for all our visitors, Balboa Park, and the City of San Diego to see. Similarly, the day after the 2016 presidential election, in an effort to offer up a safe space for our visitors, we changed our name to "The Museum of Humankind," made our offerings free for the day, gave our staff the day off if they felt they needed it, and held a staff "council" for those who worked that day. Not all of our stakeholders agreed with our actions, but—ironically—those follow-up conversations enabled us to "deepen the hug" in meaningful ways.

Perhaps even more importantly, we realized that the more we aligned who we say we are to our visitors (the external) with who we actually are (the internal), the more authentic we grow, the more capacity we build, and the more sustainable we become. In other words, the better we could support the bend. So, we set about doing that.

We created an initiative called "World Peace Starts @ Home." Using our new mission as a springboard, this new initiative articulated our commitment to create an inspired and connected human-centered workplace culture throughout the museum. Focused on how we treat and relate to one another as a staff, how we treat and relate to one another as a Board, and how we treat and relate to one another as a staff/Board community (albeit with different roles), "World Peace Starts @ Home" established mechanisms that work to actively break down silos, increase the flow of communication, and give primacy to relationships throughout the organization.

Understanding full well that we had to put our money where our mouth was, we identified a "World Peace Starts @ Home" line item in our budget. We invested in professional development, staff/Board cultural sensitivity trainings, team-building initiatives, and even employees' personal growth. We also came to the hard-fought conclusion that we could better support the bend when museum workers speak and we listen. We came to understand that we had to do more than just talk about compensation equity, and so we committed to a fair exchange with our employees and began to implement a multi-year compensation equity initiative.

We also realized that we could better support the bend if we took a hard look at our staff and our Board, and we acknowledged that talking about inclusion is not enough. We realized it was time for us to admit that we weren't doing enough and to publicly commit to doing better. So, we made equity and inclusion a priority, created a staff/Board working group, funded a line item in our budget, and began developing a strategic plan for how we were going to become a more inclusive organization.

We also realized that we could better support the bend when we look at our trustees less as often-broken ATM machines and more as fellow human beings who have much more to offer us, if we can only crack the nut on how to meaningfully partner with them, engage them, and help them help us. So we took our decades-old governance structure created for a museum that existed decades ago and replaced it with a new Board ecosystem designed to serve who we want to become, not who we once were. Among other innovations, we created a new Board role called the "trustee engagement officer," tasked with optimizing trustee engagement wherever and whenever possible.

We also realized that we could better support the bend by facing the demons in our institutional closet. We realized that it was time to own the wrongs of our past, to apologize, and to ask those who have been wronged how we can help make it right. We realized that, for us, this meant making a commitment to the never-ending process of decolonizing our museum. So, inspired by institutions such as the Abbe Museum in Bar Harbor, Maine, we began by developing a human remains policy that requires informed consent from descendent communities. Then we embarked down the long path of truly partnering with Native and other indigenous peoples about what happens to their ancestral remains, their cultural patrimony, and how their stories are told (and by whom) at the museum, if at all.

Ultimately, we realized that we could better support the bend when we feel each other's pain as if it is our own. When we embrace the fact that as long as one of us suffers, every one of us suffers. The results? Well, we have gradually transformed a musty, dusty, and tired institution in significant distress into a leading-edge museum that is thriving inside and out.

"Where do we go from here?" We continue to work in support of the bend, and we hold ourselves accountable. It is hard work, it is messy work, and it is often painful work. It is, however, the work of inspiring human connections. Let's play the long game.

SAN DIEGO MUSEUM OF MAN

Year Founded: 1915

Location: San Diego, California

Mission Statement: Inspiring human connections by exploring the human experience.

Vision Statement: To be San Diego's dynamic place to go to learn from each other, reflect on our place in the world, and build a better community.

Values Statement: At all times, we strive to be:

- **Adventurous** We try new things, push boundaries, and are fearless.
- **Passionate** We love what we do and share our enthusiasm with others.
- **Engaging** We inspire our visitors to actively participate in the museum and we have fun doing it.
- **Disciplined** We strategically evaluate everything we do for alignment with our mission, vision, and values.
- **Open** We create an inclusive environment and welcome respectful discourse.
- **Accountable** We all share equal responsibility for SDMoM's success.

Distinct Characteristics: For over one hundred years, the SDMoM has been the steward of an immense array of cultural resources, including items of material culture. In 2010, museum leadership adopted a new strategy to use contemporary social issues and popular culture as a springboard for exploring the past, present, and future of what it means to be human. This approach, among others, is helping SDMoM achieve its goal of becoming a "fourth place" (not home, not work, not the internet), a participatory museum where both locals and tourists can come together to connect with one another about subjects that matter to their everyday lives. An institutional commitment to decolonization is key to support our fundamental convictions as set forth in our mission.

Governance: Private, nonprofit 501(c)(3)

Budget: $4.2 million

Staff: Forty-one full-time, thirty-three part-time

Adoption Date of Mission and Values: 2010

SANTA CRUZ MUSEUM OF ART & HISTORY

Santa Cruz, California

Written by Nina Simon, Executive Director

A New Mission Born From Crisis

Some institutions revise their mission out of a sense of civic purpose. Others, because of new directions in their programming. In the case of the Santa Cruz Museum of Art & History (MAH), changing our mission was a matter of life and death. To survive, we had to change.

When I arrived as the MAH's new executive director in 2011, the MAH was on the brink of financial collapse. There wasn't enough money in the bank to get through the week. The Board was considering closing its doors. Yet this financial crisis masked a more important crisis: one of community relevance. The museum didn't matter enough to enough people, or to the right people, to succeed. Most people in our community didn't even know the MAH existed. And they certainly weren't ready to jump in and save it.

Before I arrived, the Board and staff envisioned the MAH as a "thriving, central gathering place" for our community. They hired me to make that vision real. I took the job because of that vision statement. I knew that *if* we could achieve it, we could do something incredible for our community—and something innovative in the museum field.

The urgency of the crisis meant we couldn't act incrementally. We couldn't plan for years before taking our first steps toward the new vision. We had to act immediately to save the museum and move toward the institution of our dreams. The vision set our goal, but the crisis pushed us courageously down the path toward it. A crisis is a terrible thing to waste.

Museum Evolution

With our backs against the wall and that vision statement in hand, we started a revolution in the MAH. Our first year was all about action. We focused on three big ideas:

1. Art and history is something you do, not just something you learn about. People make art. People make history. By inviting people to actively participate with us in co-creating programming, we empowered them as creative agents, cultural producers, and people for whom the museum became a relevant, compelling partner.
2. We build community by building bridges across our differences. We didn't want to trade our historic audience of retirees and schoolkids for a new but equally closed market. We wanted to build bridges across the diversity of our community. We worked with unexpected collaborators, from opera singers and ukulele players to knitters and graffiti artists, to catalyze new partnerships and relationships that make our community stronger and more cohesive.
3. We believe in fearless experimentation. We had to get messy, try things out, and measure the results to iterate our way to a new, adaptive model.

This revolution was hard, tiring, and successful. In 2012, attendance more than doubled. Our busiest day more than tripled. We went from five years in the red to running a generous surplus, putting us on the path to financial stability. Best of all, was the response from our community, diverse individuals and the local press, who effused about the new vitality, public value, and engagement in the museum. We had started to build that "thriving, central gathering place" the Board and staff envisioned.

More Clarity, More Resistance

By 2013, we started to hit our stride programmatically and financially. We were now living the vision of a participatory, community-based museum. Our path was clearer. But it wasn't just clearer to us. It brought into sharp focus—for supporters *and* detractors—just exactly what we were up to.

Many people loved the "new" MAH, but not everyone. In 2013, two long-time staff members and a trustee resigned because of concerns about the museum's direction. A local blogger slammed the MAH for taking participatory experiences too far.[17] Warring local newspaper editorials championed the MAH as a site of courageous experimentation and challenged our community-centered approach.[18] National bloggers and newspapers joined the dialogue, linking the MAH to broader trends in audience engagement and participation.

On one level, it was maddening to live through this controversy. But ultimately, this controversy was a gift. It helped us strengthen and clarify our values and vision.

Participatory experiences are not for everyone. Some people feel that social work means mission creep for museums. What surprised me was the argument that inclusivity is a problem. Our detractors argued that participatory and community-centered initiatives—offered alongside many other interpretative strategies, program types, and projects—erodes the value of an institution and the experiences it provides. This argument felt ungenerous and close-minded. Why should a comment wall in an exhibition be more threatening than a label? Why is a crowded Friday night event in conflict with a quiet Saturday in the galleries? Why should any one type of experience in the museum have veto power over others?

The fundamental issue had little to do with participation. It was about the complexity of "and." I'm a big believer in the "museum of 'and'" premise, as championed by Elaine Heumann Gurian and the museum professionals who crafted the seminal publication, *Excellence and Equity* in 1992.[19] The strongest museums fearlessly seek out, test, and iterate many ways to achieve their missions. The diversity of the human experience necessitates an approach that values multiple forms of learning and meaning-making.

The MAH emerged from this controversy as a museum of "and"—a place where people come together from all over our community to engage with art and history through quiet contemplation *and* active participation. Value is reflected in the diversity of the people who participate, the power of the experiences we offer, and their ripple effects throughout the county. The stronger our value, the stronger our finances, the stronger our ability to expand all our offerings —the contemplative *and* the participatory. In 2013, during this philosophical tumult, a visitor posed a question on a comment card left in our lobby: "What is this—a museum or a community center?" Another person wrote beneath it, "Why can't it be BOTH?" We agreed.

Stabilizing Strategy

The MAH came out of the controversies in 2013 stronger. It was time to clarify the institution's strategic underpinnings and evaluation strategies. We wanted people to know we were serious, focused, and ready to be held accountable to our goals.

We were ready to rewrite the twenty-year-old mission statement, "The Museum of Art & History promotes a greater understanding of contemporary art and the history of Santa Cruz County, through its exhibitions, collections, and programs, for the benefit of residents and visitors to Santa Cruz County."

We were ready for a mission statement that reflected the museum's current direction. Our mission statement work was a process of "naming and claiming" our existing purpose, not developing a *new* mission. In the end, we were debating two options: "ignite shared experiences" and "ignite unexpected connections." "Ignite" reflected our creative, participatory, fun approach to art and history—and the fact that we emphasize being the start, but not the end, of your encounter with art and history. "Shared experiences" speaks to the sense of gathering and coming together as a community. "Unexpected connections" speaks to the diversity of activities and people engaged and the importance of bridging across our differences. Ultimately, we decided we wanted both, "to ignite shared experiences and unexpected connections."

More Than a Mission Statement

Our new mission statement is short, memorable, and inspiring. But our staff needed more than seven words to take action. We decided to develop three supporting elements:

- Organizational values that defined how we approach our work
- Engagement goals that defined what mission-aligned community engagement looks like
- A theory of change to connect what we do to the impact we seek

In early 2014, all staff worked together to establish five engagement goals: Relevant, Sustainable, Bridging, Participatory, Igniting. We use these goals to evaluate existing and new engagement strategies, and to guide productive discussions about how to improve our work. We created broad goals that made sense across the entire museum and our diverse work. These goals gave us common language about what we are trying to achieve with our various programs, projects, and exhibitions. This was the first step on our path to creating a coherent, valued strategic framework.

Our next step—and ultimately the most important—was to develop a theory of change that connects the activities we do, to the outcomes they affect, to the impact we seek to create in the world.

We wanted to build a theory of change for two reasons:

1. Externally, we sought strong, data-driven arguments for support. We can't just say, "fund this exhibition and the community will grow stronger." We have to prove it. Donors want to understand the logic of how their dollars will translate into impact. A strong theory of change can make that case.
2. Internally, everyone needs to know what "good" looks like and how their work helps contribute to the overall goals of the organization. A clear theory of change helps staff make strategic choices at every level.

With assistance from a consultant, we built theories of change specific to MAH defined in two directions: up from our activities to our intended impact, and down from the intended impact to the activities that fuel it. The "down" side was the most interesting, because it helped us understand the role we could play in our desired impact—and the community partners we would need to engage and support to see the impact realized to its fullest. We refined this theory by tapping into social psychology research that proved the causal linkages within it. This increased the rigor of the theory, and it also helped us hone in on the parts of it that were most untested—the parts we would have to test ourselves.

The final theory of change was a PowerPoint slide deck. It was technical, precise, well-researched . . . and ugly. We commissioned an illustrator, to make an artistic rendering of it. Her version—one page, attractive, easy-to-read—hangs at every desk at the MAH. It was worth the extra time and money to make our most important strategic document beautiful as well as functional. Three years later, few staff members could tell you what our engagement goals are. Engagement handbooks pick up dust on our shelves. But everyone can explain the theory of change.

What's in the Theory Of Change?

The single most important part of the MAH theory of change is the impact statement to "build a stronger, more connected community" through our work. At the end of the day, everything we do drives toward this goal. Over time, this impact statement effectively replaced our 2011 vision statement. We had achieved "central" and "thriving." Now we were aiming for building community. We couldn't achieve this impact on our own. A stronger, more connected community requires economic justice. Good public transportation. Public space. Public safety. We partner with diverse collaborators because we know that all these actors are essential to creating the impact we seek.

The MAH's slice of this work focuses in three areas:

1. Empowering individuals to share their own creative voices and cultural stories. We empower visitors through welcoming, participatory experiences, and we empower partners by making the MAH a platform for them to shine. When we empower individuals—especially those who are often marginalized—it leads to a stronger community.
2. Supporting social bonding among families and friends. When people connect with their loved ones at the museum, it strengthens existing community relationships.
3. Encouraging social bridging among people from different walks of life. When people celebrate and learn with strangers, it builds a more connected community.

We focus most of our energy on social bridging. Sociologists have demonstrated the extent to which most contemporary Americans live in bubbles. Most of us experience community in isolation, moving through a small cluster of bubbles: Work. School. Neighborhood. Soccer. We spend most of our days with people who look like us, who share our culture, background, and class. Bubbles protect, empower, and insulate us. But they can also lock us into fear, judgment, and insecurity.

When we break out of these bubbles and build bridges across our differences, we build stronger communities. We bridge through experiences that bring together people from all walks of life, in shared celebration, respect, and learning. Research shows that social bridges decrease racism, increase public safety, and improve community health. Building bridges makes communities more equitable. Bridges shrink gaps in housing, health care, and quality of life. And they make all our lives richer as we expand beyond the bubbles of our personal experiences. Our unique value is not in targeting people but bridging across differences. Our staff are matchmakers for unlikely partners across the county: engineers and folkloric dancers presenting at monthly festivals. Artists and activists exhibiting their work. Homeless adults and history buffs improving a historic cemetery. Business leaders and street performers designing a new community plaza on the museum's front porch.

We measure social bridging via studies of participant diversity and attitudes toward strangers. MAH visitors now tell us that "meeting new people" and "being part of a bigger community" are two of the things they love most about our museum. We're programming the museum as a place of bridging, and participants are reflecting those values back to us.

Santa Cruz Museum of Art & History

Written by Nina Simon, Executive Director

From Strategy to Bold Action

Our biggest step forward since the founding of the museum in 1992 is Abbott Square, a five-million-dollar capital project opened in summer 2017. Like most capital campaigns, our goal was to strengthen the organization and expand the MAH's impact. But this was not your typical museum expansion. We raised five million dollars to transform an underutilized downtown plaza next to the MAH, Abbott Square, into a creative town square. We gutted an adjacent office building to host a new public market with six mini-restaurants and two bars. We planted gardens, painted murals, built performance stages, set out tables and chairs, and hung market lights. The goal was for Abbott Square to become a new creative heart of our county, a town square that brings together art, history, food, play, and community.

The Abbott Square project stemmed directly from the MAH's theory of change and overall strategic direction. Through the lens of our theory of change, Abbott Square was core to our overall institutional strategy. Just as we had opened the MAH up to more diverse people, perspectives, art forms, and historical narratives, now we were physically opening our facility with new offerings that are accessible and appealing to a much wider audience—including thousands of people who might not ever set foot in a museum. The people who enjoy Abbott Square's whimsical Secret Garden, locally rooted public market, and free outdoor performances all experience the MAH—whether they also visit exhibition galleries or not. This intersection is not entirely a coincidence—the MAH and the Abbott Square project grew up together—but it was reassuring to realize that the community's interest in Abbott Square was in our strategic best interest, too.

More museums should be in the public space business. If we care about building community, we can't just do it within our walls. We live in a time—especially in the United States—when people are more divided than ever. Space is contested, privatized, and segregated. Many people call this work "creative placemaking." The idea is that creativity—not just sculptures or murals but events, art-making, art-sharing, commerce—can help turn an intersection or a riverfront or a concrete wedge into a place with a story and an identity. Creativity and culture connect us to place and to each other.

I want to imagine a future of downtown Santa Cruz in which creativity, commerce, and community are all welcome. I want to imagine a future in which the spirit of welcome and inclusivity that permeates the MAH spreads throughout our whole town. We're trying to build a slice of that future in Santa Cruz County. What future do you want to build in your community?

SANTA CRUZ MUSEUM OF ART & HISTORY

Year Founded: 1992

Location: Santa Cruz, California

Mission Statement: To ignite shared experiences and unexpected connections.

Impact Statement: To build a stronger, more connected community.

Distinct Characteristics: We're a different kind of museum, one that focuses on building community in Santa Cruz County through exhibitions, events, and projects that connect people to art, history, ideas, and each other. We believe that art and history are for everyone, and we work hard to offer experiences that connect people from many walks of life: across generations, ethnicity, and background. Multicultural festivals, exhibitions, and partnerships throughout the county create surprising fun connections with people and ideas across our community.

Governance: Private, nonprofit 501(c)(3)

Budget: $3 million

Staff: Thirty-four full-time, fourteen part-time

Adoption Date of Mission and Impact: 2014

TAMÁSTSLIKT CULTURAL INSTITUTE
Pendleton, Oregon
Written by Roberta Conner, Director

The Tamástslikt Cultural Institute is one manifestation of the dreams and prayers of our ancestors. The Cultural Institute is the embodiment of a tribe's commitment to its own teachings and way of life. The Cultural Institute is a monument to our survival. When you come inside the facility, our world begins to unfold. It is not just a love for land but a love of who you are, what you are, and where you came from.

The most important measures of success will be determined generations from now. Did we collect the right materials? Take care of the things that can teach us? Our way of thinking about the collection—artifacts and documents—is that these are all teachers and they will teach when we are not here to do it. It a repository of the collective memory of a people.

Men and women. Day and night. Abundance and scarcity. Good and bad. We learn from it all. We learn especially when things are out of balance. When things are out of balance more scarcity occurs—more for some and less for others. It is important for us to know where the balance is. It is also important to understand what these languages can teach us. This indigenous culture I come from, the Columbia River Plateau people, is at a crossroads.

We are in the midst of laying to rest our elders who were born as speakers of their languages, passed on by those who went before, not learned in classrooms. The next generations will decide whether these languages live or die.

Indigenous cultures are trying to keep their cultures alive to perpetuate the knowledge from thousands of years—we are not trying to take anything away nor are we trying to give it away. We are trying to protect an enormous database of ecological information that could benefit all of us.

We don't have a word for wilderness because every place is known. A place might be wild, but it is not a wilderness. It is always someone's home.

If all of us look deep enough, we are all tribal in origin, a long time ago. Our culture teaches us that we aren't the most important thing. We are trying to keep knowledge of how to live with the land alive in modern times.

TAMÁSTSLIKT CULTURAL INSTITUTE

Year Founded: 1998

Location: Umatilla Reservation, near Pendleton, Oregon

Mission Statement: To preserve, perpetuate, and educate audiences about the diverse cultures and histories of the Indigenous people now known as the Cayuse, Umatilla, and Walla Walla Tribes.

Vision Statement: We are a trusted and accessible source of knowledge about the cultures, histories, and contemporary lives of the Confederated Tribes of the Umatilla Indian Reservation.

Distinct Characteristics: Only tribally owned and operated museum along the Oregon National Historic Trail, and one of a handful along the National Lewis and Clark Historic Trail. The Cultural Institute was honored in 2016 by Harvard Honoring Nations program for Tribal Governance for Čáw Pawá Láakni and honored in 2007 for a Guardian Award by the Association of Tribal Archives, Libraries, and Museums. We tell the story of Western expansionism from the tribal point of view better than anyone else.

Governance: Owned and operated by the Confederated Tribes of the Umatilla Indian Reservation. Tamástslikt Trust Board advises and oversees endowments, strategic planning, and fundraising.

Budget: $3 million

Staff: Twenty full-time, three part-time

Adoption Date of Mission, Vision, and Values: 2007

THE WILD CENTER

Tupper Lake, New York

Written by Stephanie Ratcliffe, Executive Director

What Happens When a Mission Statement is Ignored?

The Wild Center is a young, place-based natural science museum that was founded on the passion to share knowledge of the natural world of the Adirondack region in northern New York State. The Adirondacks is a wild place, and written into the landscape is the story of how people have cared for, restored, and protected the natural world. Late in the eighteenth century, the Adirondacks were ravaged by extractive industries. Then, in 1892, visionary lawmakers passed what is believed to be the first piece of environmental legislation, establishing the Adirondack State Park. Unlike the national park model, communities live clustered inside the park under a set of highly restrictive regulations in a patchwork of public and private lands. Public lands are deemed forever wild and are "owned" by the citizens of New York State. Now, over 126 years later, the Adirondack Park natural areas have recovered, and it is known as a model of preservation throughout the world. The Wild Center was created to interpret the natural world of this special place.

Although there were other early versions of mission statements, the one that provided a guiding light during the latter part of the start-up phase and through the first ten years of operation was this aspirational statement:

Ignite an enduring passion for the Adirondacks where people and nature thrive together and set an example for the world.

Our Ethos—and Our Inability to Explain It

Now, and throughout our first ten years after opening in 2006, we are determined to not be tethered by the standard model of science centers and museums—experimentation and risk-taking by staff is encouraged and valued. Some early experiments were successful, and after years of iterative improvements we now have a solid set of signature programs. Experiments also failed and were abandoned but never punished because as the executive director, I was intent on building and nurturing a culture comprised of honest critique, reflection, and learning.

At the end of our first decade by all traditional measures, The Wild Center was succeeding. We had solid indoor and outdoor exhibits on our now expanded 115-acre campus, provided a series of programs that worked, and were considered a quintessential "Wild Center." The results of our decade of experimentation and organic process of program development made sense to founding staff, but we struggled to succinctly express to external audiences how we had evolved and who we had become. Truth be told, we were most often guided by our passion for the Adirondacks and our instincts and desire to rethink what a museum could mean to a community. While we set revenue goals, simultaneously we started asking ourselves if every interaction with the public has to be transactional. Our staff-to-visitor ratio (which we call the human interface) is quite high and will never pass the traditional return on investment metrics. We think of it more like the *return on inspiration*. Our building and campus is a community asset that we share in a nontransactional way whenever practical and possible. The creation of our name, The Wild Center, was intentional—we can become a center for many things, and we can redefine what that means today and might mean in the future.

If we have one guiding principle, it is captured by Seth Godin's concept of the "Purple Cow." This notion is based on the idea that to be noticed in today's noisy and crowded world, offerings (e.g., programs and exhibitions) must be surprising, unexpected, and remarkable. People do not notice brown cows; they only notice purple ones. We challenged ourselves to explore a new twist on almost everything we offered. Creativity and innovation remains strong today and was in our early years but what had continued to challenge and unsettle us is that we were not able to tie the pieces of our work together with a cohesive philosophy and explain *why* our work mattered. Each program stood strong on its own isolated set of goals and rationale, but naming the strategy that made the programs work was elusive. Board members in particular voiced concern that they were not able to adequately tell our story to others to garner more support. Although each signature program was original and something to be proud of, we lacked a cohesive narrative. The mission statement at that point had not been abandoned, but it had become only useful for publications and grant wallpaper. It sounded good but it was no longer guiding our decisions and was certainly not helping us edit our creative energies. I believe this perhaps was one of the best things that could have happened—benign neglect. If we had filtered all our ideas through the mission, it would have constrained us from evolving and innovating.

Prompted by gentle Board pressure, we took a step back. We needed to reflect on our signature programs to determine what made them successful, and we needed to understand what unified them. In internal parlance we would say to each other "that is so Wild Center" or "that is old school, and not our brand." But if challenged to explain "why," we simply could not do it. We worked with a consultant to guide us through an intentional planning process that would help us articulate what was "so Wild Center" about our work. Program staff were guided through a process of stating the intended outcomes for each program. (Yes, that is right. We did not have them from the outset. We had been practicing a very organic iterative process directing our program development.) From there we looked across the outcomes and with much debate and discussion our consultant helped us articulate our impact statement.

People deepen their connection to nature and consider their role in sustaining their natural world for future generations.

What We Learned about Our Programs and Audiences Through Intentional Reflection

Several of our early programmatic experiments involved convening the community around climate change. We began this work in 2007, a year after we opened. This was a risky endeavor at the time, as scientific opinion was not fully accepted by the public and the topic was already highly politicized. We took the approach of convening and carefully constructed dialogue formats to present the science and then asked participants to draw their own conclusions about action. One of the lines we did not cross in our convening work was not to be prescriptive and ever say "you should" take a specific action. Action, if any, was up to the individual.

Over time in some cases we helped to develop community consensus on issues, in other cases people decided their own actions. One of these convening models was the creation of an annual Youth Climate Summit. Although expertly facilitated and structured by our staff, the content and approach was student-driven. The model can be replicated in other locations so we developed a toolkit to share the format with others. In the past ten years, The Wild Center has supported and led summits throughout the United States and in four international locations. As we reflected about how this work could exist under the phrase "Ignite and enduring passion for the Adirondacks," we quickly realized it no longer fit—a problem that we addressed. (See the following explanation.) This work has taken our programs well beyond the Adirondack Mountains. We had no intention of ending this critically important work that had reached thousands because of twenty words that had been strung together over a decade ago.

We learned a lot about our audience in the first ten years of operation. Located in a highly seasonal tourist region, it turned out that our audience was comprised of 60 percent new visitors each year. Unlike urban areas with a much larger audience base to draw from, almost two-thirds of our audience is transient. We had carefully created an interpretative style of not only offering information about our local region but tying that information to larger concepts in natural science that could be applied in other locations. Visitors could learn about the Adirondacks, but also something about their own backyard. Through other programmatic and exhibit experiments, we also came to understand that each person connects with nature on their own terms, having taken their own individual pathways. We exploited this basic premise and used science, live animals, art, music, technology, green building concepts, and outdoor recreation as approaches to invite visitors to reconnect and deepen their personal connection with nature. We believe this is an essential building block for taking individual action on nature's behalf.

Mission/Impact Relationship

Our mission statement is about The Wild Center; the impact statement is about our audiences' experiences. Both should be reflective of what we do and aspire to achieve. The process of developing an impact statement felt grounded and satisfying. But when we looked at our impact statement and its relationship to the mission statement, staff saw a disconnect. To reconcile the newly articulated impact statement with our existing mission statement, staff felt some modifications were required and drafted a new version of the mission statement. Staff operated under the new version as a draft for a year but when we brought it to a formal vote of acceptance it sparked a lively debate with the Board of Trustees. Some trustees did not feel a change was needed, and staff learned some members interpreted the meaning of the mission differently. Our climate change convening work that took place outside the Adirondacks was seen as "setting an example for the world" by some trustees, whereas staff felt like the first phrase "Ignite and enduring passion for the Adirondacks" was constraining our ability to reach out beyond the region and by doing so with our Youth Climate Summits we were not being true to our mission.

The staff felt constrained and worried about mission drift, whereas the trustees felt we were actually achieving our mission!

As with any mission statement discussion, debating each word of the statement is coupled with moments of overthinking and often results in pounding headaches. In the end one word was changed. Instead of the word "set" in the last phrase we settled on "offer an example for the world." Staff felt strongly that this small change was significant and important. That one word shifts to a humbler tone about what we can offer the world—not emphatically tell the world. We know the Adirondack Park is a wonderful model for others to know and consider, but it is a working model and certainly not perfect. That one word also implicitly reflected our philosophy of allowing everyone to make their own decisions about action. Offering versus setting an example for the world is what distinguishes our approach from advocacy organizations. Advocacy organizations often believe they have the answers and tell the rest of us to join in with them. Informal education is a free choice environment, and we believe people can make their own decisions. In the end, trustees accepted our need for the word change, and we accepted the new interpretation of how our climate work is living the mission.

We also wanted to capture what we felt made our programs and interpretation unique, as described previously, so we created a list of distinctive qualities and added that to our intentional planning framework. This has proven helpful in communicating our interpretative DNA to new staff.

Slightly Revised Mission Statement:
Ignite an enduring passion for the Adirondacks, where people and nature thrive together, and offer an example for the world.

Other elements in the intentional planning framework include how we do our work and our distinct qualities:

Our deep respect for nature and people drives the methodology in all we do—from igniting curiosity about the natural world, to learning from nature's intelligence to convening so people use their personal passion to work on nature's behalf. We learn alongside whom we seek to serve. We serve others to serve nature.

Our distinct qualities:

- We continue to reimagine what a museum is and what museum-like entities can do for a community and a region.
- We take risks in our work and seek to learn from our work.
- We are small, take on big ideas, and inspire many to carry out important work.
- We relinquish authority and value other perspectives and ways of knowing the natural world.
- We practice humility.

Considering Our Future

Now more than ever, museums and science centers must respond to external societal shifts and evolve quickly, or they will not make it to the end of this century. External pressures, changing demographics, and shifts in how we choose to learn are requiring us to rethink how we do things. Now is the time to question if we are really serving all of our communities and deserve to retain the high acclaim and respect afforded to museums in the past. One approach to embracing rapid change is through experimentation and not allowing our stated mission statements to confine our thinking. Our story demonstrates good things can happen if you purposefully ignore your mission statement every once in a while, in your pursuit of the greater good.

THE WILD CENTER

Year Founded: 2006

Location: Tupper Lake, New York

Mission Statement: Ignite an enduring passion for the Adirondacks where people and nature can thrive together and offer an example for the world.

Distinct Characteristics: We are committed to a future where people and the natural world thrive together. Visitors discover the story of the Adirondacks and explore new ways that people and nature can thrive in the same place. Place-based interpretation of the Adirondacks, living collection, indoor and outdoor exhibits on a 115-acre campus, elevated walkway over the forest, interpreted canoe and stand-up paddle trips—all urge visitors to embrace art as interpretive technique to connect people with nature.

Governance: Private, nonprofit 501(c)(3)

Budget: $4 million

Staff: Thirty-three full-time; seventeen part-time

Adoption Date of Mission: 2009, with slight revision in 2018

NOTES

1. Jamie Bissonette Lewey, Abenaki formerly coordinated the Healing Justice Program for the American Friends Service Committee in New England, and she is the chair of the Maine Indian Tribal State Commission. She is one of the founders of the Healing and Transformative Justice Center that gathers, supports, and shares essential healing methodologies. She also sits on the board of the Louis D. Brown Peace Institute, which focuses on the needs of families who have lost their children to gun violence in Boston. Since this board retreat, Jamie has joined the Abbe's board of trustees and continues as a key resource for developing decolonizing museum practice.

2. Portions of this case study are excerpted from Cinnamon Catlin-Legutko, "History that Promotes Understanding in a Diverse Society," in *The Future of History: Historians, Historical Organizations, and the Prospects for the Field*, ed. Conrad Edick Wright and Katheryn P. Viens (Boston: Massachusetts Historical Society, 2017).

3. For a full history of the CLGA, please see Rebecka Sheffield's 2015 thesis *The Emergence, Development and Survival of Four Lesbian and Gay Archives* from the University of Toronto.

4. Emlyn Koster, "From Apollo into the Anthropocene: The Odyssey of Nature and Science Museums in an External Responsibility Context," in *Museums, Ethics and Cultural Heritage*, ed. B. Murphy (New York: Routledge, 2016), 228–41.

5. Martin Margaret, *A Long Look at Nature: the North Carolina Museum of Natural Sciences*. (Chapel Hill: University of North Carolina Press, 2001).

6. Tom Earnhardt, *Crossroads of the Natural World: Exploring North Carolina* (Chapel Hill: University of North Carolina Press, 2013).

7. Jamie Bell, David Chesebrough, Jason Cryan, and Emlyn Koster, "Museum-University Partnerships as a New Platform for Public Engagement with Scientific Research," *Journal of Museum Education*, 41, no. 4, (October 2016): 293–306.

8. Emlyn Koster and L. Pendergraft, "Bringing the Mission to the Community: State Museum Opens a Satellite in an Underserved Rural Region," *Informal Learning Review*, 131, (2016): 11–15.

9. Ingrid K. Williams, "36 Hours in Raleigh," *New York Times*, (March 6, 2014).

10. Liza Roberts, "On a Global Stage: A Day in the Life of the N.C. Museum of Natural Sciences," *Walter, Raleigh's Life & Soul*, (October 2014).

11. Emlyn Koster, S. Yalowitz, and B. Watson, "Natural History: Past, Present, Future." *Informal Learning Review*, 113, (2012): 22–24.

12. Stephen Weil, "From Being About Something to Being for Somebody: The Ongoing Transformation of the American Museum." *America's Museums*, 128, no. 3, (1999): 277–96; Stephen Weil, "Beyond Management: Making Museums Matter." *International Council of Museums, International Committee on Management Study Series*, 12, (2006): 4–8; Emlyn Koster, "Evolution of Purpose in Science Museums and Science Centers," in *Hot Topics, Public Culture, Museums* (Newcastle-upon-Tyne: Cambridge Scholars Publishing, 2010): 76–94; Emlyn Koster, "Broadening the Reflections on Science Center Attendance." *Informal Learning Review*, 113, (2012): 26–28.

13. Emlyn Koster, "The Anthropocene as Our Conscience," in *Designing for Empathy, Perspectives on the Museum Experience* (Lanham, MD: Rowman and Littlefield, 2019).

14. Stephen Weil, *Making Museums Matter*. (Washington, DC: Smithsonian Institution Press, 2002).

15. Emlyn Koster and J. Schubel, "Raising the Relevancy Bar for Aquariums and Science Centers," in *In Principle, In Practice* (Lanham, MD: AltaMira Press, 2007): 197–220.

16. Emlyn Koster, E. Dorfman, and T. Nyamb, "A Holistic Ethos for Nature-Focused Museums in the Anthropocene," in *The Future of Natural History Museums* (New York: Routledge, 2018), 29–48.

17. Judith H. Dobrzynski, "Trouble in Paradise: Santa Cruz's Museum Loses Its Way." *Real Clear Arts* (blog), September 22, 2013, http://www.artsjournal.com/realcleararts/2013/09/trouble-in-paradise-santa-cruzs-museum-loses-its-way.html.

18. Stephen Kessler, "Stephen Kessler: An Art Museum's Purpose is Worth Contemplating." *Santa Cruz Sentinel.* September 11, 2018. Accessed May 2018. https://www.santacruzsentinel.com/2013/10/26/stephen-kessler-an-art-museums-purpose-is-worth-contemplating/.

19. Ellen Cochran Hirzy, *Excellence and Equity: Education and the Public Dimension of Museums* (Washington, DC: American Alliance of Museums, 2008).

6

Mission Statement Examples

The best way to illustrate inspirational mission statements is to highlight examples from a wide range of museums here in the United States and abroad. The process for collecting mission statements was a multi-pronged effort: some institutions submitted their mission statements for consideration; conversations with colleagues, both in the United States and abroad, identified museums doing meaningful work; and extensive research was conducted through the Internet. There were many rounds of review, culling, and selecting the most representative examples possible. The eighty examples featured in this volume were culled from more than three hundred mission statements.

The process of reviewing and determining inclusion was guided by a commitment to feature institutions representing diverse characteristics in numerous ways including location in the United States and abroad, size and type of museum, urban, suburban and rural, and a range of types of institutions. It is important to point out that the research for this publication did not include onsite visits to the featured institutions to verify whether their mission statements reflect all aspects of their respective museum operations.

Further, as stated in chapter 4, an ideal mission statement is short, crisp, and relevant. The reader will note a few examples achieve this sought-after characteristic; most are longer or have a brief explanation as to the reason for their existence. However, all of the mission statements featured have distinguishing and redeeming qualities and a commitment to make a difference, connect to communities, and achieve a relevant role. It is also important to acknowledge that longer mission statements are often common when a museum is in the nascent stages of development necessitating justification for the new institution. Some, like the National Museum of African American History and Culture, a museum within the Smithsonian Institution, are examples of a longer mission due to the legislation presented to Congress for the adoption and support of this new museum.

It is the hope that anyone using this volume can see themselves in this compendium of mission statements, be inspired, and find examples helpful to spur institutional discussion and consideration for refining their institutional mission and correlating work. It is the hope that some museums decide it is time to review their missions and invest in ensuring that their institutions are relevant and dynamic. Review and refinement of the mission statement is one important step in codifying the role of a museum in today's society. For emerging leaders and students of museum practice, it is the goal that these examples will be instructive.

The rubric for grouping the mission statements required new thinking and a different organizing principle reflective of contemporary museum thinking. Grouping museums by discipline such as art, history, or anthropology, for example, based on early nineteenth century academic disciplines and thinking, was deemed less useful in the context of the twenty-first century. Such categories pigeonhole museums into a defining mechanism that can be limiting and impose assumptions about the museum and its role, often at the expense of innovative and more relevant approaches. Today, more than ever before, museums are embracing cross-disciplinary connections, integrating issues-based dialogue, and featuring cultural experience-based offerings that tap into a range of perspectives and content areas, all of which expand beyond the limitations of museums defined by a singular discipline or content area. Many museums today are redefining their organizing principles, their identity, and the nature of their work to reposition their institutions for greater community and public engagement, and away from the singular discipline identity concept. As a result, the lexicon used for grouping the mission statements reflects an alternative and more apt way to think about the work of many institutions. It acknowledges that the terminology about how the field talks about museums is changing.

The categories selected to group mission statements are organized around the leading characteristics of institutional work instead of by discipline or collection focus. These categories were inspired by Elaine Heumann Gurian's article entitled "Choosing Among the Options: An Opinion about Museum Definitions" of 2002, where she proposed new categories for thinking about museums and the work they do.[1] Gurian proposed five categories in which she posited a leading characteristic, advocating that any museum may fulfill characteristics of a number of the categories. She identified the object-centered museum, the narrative museum, the client-centered museum, the community-centered museum, and national (government) museums.[2] The categories used for this publication are a hybrid of her thinking and condensed to four areas. Like Gurian's proposal of thinking anew about museums' redefining characteristics, the groupings in this chapter do not mean a museum exhibits only a singular feature; rather, a museum may well exhibit or feature any of the other aspects of these categories. However, every effort was made to place a museum in the category that best fit its dominant characteristic and how the museum presents itself to the public. The other purpose of attributing categories is to make it easier for the reader to see new ways of looking at museums and hopefully provide new ways to think about their own institution and its mission. Each museum features a mission statement, and some also feature additional elements such as values and vision statements.

First, the museum mission statements are organized by museums in the United States and international museums with examples from each continent. Examples have also been drawn from other nonprofit mission statements such as the American Humane Society, National Geographic Society, Glide United Methodist Church, and American Farm Land Trust.

The categories for the museum mission statements include:

- *Community-building museums.* These are institutions who define their role in relation to their communities as primary, demonstrate a vibrant relationship with their community(s) on a range of topics and issues, and aim to make a difference in those communities. Examples include the National Anacostia Museum in Washington, DC, the Oakland Museum of California, Navajo Tribal Museum, and Ka'ala Farms in O'ahu.
- *Content-centered museums.* These museums are dedicated to revealing and highlighting diverse areas of focus such as specific collections, research, and subject areas used as a springboard for their engagement with the public. Examples include the Museum of International Folk Art, the Sixth Floor Museum, the National World War II Museum, etc.
- *Experience-focused museums.* These museums highlight interactive experiences as the primary deliverable of their work and connection with their audiences. Examples include the Bay Area Discovery Museum, Minneapolis Science Museum, the Tenement Museum, etc.
- *Issues-based museums.* These museums focus their efforts on revealing aspects and knowledge around a key historic event, societal movement, or contemporary issue. Examples includes The National Museum of Memory in Columbia, the National Civil Rights Museum, the Anchorage Museum, Remember Bhopal Museum in India, etc.

U.S. MUSEUM MISSION STATEMENTS

Community-Building Museums

Abbe Museum

Bar Harbor, Maine

Mission Statement

To inspire new learning about the Wabanaki Nations with every visit.

Vision Statement

The Abbe Museum will reflect and realize the values of decolonization in all of its practices, working with the Wabanaki Nations to share their stories, history, and culture with a broader audience.

Smithsonian Anacostia Community Museum

Washington, DC

Mission Statement

The mission is to enhance understanding of contemporary urban experiences and strengthen community bonds by conserving the past, documenting the present, and serving as a catalyst for shaping the future.

Vision Statement

Our vision of the Smithsonian's Anacostia Community Museum is to challenge perceptions, generate new knowledge, and deepen understanding about the ever-changing concepts and realities of communities.

Gadsden Arts Center & Museum

Quincy, Florida

Mission Statement

The Gadsden Arts Center & Museum's mission is to foster understanding and appreciation of the visual arts to improve the quality of life in Gadsden County and the region. The organization works to enhance arts education, provide cultural opportunities, and stimulate economic growth in the community.

Ka'ala Farm

Wai'anae Valley, Hawai'i

Mission Statement

The mission of Ka'ala Farm, Inc. is to reclaim and preserve the living culture of the Po'e Kahiko (people of old) in order to strengthen the kinship relationships between the 'aina (land, that which nourishes) and all forms of life necessary to sustain the balance of life on these venerable lands.

Values Statement

KFI's restorative work is embodied by the saying: "If you plan for a year, plant kalo. If you plan for ten years, plant koa. If you plan for a hundred years, teach the children aloha 'aina.'"

Levine Museum of the New South
Charlotte, North Carolina

Mission Statement
Levine Museum's mission is to engage a broad-based audience in the exploration and appreciation of the diverse history of the South since the Civil War, with a focus on Charlotte and the surrounding Carolina Piedmont. Through the museum we collect, preserve, and interpret the materials, sights, sounds, and ideas that illuminate and enliven this history. The museum presents opportunities for lifelong learning about this history for the benefit, enjoyment, and education of children and adults, and provides historical context for contemporary issues and a community forum for thoughtful discussion.

Core Values
Scholarship, Education, Collaboration, Inclusion, and Fiscal Responsibility

Guiding Principle
We believe in and are committed to **using history to build community**.

Minneapolis Institute of Art (Mia)
Minneapolis, Minnesota

Mission Statement
The Minneapolis Institute of Art enriches the community by collecting, preserving, and making accessible outstanding works of art from the world's diverse cultures.

Vision Statement
Inspiring wonder through the power of art.

Navajo National Museum
Arizona

Mission Statement
Striving to achieve Hózho through contemporary and traditional exhibits, programs, and tours; to promote our Diné culture, language, history, and sovereignty.

Oakland Museum of California
Oakland, California

Mission Statement
To inspire all Californians to create a more vibrant future for themselves and their communities.

Vision Statement
OMCA is the heart of a thriving community and a statewide leader.

Values Statement
These values are fundamental to our institutional culture and guide our work together:

Excellence:
We are committed to excellence and working at the highest standards of integrity and professionalism.

Community:

We believe everyone should feel welcome and part of our community, both within the museum and with our visitors and neighbors.

Innovation:

We embrace innovation and calculated risk-taking to achieve our mission.

Commitment:

Our work at the museum demonstrates a sense of purpose and a shared accountability for the institution's success.

Santa Cruz Museum of Art and History
Santa Cruz, California

Mission Statement

To ignite shared experiences and unexpected connections.

Impact Statement

To build a stronger, more connected community.

San Diego Museum of Man
San Diego, California

Mission Statement

Inspiring human connections by exploring the human experience.

Vision Statement

To be San Diego's dynamic place to go to learn from each other, reflect on our place in the world, and build a better community.

Values Statement

At all times, we strive to be:

- **Adventurous** We try new things, push boundaries, and are fearless.
- **Passionate** We love what we do and share our enthusiasm with others.
- **Engaging** We inspire our visitors to actively participate in the museum, and we have fun doing it.
- **Disciplined** We strategically evaluate everything we do for alignment with our mission, vision, and values.
- **Open** We create an inclusive environment and welcome respectful discourse.
- **Accountable** We all share equal responsibility for San Diego Museum of Man's success.

State Historical Society of Iowa
Des Moines, Iowa

Mission Statement

We empower Iowa to build and sustain culturally vibrant communities by connecting Iowans to the people, places, and points of pride that define our state.

Sonoma Valley Museum of Art
Sonoma, California

Mission Statement
Building community around art.

Tamástslikt Cultural Institute
Pendleton, Oregon

Mission Statement
To preserve, perpetuate, and educate audiences about the diverse cultures and histories of the Indigenous people now known as the Cayuse, Umatilla, and Walla Walla Tribes.

Vision Statement
We are a trusted and accessible source of knowledge about the cultures, histories, and contemporary lives of the Confederated Tribes of the Umatilla Indian Reservation.

Content-Centered Museums

Arizona-Sonora Desert Museum
Tucson, Arizona

Mission Statement
The mission of the Arizona-Sonora Desert Museum is to inspire people to live in harmony with the natural world by fostering love, appreciation, and understanding of the Sonoran Desert.

Burke Museum of Natural History and Culture
Seattle, Washington

Mission Statement
The Burke Museum cares for and shares natural and cultural collections so all people can learn, be inspired, generate knowledge, feel joy, and heal.

El Museo del Barrio
New York, New York

Mission Statement
The mission of El Museo del Barrio is to present and preserve the art and culture of Puerto Ricans and all Latin Americans in the United States. Through its extensive collections, varied exhibitions and publications, bilingual public programs, educational activities, festivals, and special events, El Museo educates its diverse public in the richness of Caribbean and Latin American arts and cultural history. By introducing young people to this cultural heritage, El Museo is creating the next generation of museum-goers, while satisfying the growing interest in Caribbean and Latin American art of a broad national and international audience.

Fallingwater
Mill Run, Pennsylvania

Mission Statement

Fallingwater preserves Frank Lloyd Wright's masterpiece, conserves the site for which it was designed, and interprets them and their history for present and future generations of the world community. In pursuing its work, Fallingwater demonstrates leadership and creativity, engages the public, and celebrates the power of design in harmony with nature. Its approach is collaborative, and it meets the highest recognized standards of museum and preservation practices.

Iolani Palace
Honolulu, Hawai'i

Mission Statement

E malama, hoihoi hou, wehewehe, kaana a hoohiwahiwa i keano laha ole o ka moomeheu, ka moaukala a me ka mana o ka Hale Alii o Iolani a me kona pa no ka pono o ke kanaka oiwi a me ka poe o Hawai'i nei a me ko ke ao nei. To preserve, restore, interpret, share, and celebrate the unique cultural, historical, and spiritual qualities of Iolani Palace and its grounds for the benefit of native Hawaiians, the people of Hawai'i, and the world.

Japanese American National Museum
Los Angeles, California

Mission Statement

The mission of the Japanese American National Museum is to promote understanding and appreciation of America's ethnic and cultural diversity by sharing the Japanese American experience.

Museum of International Folk Art
Santa Fe, New Mexico

Mission Statement

The mission of the Museum of International Folk Art is to foster understanding of the traditional arts to illuminate human creativity and shape a humane world.

Smithsonian National Museum of African American History and Culture
Washington, DC

Vision Statement

The National Museum of African American History and Culture is the only national museum devoted exclusively to the documentation of African American life, history, and culture. It was established by Act of Congress in 2003, following decades of efforts to promote and highlight the contributions of African Americans. To date, the museum has collected more than thirty-six thousand artifacts and nearly one hundred thousand individuals have become members. The museum opened to the public on September 24, 2016, as the nineteenth and newest museum of the Smithsonian Institution.

There are four pillars upon which the National Museum of African American History and Culture stands:

1. It provides an opportunity for those who are interested in African American culture to explore and revel in this history through interactive exhibitions.
2. It helps all Americans see how their stories, their histories, and their cultures are shaped and informed by global influences.
3. It explores what it means to be an American and share how American values like resiliency, optimism, and spirituality are reflected in African American history and culture.
4. It serves as a place of collaboration that reaches beyond Washington, DC, to engage new audiences and to work with the myriad of museums and educational institutions that have explored and preserved this important history well before this museum was created.

The National Museum of African American History and Culture is a public institution open to all, where anyone is welcome to participate, collaborate, and learn more about African American history and culture. In the words of Lonnie G. Bunch III, founding director of the museum, "there are few things as powerful and as important as a people, as a nation that is steeped in its history."

National Museum of Mexican Art
Chicago, Illinois

Mission Statement
To showcase the beauty and richness of Mexican culture by sponsoring events and presenting exhibitions that exemplify the majestic variety of visual and performing arts in the Mexican culture; to develop, conserve, and preserve a significant permanent collection of Mexican art; to encourage the professional development of Mexican artists; and to offer arts education programs.

The National WWII Museum
New Orleans, Louisiana

Mission Statement
The National WWII Museum tells the story of the American Experience in *the war that changed the world*—why it was fought, how it was won, and what it means today—so that all generations will understand the price of freedom and be inspired by what they learn.

Values Statement
Commitment to the defense of freedom, courage, optimism, determination, sacrifice, teamwork, generosity, volunteerism.

The Nevada Museum of Art
Reno, Nevada

Mission Statement
We are a museum of ideas. While building upon our founding collections and values, we strive to offer meaningful art and cultural experiences, and foster new knowledge in the visual arts by encouraging interdisciplinary investigation. The Nevada Museum of Art serves as an educational resource for everyone.

New York Botanical Garden
Bronx, New York

Mission Statement

The New York Botanical Garden is an advocate for the plant kingdom. The garden pursues its mission through its role as a museum of living plant collections arranged in gardens and landscapes across its National Historic Landmark site, through its comprehensive education programs in horticulture and plant science, and through the wide-ranging research programs of the International Plant Science Center.

Peabody Essex Museum
Salem, Massachusetts

Mission Statement

The mission of the Peabody Essex Museum is to celebrate outstanding artistic and cultural creativity by collecting, stewarding, and interpreting objects of art and culture in ways that increase knowledge, enrich the spirit, engage the mind, and stimulate the senses.

Royall House and Slave Quarters
Medford, Massachusetts

Mission Statement

The Royall House Association explores the meanings of freedom and independence before, during, and since the American Revolution, in the context of a household of wealthy Loyalists and enslaved Africans.

Sixth Floor Museum
Dallas, Texas

Mission Statement

The Sixth Floor Museum at Dealey Plaza chronicles the assassination and legacy of President John F. Kennedy, interprets the Dealey Plaza National Historic Landmark District and the John F. Kennedy Memorial Plaza, and presents contemporary culture within the context of presidential history.

Vision Statement

To be an impartial, multi-generational destination and forum for exploring the memory and effects of the events surrounding the assassination of President Kennedy, through sharing his legacy and its impact on an ever-changing global society.

Umbrella Cover Museum
Portland, Maine

Mission Statement

The Umbrella Cover Museum is dedicated to the appreciation of the mundane in everyday life. It is about finding wonder and beauty in the simplest of things, and about knowing that there is always a story behind the cover.

Experience-Focused Museums

Bay Area Discovery Museum

Sausalito, California

Mission Statement

Our mission is to transform research into early learning experiences that inspire creative problem-solving.

Vision Statement

It is our vision that all children will have early learning experiences that unlock their full potential.

Boston Children's Museum

Boston, Massachusetts

Mission Statement

Boston Children's Museum engages children and families in joyful discovery experiences that instill an appreciation of our world, develop foundational skills, and spark a lifelong love of learning.

Vision Statement

Boston Children's Museum's vision is to be a welcoming, imaginative, child-centered learning environment that supports diverse families in nurturing their children's creativity and curiosity. We promote the healthy development of all children so that they will fulfill their potential and contribute to our collective wellbeing and future prosperity.

The Contemporary Jewish Museum

San Francisco, California

Mission Statement

The Contemporary Jewish Museum makes the diversity of the Jewish experience relevant for a twenty-first-century audience. We accomplish this through innovative exhibitions and programs that educate, challenge, and inspire. The museum's Daniel Libeskind–designed facility enables and inspires its mission. Dynamic and welcoming, it's a place to experience art, music, film, literature, debate, and—most importantly—people.

Detroit Institute of Art

Detroit, Michigan

Mission Statement

The town square of our community, a gathering place for everybody.

di Rosa Center for Contemporary Art

Napa, California

Mission Statement

di Rosa Center for Contemporary Art is a catalyst for transformative experiences with contemporary art of Northern California.

The Hammer Museum at the University of California, Los Angeles
Los Angeles, California

Mission Statement

The Hammer Museum at the University of California, Los Angeles believes in the promise of art and ideas to illuminate our lives and build a more just world.

Minneapolis Science Museum
Minneapolis, Minnesota

Mission Statement

Turn on the science: Inspire learning. Inform policy. Improve lives.

Vision Statement

We envision . . . a world in which all people have the power to use science to make lives better.

Values Statement

We value . . .

Science as an essential literacy
The ability to understand and use science is essential to educational success and full civic and economic participation in the world.

Fun, accessible learning
We engage learners by sparking interest and supporting deep science learning through wonder, play, hands-on exploration, and experimentation.

Authenticity and relevance
We present real objects and phenomena, solid scientific research, and compelling stories and insights from diverse perspectives.

Inclusion inside and out
Our museum and our people reflect and respond to the diverse needs and cultures of our community.

Remaining vital to our community
We serve a vital role in the community, providing resources and opportunities for learning that are valued by families, educators, funders, and policy makers.

Leadership through collaboration
We collaborate with organizations near and far, improving our own work, benefitting our partners, and setting an example for others.

The Tenement Museum New York City
New York, New York

Mission Statement

The Tenement Museum preserves and interprets the history of immigration through the personal experiences of the generations of newcomers who settled in and built lives on Manhattan's Lower East Side, America's iconic immigrant neighborhood; forges emotional connections between visitors and immigrants past and present; and enhances appreciation for the profound role immigration has played and continues to play in shaping America's evolving national identity.

Yerba Buena Center for the Arts

San Francisco, California

Mission Statement

We generate culture that moves people.

Issues-Based Museums

Anchorage Museum

Anchorage, Alaska

Mission Statement

The Anchorage Museum connects people, expands perspectives, and encourages global dialogue about the North and its distinct environment.

Vision Statement

The Anchorage Museum is recognized as a leading center for scholarship, engagement, and investigation of Alaska and the North.

Boston Science Museum

Boston, Massachusetts

Mission Statement

The museum's mission is to play a leading role in transforming the nation's relationship with science and technology.

Coastal Discovery Museum

Hilton Head, South Carolina

Mission Statement

The Coastal Discovery Museum inspires people to care for the Lowcountry.

Vision Statement

The Coastal Discovery Museum is a national model for demonstrating how local stories inspire action for better stewardship.

Eastern State Penitentiary Historic Site

Philadelphia, Pennsylvania

Mission Statement

Eastern State Penitentiary Historic Site interprets the legacy of American criminal justice reform, from the nation's founding through to the present day, within the long-abandoned cell blocks of the nation's most historic prison.

Vision Statement

Eastern State Penitentiary's innovative preservation, interpretation, and public programs will move visitors to engage in dialogue and deepen the national conversation about criminal justice.

Lindsay Wildlife Experience

Walnut Creek, California

Mission Statement

Connecting people with wildlife to inspire responsibility and respect for the world we share.

Harriet Beecher Stowe Center

Hartford, Connecticut

Mission Statement

The Harriet Beecher Stowe Center preserves and interprets Stowe's Hartford home and the center's historic collections, promotes vibrant discussion of her life and work, and inspires commitment to social justice and positive change.

Monterey Bay Aquarium

Monterey, California

Mission Statement

The mission of the nonprofit Monterey Bay Aquarium is to inspire conservation of the ocean.

National Building Museum

Washington, DC

Mission Statement

Our mission is to advance the quality of the built environment by educating people about its impact on their lives.

National Civil Rights Museum

Memphis, Tennessee

Mission Statement

The National Civil Rights Museum, located at the Lorraine Motel, the assassination site of Dr. Martin Luther King Jr., chronicles key episodes of the American Civil Rights Movement, examines today's global civil and human rights issues, provokes thoughtful debate, and serves as a catalyst for positive change.

National Underground Railroad Freedom Center

Cincinnati, Ohio

Mission Statement

We reveal stories about freedom's heroes, from the era of the Underground Railroad to contemporary times, challenging and inspiring everyone to take courageous steps for freedom today.

North Carolina Museum of Natural Sciences

Raleigh, North Carolina

Mission Statement

To illuminate the natural world and inspire its conservation.

Values Statement

Foundation:

Integrity, professionalism, and commitment.

Approach:

Inclusive, innovative, and collaborative.

Outcomes:

Engagement, impact, and sustainability.

Phipps Conservatory and Botanical Gardens

Pittsburgh, Pennsylvania

Mission Statement

To inspire and educate all with the beauty and importance of plants, to advance sustainability and promote human and environmental well-being through action and research, and to celebrate its historic glasshouse.

President Lincoln's Cottage

Washington, DC

Mission Statement

Reveal the true Lincoln and continue the fight for freedom.

Vision Statement

Plant the seeds of Lincoln's brave ideas around the world so that all people, everywhere, can be free.

Shedd Aquarium

Chicago, Illinois

Mission Statement

Sparking compassion, curiosity, and conservation for the aquatic animal world.

The National September 11 Memorial Museum

New York, New York

Mission Statement

The National September 11 Memorial Museum at the World Trade Center bears solemn witness to the terrorist attacks of September 11, 2001, and February 26, 1993. The museum honors the 2,983 victims of these attacks and all those who risked their lives to save others. It further recognizes the thousands who survived and all who demonstrated extraordinary compassion in the aftermath. Demonstrating the consequences of terrorism on individual lives and its impact on communities at the local, national, and international levels, the museum attests to the triumph of human dignity over human depravity and affirms an unwavering commitment to the fundamental value of human life.

The Wild Center
Tupper Lake, New York

Mission Statement

Ignite an enduring passion for the Adirondacks where people and nature can thrive together and offer an example for the world.

Woodland Park Zoo
Seattle, Washington

Mission Statement

To save wildlife and inspire everyone to make conservation a priority in their lives.

INTERNATIONAL MUSEUM MISSION STATEMENTS
Community-Building Museums

Science Gallery of Dublin
Dublin, Ireland

Mission Statement

A new type of venue where today's white-hot scientific issues are thrashed out and you can have your say. A place where ideas meet and opinions collide.

Derby Museums
Derby, United Kingdom

Mission Statement

Derby Museums' mission is to positively affect the way in which Derby is understood, the way in which the city projects itself, and the way in which people from all places are inspired to see themselves as the next generation of innovators, makers, and creators.

Te Papa Museum
Wellington, New Zealand

Vision Statement

Te Papa's vision for the future is to change hearts, minds, and lives. Our role is to be a forum for the nation to present, explore, and preserve the heritage of its cultures and knowledge of the natural environment. Te Papa was established with this role by the Museum of New Zealand Te Papa Tongarewa Act 1992.

Haida Gwaii Museum
British Columbia, Canada

Vision Statement

Suuda ganunsid ad gina 'waadluxan ganyahguudang xaayda gwaay. Yaay iiji Xaayda gwaay 'ahl tl'a gan unsiideel-gang isgyaan yahgudang. Gang giigang.

To inspire understanding and respect for all that Haida Gwaii is.

Western Australian Museum
Northbridge, Australia

Mission Statement
To inspire and challenge people to explore and share their identity, culture, environment, and sense of place, and to contribute to the diversity and creativity of our world.

Call to Action
Rethink your world.

Content-Centered Museums

Museum of Anthropology at University of British Columbia
Vancouver, British Columbia

Mission Statement
To inspire understanding of and respect for world arts and cultures.

Vision Statement
The Museum of Anthropology will become one of the world's principal hubs for exhibition, teaching, and research of international visual, intangible, and performative culture. It will provide a transformative environment for visitors to learn about themselves and others, and to consider contemporary and historical events and issues from multiple perspectives. It will enhance its international profile while working locally, maintaining and strengthening its focus on First Nations peoples of British Columbia as well as diverse cultural communities. It will embrace interdisciplinarity and champion collaboration. It will provide innovative and imaginative exhibits and programs, and encourage full academic and student participation while promoting the University of British Columbia's values, commitments, and aspirations.

Kenya Wildlife Service
Nairobi, Kenya

Mission Statement
To sustainably conserve, manage, and enhance Kenya's wildlife, its habitats, and provide a wide range of public uses in collaboration with stakeholders for posterity.

Vision Statement
To save the last great species and places on earth for humanity.

Powerhouse Museum: Museum of Applied Arts and Sciences
Ultimo, Australia

Mission Statement
To be a catalyst for creative expression and curious minds.

Vision Statement
To be the leading museum of applied arts and sciences, inspiring people and communities to transform our world.

Values Statement
Integrity. Courage. Passion.

POLIN—Museum of the History of Polish Jews
Warsaw, Poland

Mission Statement
To recall and preserve the memory of the history of Polish Jews, contributing to the mutual understanding and respect among Poles and Jews as well as other societies of Europe and the world.

Vision Statement
To create a modern museum—an educational and cultural center, a platform for social dialogue; an institution offering a profound, transformative experience and promoting new standards of relating to history.

Experience-Focused Museums

Museo Interactivo Economía
Mexico City, Mexico

Mission Statement
We use economics as a lens for people to discover how the world works.

Vision Statement
We ignite critical and creative thinking to enhance well-being for all.

Australian Center for the Moving Image
Melbourne, Australia

Mission Statement
To enrich our lives and foster our creative industries by illuminating the moving images and technologies that define our age.

Issues-Based Museums

The Arquives (formerly The Canadian Lesbian and Gay Archives)
Toronto, Ontario, Canada

Vision Statement
The Canadian Lesbian and Gay Archives aspires to be a significant resource and catalyst for those who strive for a future world where lesbian, gay, bisexual, and trans people are accepted, valued, and celebrated.

Mandate
The Canadian Lesbian and Gay Archives was established to aid in the recovery and preservation of our histories. Its mandate is to:

- acquire, preserve, organize, and give public access to information and materials in any medium, by and about LGBTQ2+ people, primarily produced in or concerning Canada; and
- maintain a research library, international research files, and an international collection of LGBTQ2+ periodicals.

Ditsong Museums
Gauteng Province, South Africa

Mission Statement
To transform and enhance museums and heritage sites as vehicles for nation building and social cohesion through active conservation, innovative research, and relevant public programs for the benefit of present and future generations.

Vision Statement
Sustainable museums accessible to all.

The Jewish Museum
London, United Kingdom

Mission Statement
Our mission is to surprise, delight, and engage all people, irrespective of background or faith, in the history, identity, and culture of Jews in Britain: by inspiring discovery, provoking questions, and encouraging understanding.

Vision Statement
Our vision is of a world where cultural diversity and the contribution of minority communities are explored, valued, and celebrated for the enrichment of society as a whole.

Hiroshima Peace Memorial Museum
Hiroshima, Japan

Mission Statement
Hiroshima Peace Memorial Museum shall be established to convey to the world actual facts of the atomic bombing, and to contribute to the abolition of nuclear weapons and realization of lasting world peace.

Malmö Museer (Malmö Museums)
Malmö, Sweden

Mission Statement
Malmö Museums creates the opportunity for insight into and empathy for our natural and cultural heritage so that it can be preserved, used, and developed and concern everyone.

Vision Statement
To be the best at arousing curiosity and encouraging involvement.

Museum of International Democracy
Rosario, Argentina

Mission Statement
The Museum for International Democracy will be a place to reflect on what democracy means. The intention is to encourage visitors to work toward a better quality of life, promoting free speech, debate, mutual respect, and analyzing democratic values.

National Museums Liverpool
Liverpool, United Kingdom

Mission Statement
To be the world's leading example of an inclusive museum service.

Values Statement
1. We are an inclusive and democratic museum service; we aim to maximize social impact and educational benefit for all—museums change lives.
2. Museums are fundamentally educational in purpose.
3. Museums are places for ideas and dialogue, that use collections to inspire people; we do not avoid contemporary issues or controversy.
4. Museums help promote good citizenship and act as agents of social change: the National Museums of Liverpool believes in the concept of, and campaigns for, social justice.
5. We believe in sustainable development, and we have a role to play in the conservation and protection of the built and natural environment.
6. We believe in innovation so as to keep our public offer fresh and challenging, while behaving ethically, and working with partners who support our values.

National Museum of Memory
Bogotá, Colombia

Mission Statement
To achieve the strengthening of the collective memory regarding Colombia's recent history of violence, making sure to combine efforts from the private sector, civil society, international cooperation, and the state.

Natural History Museum
London, England

Purpose Statement
The museum's purpose is to challenge the way people think about the natural world—its past, present, and future. We aim to stimulate public debate about humanity's future and equip our audiences at every level with an understanding of science. We focus on three themes:

- **Origins and evolution:** the 4.5-billion-year history of our solar system, the Earth, and life.
- **Diversity of life:** today's natural diversity among species, habitats, and ecosystems.
- **Sustainable futures:** the future of the natural systems that our society depends on.

The Remember Bhopal Museum
Bhopal, India

Mission Statement
The Remember Bhopal Trust will organize commemorative activities and its first project is to build the Remember Bhopal Museum in the city.

The Remember Bhopal Museum is a survivor-led effort at collecting, archiving, and exhibiting memories, artifacts, and oral histories of the experience of the communities affected by the aftermath of what has come to be known as the world's worst industrial disaster.

It is perhaps the first museum in independent India that is collectively curated by a community of survivors and activists and tells the story of a contemporary people's movement.

The museum will display artefacts, oral histories, photographs, protest songs, and campaign posters that have emerged in the movement for justice.

Svendborg Museum (The Danish Welfare Museum)
Svendborg, Denmark

Mission Statement
The Danish Welfare Museum strives to be an important cultural institution that addresses contemporary social issues and engages in and qualifies debates about the welfare state. We have created a dynamic museum through a close collaboration with people who have spent part of their lives in institutions and/or have experienced social vulnerability, exclusion, severe personal downturns, or stigmatization.

Vision Statement
It is our ambition to continuously strengthen the collaborative impetus in the museum's efforts to anchor the following: The Danish Welfare Museum aims to be the historical consciousness of the social welfare system and contribute to the cohesion of society.

Museo Memoria y Tolerancia
Mexico City, Mexico

Mission Statement
Disseminate the importance of tolerance, nonviolence, and human rights. Create awareness through historical memory, particularly from genocides and other crimes. Alert about the danger of indifference, discrimination, and violence to create responsibility, respect, and conscience in each individual that grows into social action.

Vision Statement
Transcend as an institution that is an authority on the subject related to the historical memory of genocides, tolerance, and human rights, both nationally and internationally.

Aims
- Promote the values of tolerance and respect.
- Encourage new generations to seek a healthier coexistence and commitment to society.
- Confront the visitor in order to create an introspection and a change of attitude.
- Promote inner reflection that activates social action.
- Educate and create sense of responsibility toward the needs of the most vulnerable.

War Childhood Museum
Logavina, Sarajevo, Bosnia, and Herzegovina

Mission Statement
The mission of the War Childhood Museum is to continuously and in accordance to the highest standards document and digitize materials related to growing up in the war, and to present the archived materials throughout various media channels in order to educate a broad audience about this experience.

Vision Statement

The vision of the War Childhood Museum is to help individuals overcome past traumatic experiences and prevent traumatization of others, and at the same time advance mutual understanding at the collective level in order to enhance personal and social development.

OTHER NONPROFIT MISSION STATEMENT EXAMPLES

American Humane Society

Washington, DC

Mission Statement

Celebrating animals, confronting cruelty.

Amnesty International

London, United Kingdom

Mission Statement

Amnesty International is a global movement of people fighting injustice and promoting human rights.

American Farmland Trust

Washington, DC

Mission Statement

The mission of American Farmland Trust is to save the land that sustains us by protecting farmland, promoting sound farming practices, and keeping farmers on the land.

GLIDE United Methodist Church

San Francisco, California

Mission Statement

GLIDE's mission is to create a radically inclusive, just, and loving community mobilized to alleviate suffering and break the cycles of poverty and marginalization.

Greenpeace

Washington, DC

Mission Statement

Greenpeace is the leading independent campaigning organization that uses peaceful protest and creative communication to expose global environmental problems and promote solutions that are essential to a green and peaceful future.

National Geographic Society

Washington, DC

About Section

At National Geographic, we believe in the power of science, exploration, and storytelling to change the world.

National Park Services
Washington, DC

Mission Statement

The National Park Service preserves unimpaired the natural and cultural resources and values of the National Park System for the enjoyment, education, and inspiration of this and future generations. The Park Service cooperates with partners to extend the benefits of natural and cultural resource conservation and outdoor recreation throughout this country and the world.

NOTES

1. Elaine Heumann Gurian, "Choosing Among the Options: An Opinion about Museum Definitions," in *Civilizing the Museum: The Collected Writings of Elaine Heumann Gurian*, (London and New York: Routledge, 2006), 48.

2. Heumann Gurian, "Choosing Among the Options: An Opinion about Museum Definitions," 48–56.

A Mission Statement Development Process

When to Tackle Working on the Mission

Timing and readiness are key to a productive and inspiring mission revision or development process. There is no one best time, but there are decidedly better times, and moments when it is not wise to undertake a revision of the mission.

The organizational perspectives in chapter 5 capture the importance of timing. Some museums changed their mission after they dramatically changed the work of the museum. This was true for the Oakland Museum of California. Some museums, such as the San Diego Museum of Man, used mission reevaluation as a galvanizing moment to instigate change and revitalization. Others used the process of rethinking the mission to initiate decolonization initiatives, as did the Abbe Museum in Maine.

Determining the right timing for an institution is predicated on an honest assessment of factors from leadership capacity to status of financial health to changing external factors.

Some Ideal Times to Reshape a Mission

Moments like these tend to reveal both readiness and a commitment to do the work:

- *When a new director or chief executive officer has been appointed.* This moment can bring everyone together to dream, aspire, and envision the future together. Nevertheless, it is best to wait about six months after the new director has been onsite before kicking off a process. This acclimation period gives the new leader a chance to learn some of the nuances of the institution, the Board and staff, and the community.

- *Leadership at the governance and executive level concur that it is time to revise the mission and agree to participate in the process.* Together, the Board president or chair and the director exhibit a healthy partnership, an understanding of their distinct and appropriate roles and responsibilities, and a commitment to do the work. Not to be underestimated is having the staff leadership capacity in place, at least with the majority of the staff. Given that the staff will shoulder the lion's share of any work that emanates from a changed mission, their participation in shaping the mission is essential, as is their understanding of how their work will change.

- *The last strategic plan is nearing completion.* There is a level of readiness to look anew at the mission and ensure that it still aligns given the changing landscape in which the museum operates, and internal shifts occurring within the organization.

- *The museum's work no longer aligns with the mission.* This moment can be a positive one as the work of the museum has evolved beyond the intention of the existing mission, as with the Santa Cruz Museum of Art & History, described in chapter 5.

- *The mission statement is so old that no one knows it, knows where it is, or understands how to use it.* Some missions are so out of sync with contemporary life and the realities of the museum that they reflect badly on the institution. Disregarding the mission, not using it, and not recreating a relevant mission are detrimental to the health and success of any museum. It is a rudderless way to lead and guide an institution forward.

- **Early warning signs indicate that the museum is in trouble and needs a reorientation to its role and purpose.** Signs of trouble might include declining attendance and limited public participation, declining funding support or earned revenue activities, or an unclear role and brand in the eyes of the public. If there is strong leadership at the helm, and it is not the leadership that led the museum into this vulnerable place to begin with, such an institution may be poised to revise and reshape the mission. There has to be enough confidence to proceed, or this example is bumped into the category of not a good time.

When Not to Tackle Reworking the Mission

Not proceeding is highly recommended if:

- **Top institutional leaders do not agree on the importance of revisiting the mission.** This situation may reveal some issues around the leadership of the institution board's make-up and the strength and vision of the director, or it is a situation where the two are simply not in sync.

- **The institution is in financial or leadership crisis or amid a controversy.** These matters require attention first. While enmeshed in stressful situations and navigating out of an institutional crisis, there is no bandwidth to discuss issues like the mission. Take care of the pressing issues first.

- **The institution has lost its way, evidenced by conditions such as a weak financial profile, limited public engagement, or lack of community interest.** This is a moment when remedial actions are needed first. It all has to do with the severity of the situation. If the ship is sinking, stop taking on water, repair the leaks, and determine if the institution is still a going concern, then do some course correction. The issues may stem from poor management, lack of connectedness to the community, lack of a relevant vision, or a weak financial position. See the perspective of the Santa Cruz Museum of Art & History for a carefully described recovery effort to rescue the institution followed by revisiting the mission years later (chapter 5).

- **Leadership wants to revisit the mission quickly so the item can be checked off on a grant proposal, an accreditation review, or another externally triggered requirement.** This course of action just isn't advisable. As described later in this chapter, a quick wordsmithing of the mission will create new problems. It also reveals a lack of understanding of the value of a well-crafted mission as institutional compass.

- **The museum is undergoing an executive transition and has an interim leader.** When an institution has an interim director to guide the institution forward until a permanent hire can be made, it is not the time to revise the mission. Focus on the transition and the upcoming search for the new director.

THE POWER OF MISSION REVISION: CONSIDERATIONS BEFORE BEGINNING

Common Missteps in Mission Revision

Before deciding to undertake mission revision, hit the pause button and reflect on a few key indicators: readiness and timing, leadership capacity, a commitment to take the time to undertake quality work, an understanding what the implications of revision mean to the institution, and stakeholders overall. Mission revision can be a galvanizing moment for any museum. The following are some common missteps observed over the years.

- *Revising the mission in a hurry.* Assuming that a few quick word changes will do the trick is not the answer, and it never is. A truncated process falls short of an inspired process, can initiate new problems, and will eventually bring the mission back to the table for more work later. Take the time to do it right.

- *Misjudging the implications of a revised mission statement and considering it an exercise in wordsmithing.* Revising a mission isn't an academic exercise. It involves reframing and defining the role of a museum. It affects the institution from top to bottom, from the inside out and the outside in, all the people involved with the museum, and the public. All aspects of institutional operations can and should be traced back to the mission.

- *Undertaking a reframing of the mission with limited stakeholder feedback and involvement.* If the Board revises the mission without the staff, there will be pushback and issues will arise because the staff has to translate the mission into their daily work and their effects engaging the public. Stakeholder involvement also means collecting viewpoints from outside the walls of the institution such as funders, city officials, community representatives, teachers, and current supporters. Hearing these voices is essential. What they say may surprise you and will certainly be helpful in moving toward a relevant mission statement.
- *Giving the lead to one or two institutional leaders and not a cross-section of trustees and staff and representative external stakeholders.* This situation is a variation on the example just described. Sometimes a strong Board member or executive director feels that they know what should be revised and why. By not engaging wider institutional representation, the aspirations rest with one or two people, making the institution vulnerable to a singular voice rather than a direction shaped with broader internal and external involvement. Single-handed mission revision is a grave error, and it does not take the institution into a process that builds a holistic engagement with public input. If done by a committee of one, two, or a handful of people, the process will be flawed and it will not galvanize the institution in a direction relevant for the twenty-first century. In fact, it will likely trigger resentment and pushback, create institutional divisions, and further harm the role of the institution relative to its current and potential audiences.
- *Misunderstanding the need for a balanced and thoughtful mission revision process.* If a process is not outlined and it is not clear who will be involved and when, the results will be compromised. Further, a thoughtful process takes time—typically over four to eight months if not longer.

Assessing of Institutional Readiness

Ask these questions to determine if this is the right time to retool a mission.

- Why does our institution want to revise our mission statement?
- Do we have the right leadership in place to guide this process and see through the institutional changes that the work will instigate?
- Is this a singular activity or a part of strategic planning or another institution-wide process?
- Are we clear how a changed mission will affect the institution overall?
- Have we decided this is the right time to undertake revising a mission?
- Does undertaking a mission review process make sense given where the museum is today? The issues in front of the museum? Current priorities?
- Is the current mission out of sync with the nature of the work of the institution?

Consider these questions regarding the process itself:

- Do we understand the time needed to do this right, and are we prepared to dedicate the necessary time and resources?
- What should the process look like and who should be involved and when?
- Do we undertake this process ourselves or do we seek guidance from someone outside the institution?
- Are we prepared to shape the other strategic framework elements to create a solid management tool for the museum or build a new strategic plan?
- Do the trustees, director, and staff understand that a revised mission will impact the institution? To that end, are we prepared to make the changes to support and advance a revised mission?

Recommendations for the Mission Development Process

When the Board and director agree that the institution is ready and the time is right, the mission development process can begin. Each museum will determine the best approach based on current circumstances, realities, and budgets, but most will follow the steps described here. It is recommended that the following aspects of the process be clarified, and together, the results woven into the timeline and efforts that will be undertaken.

Step 1: Outline mission development process

Determine who will lead and guide the process

Some museums engage an external facilitator, while others guide the process themselves:

- When working with an external facilitator, be sure that museum leadership and the facilitator work together to co-create the process, ensure regular communication, and reviews of drafts during the process. The facilitator should be your partner and provide constructive feedback.
- An internal leadership team should reflect representation of Board leaders, the director, and a cross-section of staff. Consider appointing one or two external representatives to this team. This group ensures the process stays on track, problem-solves as issues arise, and adjusts the timeline in accordance with what is needed. This smaller group may work and review drafts, but the drafts should be shared more widely internally to provide checks and balances and more broadly with external stakeholders at key times for feedback.

Identify stakeholder involvement

Key to a successful inclusive mission development process is identifying who should be involved, and when and how each stakeholder group will be included.

- Internal stakeholders typically include Board leadership and members, the director, staff, and volunteers. Some institutions consider past Board leadership, members, donors, and significant supporters as part of the internal stakeholder family. For university museums, obviously university officials and representatives are essential participants, and similarly governmental museums need to include appropriate city, county, or other representatives.
- External stakeholders represent the voices in the greater community and should be diverse in expertise, ethnic, and cultural background. Examples of external stakeholders include but are not limited to current users, representatives of specific communities, teachers and educators, university representatives, students, local government representatives, other cultural and educational institutions in the area, visitor and tourist bureau representatives, business leaders, and organizations unique to the area (such as technology experts research leaders and artist groups).
- Typically, internal stakeholders are engaged throughout the process. Some institutions bring on select external representatives to sit on the leadership group but at a minimum, external stakeholders should be included in one or two reviews of the mission drafts.

Determine the process timeline

A timeline takes into consideration the steps in the process, review and analysis of findings, work sessions, review of mission drafts, and time for reflection. Letting a mission draft sit for a while gives participants time to pause, then review it again, often seeing ways to improve the mission.

Step 2: Undertake institutional assessment

An institutional assessment typically includes these activities:

- Gather and review internal documents to gain a perspective on basic documents, practices, procedures, and programs, including, but not limited to, board documents (such as by-laws, policies, and board member expectations), recent annual budgets, financial audits, organizational charts, policies and procedures (such as hiring practices and human resource documents); educational programs; exhibitions and other external public offerings; interpretive plans, marketing plans, decision-making tools; and the most recent strategic plan.
- Create a brief history of the museum, noting benchmarks such as any name changes, capital campaigns, new facilities, hiring of the first director, significant community involvement, and introduction of new programs and initiatives.
- Complete an institutional profile as of a certain date, in sync with the fiscal year. Include facts such as budget size, Board and staff, all the public offerings, attendance and participant profiles, physical plant, collections, etc. This becomes the snapshot and baseline from which forward decisions will be made and will accompany the review using the Mission Alignment Framework (see chapter 4).
- Undertake confidential interviews with internal and external stakeholders with carefully crafted questions focused on listening and understanding the range of perspectives.
- Assess the institution using the Mission Alignment Framework with guiding questions.
- Create a profile of the local community that includes facts and trends related to demographics, the economy, leading employers, government, education, cultural life, and other indicators.
- Assess and analyze the findings in preparation for the retreat.

Step 3: Hold a retreat to launch mission development

Craft a highly interactive session with key stakeholders with adequate time to:
- Review research and interview findings, discuss takeaways, and define areas for further research and exploration.
- Assess current mission against findings to begin to shed light on what no longer aligns given the external environment and the community realities. This is the starting point for shaping the relevant role for the museum.
- Use the Mission Alignment Framework as a discussion tool to identify areas for further work in each of the four alignment areas. Design this discussion as an interactive work session, noting the results.

Use a brainstorming process during the retreat to trigger initial thinking about the mission and core strategic framework including values and vision
- Start playing with concepts for the mission and document thinking about values and vision given that they inform each other.
- Identify aspects of the current mission that may be relevant moving forward.
- Sketch the key elements that define the museum to illustrate how they interrelate and inform the other. Generate multiple versions. Use images instead of words and avoid jumping ahead to wordsmithing. (See the example from di Rosa Center of Contemporary Art in chapter 6).
- Reference assessment findings to stay on track.

Test concepts against the external environment
- Determine how well the proposed mission responds to external issues and realities germane to the museum.
- Incorporate the assessment from the Mission Alignment Framework.

Test concepts against internal strengths and weaknesses
- Tie assessment to areas to strengthen using the Mission Alignment Framework (chapter 4).
- Lay out a strategy for the longer-term work.
- Fold into the deeper work of strategic planning (if you are undertaking a planning process).

Document the work of the retreat as a foundation for the upcoming work, noting words, ideas, and concepts discussed
- Do not try to create a version of the mission, values, and vision; rather, note the parameters for the work ahead, including questions to pursue, concepts that resonated with the group, etc.
- Fold into strategic planning process, if a part of a larger planning effort. If a part of a larger planning effort, there will be other work that will funnel into the shaping of the mission in the months ahead. It is ideal to undertake mission revision in sync with a strategic planning process, if possible.

Step 4: Build a strategic framework with clear mission, values, and vision
   Shape each of the strategic framework components and refine over time.

- Incorporate the shaping of vision, values, and other framework elements to complement and strengthen the mission. Recognize that reviewing and refining these elements together will make all of the strategic framework elements better, interrelated, and complementary to one another.
- Use the process to ensure that the delineation of each piece is true to its purpose and role in the framework.
- Document different versions of each of the strategic framework components including the mission. Include sketches of the mission matrix.
- Refine, test, and refine some more.

Step 5: Shape vehicles for feedback and refinement over time
Meet with key stakeholders to evolve and refine the mission and strategic framework
   Set out at least two sessions for refinement over the next few months to:

- Refine and test again for institutional alignment.
- Determine if every word is clear and defined in the mission, and if the mission imparts the essence of what the museum is committed to undertaking on behalf of the public.
- Share the mission, vision, and values for internal feedback and refinement.
- Facilitate external stakeholder feedback sessions on the mission, at the very least.

Step 6: Outline a plan to strengthen the museum to successfully deliver on the promise of the mission
- Begin identifying areas requiring refinement using the Mission Alignment Framework.
- Lay out priorities and a timeline for addressing the change.
- Clarify how all stakeholders will participate in advancing the mission, values, and vision.
- Keep the work front of the mind through Board meetings, staff and departmental meetings, and the many avenues and activities that tie to public engagement and community participation.

Step 7: Adopt the mission, values, vision, and additional strategic components

- Use the adoption of the mission as a public messaging moment and share with external stakeholders.
- Post the mission and vision of the museum at or near the entrance to the building, explaining how visitors can participate and be engaged with the museum, and how their role contributes to what the museum does and its impact.
- Post it in prominent places in the institution in staff and Board meeting areas, over the copy machine, and on business cards.
- Feature the mission statement on board agendas, on staff agendas, and keep it front of the mind.
- Develop decision tools and other guiding documents to ensure that the mission is upheld and used.
- Consider the other ways that your museum can use this moment of redefinition in publications, public messaging, partnerships, etc. This pivotal moment of redirection should permeate and influence all the museum undertakes.
- Build and ensure that the organizational culture, staff structure, methods of working and decision making, to name a few aspects of operations, truly reflect and align with the new mission.
- Understand that a shift in culture and institutional practices, integrating greater diversity into ongoing practices, takes time and requires room for trial and error. Ensuring an openness to keep the dialogue going both internally and externally as the museum continues with its own path of learning and reinvention is necessary.

Note: It is strongly advised to tie mission revision to a strategic planning process. This will ensure that the thinking around a new direction will be carried out throughout the entire institution for the greatest results.

8

Mission Matters Toolkit

INTRODUCTION

The Mission Matters Toolkit features innovative tools that are grouped into three areas: mission alignment, institution frameworks, and theories of transformational change. Some tools provide examples for shaping or clarifying the mission, some are frameworks for institutional analysis and realignment, and others illustrate an approach to undertaking change. Certain tools have been developed and used by specific institutions featured in the perspective chapter. Other tools have been identified for their simplicity and clarity, illuminating useful strategies in support of relevant missions, and still others have been carefully developed through years of work and research to help museums build new inclusive practices in their museums.

The reader is also encouraged to refer to chapter 4 dedicated to the Mission Alignment Framework, supported by a series of questions to support an assessment in an effort to define and properly support a museum's mission.

Mission Matrices

The first three tools in this section were shaped to support the work of a specific institution.

Anchorage Museum Mission Matrix created a visual depiction of the work of the mission as it relates to significant geographic areas. As a multi-disciplinary museum, they connect art with the environment to Native cultures through creative programs and exhibitions. In the boxes featured in the diagram are specific strategies and themes to illustrate ways, concepts, and approaches for advancing the mission. See chapter 5 for the perspective on Anchorage Museum.

di Rosa Center for Contemporary Art Matrix used a visual illustration to clarify the relationship of core concepts, geographic focus, relationships with artists and the community, in addition to depicting creative tension points set within the backdrop of Northern California and contemporary art. Supporting this illustration are definitions that clarify the parameters for their work precisely. By defining this realm of work, they use the tool as a touchstone for the work at di Rosa.

Minneapolis Institute of Art (Mia) has been in the process in recent years of reframing what used to be a traditional approach to art. This is one of several tools that they use. This one places the community at the center with the three circles of the Venn diagram capturing their value proposition. Some will recognize the leadership role the Minneapolis Institute of Art has taken in launching MASSAction, a gathering of leaders from across the country, that has met once a year over the past three years to grapple and discuss openly strategies for making museums diverse and inclusive institutions.[1]

Reinventing the Museum Tool, featured in *Reinventing the Museum: The Evolving Conversation on the Paradigm Shift*, features characteristics of the traditional museum and the reinvented museum with characteristics grouped by institutional values, governance, management strategies, and communication ideology.[2] The tool can be used with trustees and staff to identify where on the spectrum the museum is currently, followed by determining where the museum aims to be in the future. Each opposing characteristic can prompt conversations about subtleties and embedded practices within the institution. It can be useful before beginning to reframe the mission, vision, and values for a museum.

Dual Bottom Line: Mission Impact and Financial Sustainability is the core concept featured in the publication, *Nonprofit Sustainability: Making Decisions for Financial Viability*.[3] This tool has a variety of uses. One useful strategy is to weigh all public engagement activities offered by the museum and to place them within the grid. While a first step in assessing how effective a museum's activities are in supporting the mission, this grid also balances mission impact against financial sustainability. At the end of the day, the financial viability of an institution must be assessed against mission. While activities will fall in different quadrants, the balance of what can be sustained must be reviewed.

Institutional Frameworks

These select examples are simple reference pieces that capture an institution and its future direction, priorities, and commitment in support of the mission.

Bay Area Discovery Museum captures strategic priorities in this one-page reference sheet. See the perspective on Bay Area Discovery Museum in chapter 5.

Strategic Plan DIA is a visual that captures the relationship of the museum in the community, captures the core elements of their strategic framework, the mission, vision, goals, and values. Strategies fall into five categories of work and emphasis. This style of conveying institutional position and strategic direction is appealing for its brevity for both internal and external use.

The Impact Planning Framework for The Wild Center delineates the layers and interrelated components that guide the work. Framing the thinking around impact statements is a concept that Randi Korn has been championing through her writing and her recent book, *International Practice for Museums: A Guide for Maximizing Impact*. This is a model of thinking about impact as a core compliment to the mission to guide the work with The Wild Center.

Theories of Transformational Change

The two models dealing with transformative change both convey the personality of the institution and reveal the core orientation of the institution.

San Diego Museum of Man Model for Transformation focuses on the visitors' journey with the mission and vision at the center. It conveys the intended result of either external or internal transformation or both.

Santa Cruz Museum of Art & History Theory of Change uses a contemporary graphic style to delineate their aspirations to engage their visitors and the range of ways and directions that engagement may take.

The Empathetic Maturity Model is a multi-year project mounted by a group of seasoned professionals who frame both the instructions and the Maturity Model tool using specific characteristics to assist institutions in determining concrete ways to identify awareness and evidence of achievement through this model. The first page outlines the process, and the rubric appears on the following two pages. With such a delineated process, it is a way to capture where an institution is on its journey to be inclusive, responsive to the community, and reflect empathetic practices internally and externally. This tool was unveiled at the Museums and Race gathering at the American Alliance of Museums in Washington, DC, in 2016. The tool is also available in Spanish. The Empathetic Museum website provides additional information.

Mission Alignment Framework

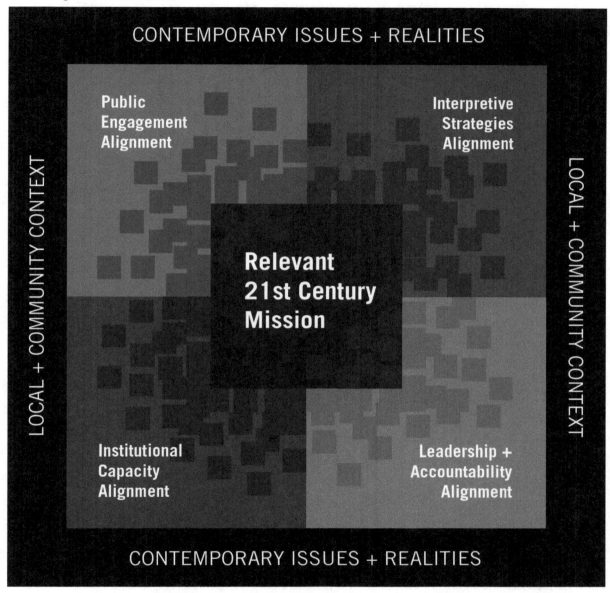

CONTEMPORARY ISSUES + REALITIES

Public
Engagement
Alignment

Interpretive
Strategies
Alignment

LOCAL + COMMUNITY CONTEXT

LOCAL + COMMUNITY CONTEXT

**Relevant
21st Century
Mission**

Institutional
Capacity
Alignment

Leadership +
Accountability
Alignment

CONTEMPORARY ISSUES + REALITIES

Mission Alignment Framework

Courtesy of Gail Anderson and Associates. Design created by Benitez Design • San Francisco.

See chapter 4 for an explanation on the concepts defining the Mission Alignment Framework, and guidelines for using the Framework for institutional assessment relative to mission.

MISSION MATRICES EXAMPLES
Anchorage Museum Mission Matrix

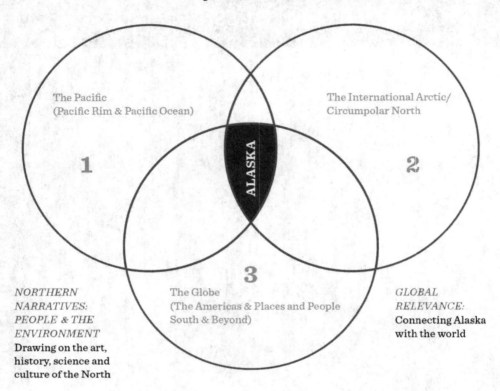

NORTHERN
NARRATIVES:
PEOPLE & THE
ENVIRONMENT
Drawing on the art,
history, science and
culture of the North

GLOBAL
RELEVANCE:
Connecting Alaska
with the world

1

The Pacific
(Pacific Rim & Pacific Ocean)
- Histories
- Byways
- Commerce
- Oceans/forests
- Geography
- International energy and
  resources
- Diverse populations

2

The International Arctic/
Circumpolar North
- Climate
- Environmental change
- Language/shared cultures
- Urgency
- Global impact
- Indigenous voices

3

The Globe
(The Americas & Places and
People South & Beyond)
- Alternate biomes/climates
- Authentic narratives to
  respond to curiosity and myths
- Parallel rural/urban
  challenges
- Disparate locations and
  cultures with shared goals
- Social and cultural globalization
- Indigenous voices

Courtesy of Anchorage Museum of Art

di Rosa Center for Contemporary Art Matrix

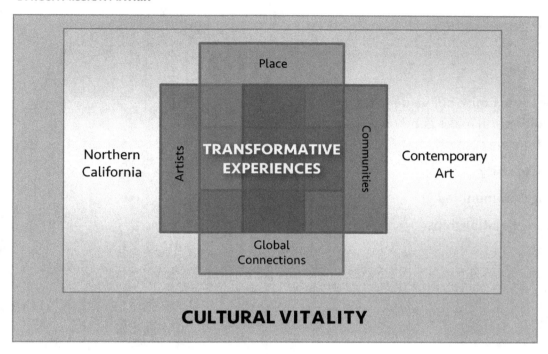

Di ROSA MISSION MATRIX

MISSION MATRIX PURPOSE AND DEFINITIONS

PURPOSE AND USE OF MISSION MATRIX
The mission matrix is a visual representation of the mission intended to guide di Rosa leadership when making decisions. The mission connects to all aspects of di Rosa operations including governance, staff leadership, public engagement strategies, the nature of exhibitions and programming, fundraising, financial management, stewardship of collections, facilities and the property, etc. Thus, this matrix should relate and inspire all facets of the work di Rosa undertakes on behalf of its many stakeholders and audiences.

MISSION MATRIX DEFINITIONS

Artists:	Professional artists at all stages of their careers.
Communities:	Communities include artists, audiences, and our neighbors. These are the communities we seek to influence and those who influence us. It is a two-way engagement.
Contemporary Art:	Art from the mid-20th century to the present.
Cultural Vitality:	The greater outcome of ongoing relationships between di Rosa and communities of artists and stakeholders as evidenced by fresh, lively, and meaningful interactions on-site, off-site, and on-line. These intersections of people, experiences and art evoke empathy and openness to others and an evolving sense of belonging and greater community.
Global Connections:	Relationships and connections that are reflective of relevant issues and trends locally and globally, bringing the greater world in and di Rosa to the world.
Transformative Experiences:	Experiences that evoke emotional and personal connections, enlarge the imagination, and expand one's sense of self, potential, and creative expression.

Courtesy of di Rosa Center for Contemporary Art Strategic Plan.

Minneapolis Institute of Art (Mia)
Mia 2021: Strategic Plan 2016–2021

In order to maximize our value to our communities and make good on our value proposition, we commit to:

Fueling Curiosity

Engaging Communities

Deepening Relationships

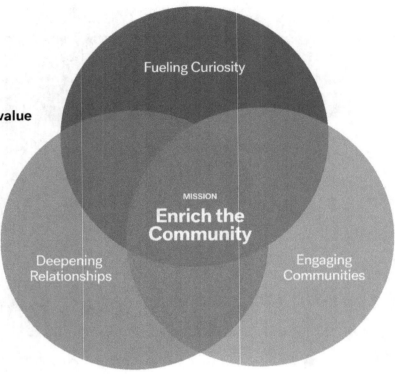

© Minneapolis Institute of Art

Reinventing the Museum Tool by Gail Anderson

REINVENTING THE MUSEUM TOOL

This tool is an excerpt from *Reinventing the Museum: The Evolving Conversation on the Paradigm Shift*, edited by Gail Anderson, + published by AltaMira Press in 2012. It is revised from the 2004 first edition.

The **Reinventing the Museum Tool** captures the essence of the paradigm shift occurring in museums. The terms on the left depict the assumptions and values that capture traditional museums. The terms on the right illustrate the characteristics typical of the reinvented museum. Museum trustees and staff are encouraged to use this tool to clarify where a museum stands in the continuum between the traditional museum and the reinvented museum, and where it wishes to be. This can trigger discussions about relevancy, institutional vitality, and responsiveness appropriate to a changing world. Each museum will determine which qualities of its operation to retain and which new approaches to adopt in support of an intentional direction. This institutional reflection may trigger varying levels of change and transformation for a museum.

TRADITIONAL MUSEUM

Institutional Values

REINVENTED MUSEUM

TRADITIONAL MUSEUM		REINVENTED MUSEUM
Values as ancillary	....	Values as core tenets
Institutional viewpoint	....	Global perspective
Insular society	....	Civic engagement
Social activity	....	Social responsibility
Collection-driven	....	Audience-focused
Limited representation	....	Broad representation
Internal perspective	....	Community participant
Business as usual	....	Reflective practice
Accepted realities	....	Culture of inquiry
Voice of authority	....	Multiple viewpoints
Information provider	....	Knowledge facilitator
Individual roles	....	Collective accountability
Focused on past	....	Relevant and forward looking
Reserved	....	Compassionate

Courtesy of *Reinventing the Museum: The Evolving Conversation on the Paradigm Shift* by Gail Anderson, 2012.

TRADITIONAL MUSEUM		REINVENTED MUSEUM
Governance		
Mission as document	....	Mission-driven
Exclusive	....	Inclusive
Reactive	....	Proactive
Ethnocentric	....	Multicultural
Internal focus	....	Expansive perspective
Individual vision	....	Institutional vision
Single visionary leader	....	Shared leadership
Obligatory oversight	....	Inspired investment
Assumed value	....	Earned value
Good intentions	....	Public accountability
Private	....	Transparent
Venerability	....	Humility
Caretaker	....	Steward
Managing	....	Governing
Stability	....	Sustainability
Management Strategies		
Inwardly-driven	....	Responsive to stakeholders
Various activities	....	Strategic priorities
Selling	....	Marketing
Assumptions about audiences	....	Knowledge about audiences
Hierarchical structure	....	Learning organization
Unilateral decision-making	....	Collective decision-making
Limited access	....	Open access
Segregated functions	....	Integrated operations
Compartmentalized goals	....	Holistic, shared goals
Status quo	....	Informed risk-taking
Fund development	....	Entrepreneurial
Individual work	....	Collaboration
Static role	....	Strategic positioning
Communication Ideology		
Privileged information	....	Accessible information
Suppressed differences	....	Welcomed differences
Debate/discussion	....	Dialogue
Enforced directives	....	Interactive choices
One-way communication	....	Two-way communication
Keeper of knowledge	....	Exchange of knowledge
Presenting	....	Facilitating
Two-dimensional	....	Multi-dimensional
Analog	....	Virtual
Protective	....	Welcoming

Dual Bottom Line: Mission Impact and Financial Sustainability

DUAL BOTTOM LINE: MISSION IMPACT AND FINANCIAL SUSTAINABILITY

Courtesy of Jeanne Bell; Jan Masaoka; Steve Zimmerman. (2010) *Nonprofit Sustainability: Making Strategic Decisions for Financial Viability*. San Francisco: Jossey-Bass (Figure 3.1, p.25).

INSTITUTIONAL FRAMEWORKS EXAMPLES
Bay Area Discovery Museum Strategic Plan

Bay Area Discovery Museum Strategic Plan

Strategic Goal 1
To demonstrate – to broad and diverse audiences at the Museum – the value of research-based learning experiences which develop creative problem solving.

Strategic Goal 2
To demonstrate – to broad and diverse audiences throughout the San Francisco Bay Area – the value of research-based learning experiences which develop creative problem solving

Strategic Goal 3
To be a nationally recognized authority on creative problem-solving for children, zero to ten, by parents, educators, and mission-aligned organizations.

Provide innovative programming and exhibits

Develop partnerships with strategic community partners

Synthesize and translate research to create proprietary CCC assets

Communicate intention and value of on-site experience

Bring museum to schools

Create and disseminate resources for parents

Evaluate efficacy of programs, exhibits and communications

Champion engineering with the Try It Truck

Build national brand awareness for BADM and CCC

Increase diversity of museum visitors and membership

Our mission is to transform research into early learning experiences that inspire creative problem solving.

Grow CCC advisory business

 Bay Area Discovery Museum

Courtesy of Bay Area Discovery Museum.

Detroit Institute of Art Strategic Plan

Our Strategic Plan

Vision
The DIA will be the town square of our community, a gathering place for everybody.

Mission
The DIA creates experiences that help each visitor find personal meaning in art, individually and with each other.

Goals
By 2021 the DIA will be **relevant to a broad and diverse audience.**
By 2021 the DIA will **lead the art museum industry in engaging people with art.**
By 2023 the DIA will be **financially independent.**

Values
Art | Accountability | Change | Collaboration | Diversity | Excellence
Great Place to Work | Learning | Scholarship | Visitor-Centered

Strategies

■ **Financial Sustainability:** We will secure long-term financial sustainability by pursuing a major endowment campaign, actively building public support, and maintaining ambitious fundraising targets.

■ **Relevance:** We will offer relevant museum experiences that authentically connect with the needs and interests of diverse, wide-ranging audiences.

■ **Leadership in the Museum Industry:** We will continue to develop next and best practices for engaging people with art.

■ **Facility and Neighborhood Presence:** We will improve and maintain the building, ground and amenities in order to enhance the visitor experience and our neighborhood.

■ **Organizational Effectiveness:** We will engage our staff to create an environment of open communication, collaboration, and high performance to enable us to reach our goals. We will align our organizational practices in order to accomplish our mission and reach our goals.

Courtesy of Detroit Institute of Art.

The Impact Planning Framework for The Wild Center

IMPACT PLANNING FRAMEWORK

WHAT What we do (aka mission)	**Revised:** Ignite an enduring passion for nature, the Adirondacks and its story--where people are working to thrive with nature and offer an example for the world **Original:** Ignite an enduring passion for the Adirondacks where people and nature thrive together and set an example for the world
HOW How we approach our work	Our deep respect for nature <u>and</u> people drives the methodology in all we do—from igniting curiosity about the natural world, to learning from nature's intelligence to convening so people use their personal passion to work on nature's behalf. We learn alongside whom we seek to serve. We serve others to serve nature.
WHY Why we do this work (aka purpose/benefit/impact)	People deepen their connection to nature and consider their role in sustaining *their* natural world for future generations.
WHO Target market and how we meet their needs (aka positioning statement)	To inquisitive minds of all ages, The Wild Center is the science-based community that cultivates and enriches your connection to nature so that you can actively engage in a future where people and nature can thrive together.
DISTINCT QUALITIES What makes The Wild Center distinct	• We continue to re-imagine what a museum is and what museum-like entities can do for a community and a region • We take risks in our work and seek to learn from our work • We are small, take on big ideas, and inspire many to carry out important work • We relinquish authority and value other perspectives and ways of knowing the natural world • We practice humility

SIGNATURE PROGRAMS / AUDIENCES   OUTCOMES

Youth Climate Summit / Teens will	VTS / 4th– 6th grade students will	Maple Project / Tupper Tappers will	BAGA / Contractors will	TWC Exhibitions / Tourist families who experience TWC campus will
Act on their climate plans in their schools/communities Become climate action leaders in their schools/communities Lead others across generations to act on climate change Deepen their awareness of climate change and associated science issues locally and globally Find purpose in being active citizens Become lifelong climate stewards	Analyze what they see (e.g., visual information) to learn about the natural world (e.g., wildlife, organisms) Respectfully talk among their peers about what they see Know that their observations are valid Accept other people's observations as valid, too Realize that thoughtful looking isn't about seeking "one right answer" Ask questions about what they see around them and seek information accordingly	Feel a sense of belonging with the Tupper community, TWC and other Tappers Feel pride by reconnecting to a local Adirondack tradition Develop a deepened affinity for this place—the Adirondacks—its land and its culture Learn about the sugaring process—from collecting sap to the newest technology for boiling sap Have new-found respect for their ancestors' participation in Adirondack sugaring Respect maple trees as a source for food, family, and fun	Become aware of green building practices, products, tools, and technologies Learn green approaches to their trade and craft and their associated efficiencies Communicate the virtues of building sustainably to their clients Implement sustainable building practices in the Adirondacks Find comradery with other contractors who are also interested in a more sustainable Adirondacks	Recognize that they are part of nature Try new experiences in and with nature while at The Wild Center Deliberately slow down and take notice of nature Share positive memories of their family enjoying the natural world Spend more family time exploring nature after visiting The Wild Center than they did before visiting The Wild Center

Courtesy of The Wild Center.

Intended Impact

Written by Randi Korn, Consultant

An impact statement is a one-sentence statement that melds together and reflects three museum-essential ideas: (1) staffs' passion for their museum work, (2) two or three characteristics that set the museum apart from other museums in the region, and (3) a vision for the kind of positive difference the museum will make in its community and among audiences. These three elements can be explored in inclusive and interactive workshops among staff, Board, and community stakeholders. These processes build a shared understanding of the museum's intended impact and model a collaborative work strategy focused on achieving an agreed-upon intended result.

An impact framework presents an impact statement as a *companion* to the mission statement; together they clarify and describe the museum's core purpose—what a museum does (mission) and the result of the museum's work on people (impact). If a museum also has a vision statement that describes what the museum aspires to become (which means that the museum would have two inwardly focused statements), consider switching the vision statement to an impact statement, thereby balancing the museum so it is mission *and* impact-focused.

As an example, consider The Wild Center, a natural history museum in the Adirondacks in upstate New York whose story is in this volume. The following is a segment of The Wild Center's Impact Framework to illustrate the interactive nature of mission and impact. In today's world where nonprofits are expected to demonstrate impact, they may need an additional statement that describes the intended result of the organization's mission-driven work. To know what The Wild Center does, the mission statement provides two important clues: the verb—ignite—and the subject—an enduring passion for the Adirondacks. The last phrase offers some clarity on *what* The Wild Center hopes its mission-driven work achieves but the impact statement clarifies the *why* and offers the beginnings of an evaluative framework for studying The Wild Center's success and shortcomings for accountability purposes. After a museum articulates what it does and what it hopes to achieve through its work, the most logical question to explore then becomes, "How will we get there?" The Wild Center responds with a bold declaration of *how* they do their work, as shown.

An impact framework is a living document, always in draft form as it is a work in progress; as the museum continues to hone its practices and weathers the changes from inside and outside the museum, staff will want to revisit, update, and alter the contents in the framework accordingly.

THEORIES OF TRANSFORMATIONAL CHANGE EXAMPLES
San Diego Museum of Man Model for Transformational Change

SAN DIEGO MUSEUM OF MAN MODEL FOR TRANSFORMATION

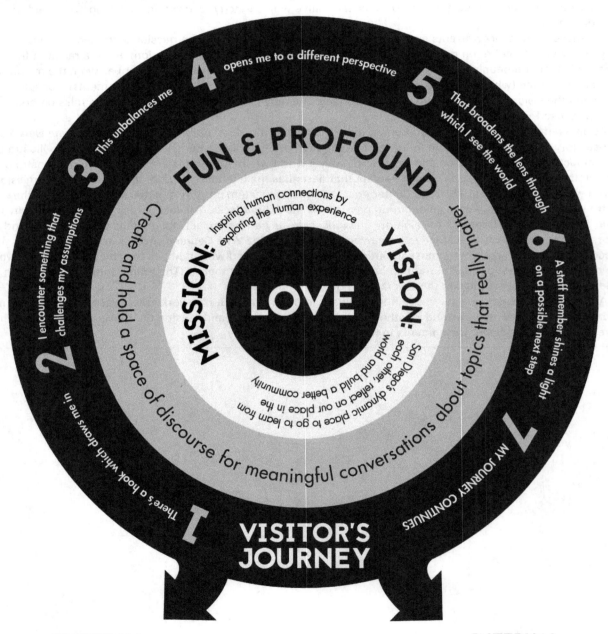

EXTERNAL TRANSFORMATION
(AWARENESS + ACTION)

INTERNAL TRANSFORMATION
(AWARENESS)

Courtesy of The San Diego Museum of Man.

Santa Cruz Museum of Art & History Theory of Change

AT THE SANTA CRUZ MUSEUM OF ART AND HISTORY, WE...

ACTIVATE THE MAH AS A **WELCOMING** GATHERING PLACE

FIND, SPARK, SHARE, AND PRESERVE **STORIES AND IDEAS**

SO THAT PARTICIPANTS...

ENJOY **SHARED EXPERIENCES**

EXPLORE ART AND HISTORY

FEEL **INVOLVED AND INCLUDED**

MAKE **UNEXPECTED** CONNECTIONS

MAKE PERSONAL CONNECTIONS

BUILD **AWARENESS AND RESPECT** FOR DIVERSE CULTURES AND PEOPLE

FEEL INSPIRED TO GO DEEPER

STRENGTHEN **BONDS**

WITH FRIENDS AND FAMILY

BUILD **BRIDGES**

ACROSS DIFFERENCES

FEEL **EMPOWERED**

TO SHARE THEIR CREATIVE AND CIVIC VOICES

OUR COMMUNITY **GROWS** STRONGER *& more connected*

Courtesy of The Santa Cruz Museum of Art and History. Design by Crista Alejandre.

The Empathetic Museum Maturity Model

A Metric for
Institutional Transformation

Empathy is one's ability to connect with others by relating to their personal experiences. It takes insight and a willingness to engage. The Empathetic Museum posits that cultural institutions can relate to their communities in the same way, and should align the work they do with the experiences, values, and needs of the communities they serve. **Our assessment tool, associated resources, and professional development workshops help organizations look within, and move towards a more empathetic future.**

Using the Maturity Model:

Materials: Overview & Characteristic Definitions (2 pgs), Rubric (2 pgs)

This rubric charts specific steps museums can take to progress towards instutional empathy in five areas: Civic Vision, Instutional Body Language, Community Resonance, Timeliness & Sustainability, and Performance Measures. Each characteristic is listed in the far left column. The columns to the right represent increasing levels of maturity in empathetic practice. This model is designed to be flexible for institutions of varying size, location, and mission (with moderate & appropriate modification).

As you examine each characteristic, evaluate the level to which your institution embodies that characteristic and check the boxes that apply. Checked boxes identify your institution's current level of achievement, ranging from Regressive to Proactive. Unchecked boxes represent goals for your institution, and can inspire organizational change, the reallocation of resources, or whatever it takes to reach the highest level of empathy for all characteristics.

If you have feedback about the maturity model rubric or would like to request information about Empathetic Museum professional development, please contact us at empatheticmuseum@gmail.com.

Key Terms:

Anchor Institution*: A key institution of civil society, such as library system, university, health system, educational system. Museums should be and should view themselves as anchor institutions. (Lord and Blankenberg 2015)
*museums are not anchor institutions by default; this position requires community buy-in

Soft Power: "The power of influence rather than of force or finance;" soft power resources are "ideas, knowledge, values, and culture." (Lord and Blankenberg 2015).

White Privilege: "An invisible package of assets that [white people] can count on cashing in each day...." Conditions that are viewed by whites as "morally neutral, normative, and average, and also ideal, so that when we work to benefit others, this is seen as work that will allow them to be more like us. "(McIntosh, 1990)

Employment Equity: Adherence to socially just guidelines for hiring in terms of race, gender, disability, sexual orientation, socioeconomic status, pay scale.

Decolonization: Deconstructing the Euro-centric, colonial origin of museums to reframe the way objects are presented, narratives constructed, and cultures privledged in interpretation, exhibition design, and educational programming.

Lord, G. D., & Blankenberg, N. (2015). *Cities, Museums and Soft Power.* American Association of Museums.
McIntosh, P. (1990) White Privilege: Unpacking the Invisible Backpack. ted. coe.wayne.edu

Empathetic Museum Contributors: Gretchen Jennings, Janeen Bryant, Stacey Mann, Jim Cullen, Kayleigh Bryant-Greenwell, Charlette Hove, Nayeli Zepeda, Matt Kirchman, Rainey Tisdale, Elissa Frankle, Jessica Konigsberg, Alyssa Greenberg, and many others who have generously shared their time and expertise.

Courtesy of Gretchen Jennings and The Empathetic Museum.

Civic Vision

Civic vision is a matter of imagination and behavior. According to Lord and Blankenberg (2015) museums, like universities, libraries, hospitals, etc. are "anchor instututions," part of the civic infrastructure of their communities. Boards and directors must have the imagination (vision) to see their institutions as such. Museums must behave as civic leaders, joining with other instututions of civil society to use their combined efforts to influence and shape (soft power) the quality of life in their community and the promotion of social justice in their municipalities.

For more information: *A discussion of museums as agents of soft power can be found in Chapter 1 of "Museums, Cities, and Soft Power," (2015) by Lord and Blankenberg (http://www.lord.ca/Pages/Cities-Museums-and-Soft-Power-Chapter1.pdf)*

Institutional Body Language

Analagous to personal body language, institutional body language (Jennings 2013, 2015) refers to the powerful messages museums convey through unspoken and unwritten manifestations of their being: the design of their buildings, the content of their advertising, the behavior of front line staff towards visitors, the demographics of their staff and boards, the choices they make in their collections, exhibitions, and programs. In the context of diversity and inclusion, museums' body language often conveys the message that the museum is for the white, the wealthy, and the powerful. Such museums may have written diversity policies and goals, but the image presented to the public by the institution in its many manifestations speaks more loudly than written goals or mission statements. People of color and other marginalized communities get the message—this place is not really for or about us—and stay away.

For more information: *Museum Commons blog posts*
http://www.museumcommons.com/2013/06/the-empathetic-museum-institutional.html
http://www.museumcommons.com/2015/06/charleston-the-cultural-landscape.html
Incluseum article
https://drive.google.com/file/d/0B2mitjKPAu6yVk9HV0ZwRkRIT0E/view

Community Resonance

Just as an empathetic individual resonates with the thoughts, feelings, and experiences of another group or person, an empathetic museum is so connected with its community that it is keenly aware of its values, needs, and challenges. The best way to achieve this is through a board and staff that reflect the diversity of a community; advisory boards, collaborations, and partnerships also help a museum's ability to be in touch with and responsive to its community.

For more information: *Incluseum Blog (www.incluseum.com)*
Joint statement from Museum Bloggers and Colleagues on Ferguson and Related Events
http://www.museumcommons.com/2014/12/joint-statement-museum-bloggers-colleagues-ferguson-related-events.html

Timeliness and Sustainability

Because an Empathetic Museum is so connected to its community (see Community Resonance), it is able to assess and respond to particular events or crises that affect its community (and beyond) in a timely and sustainable way. For example, if a museum is aware of racial tension in its community because of the racial diversity of its staff and/or strong collaborative community relationships, it can be well informed about what programs, exhibits, social media and other initiatives it might take within its mission and vision to address this civic issue. And it is aware that one-off efforts are not effective. It maintains a continuous and sustained awareness of and collaborative spirit towards its community and its needs.

For more information: *Elaine Gurian on Timeliness*
http://www.egurian.com/omnium-gatherum/museum-issues/timeliness
Museum Commons blog
http://www.museumcommons.com/2015/04/museumsrespondtoferguson-whats-authentic.html
Incluseum article
https://drive.google.com/file/d/0B2mitjKPAu6yVk9HV0ZwRkRIT0E/view

Performance Measures

A museum working to develop the characerics discussed above also incorporates them into its strategic planning. It creates tools to assess the level of achievement of each characteristic and its related goals. An Empathetic Museum commits resources to regular assessment, not only of its revenues and attendance, but also of its public and social impact.

For more information: *Scott, C.A., ed. (2013). Museums and Public Value. Chapter 3, "Creating Public Value Through Intentional Practice," by Randi Korn.*

Characteristic	Regressive (Lowest Maturity)	Emergent (Low Maturity)	Planned (Medium Maturity)	Proactive (Advanced Maturity)
Civic Vision i.e. How the museum expresses empathy externally through its civic role. *An "anchor institution" of civil society (like universities, libraries, etc.); exercises "soft power"(influence for social good) in community.*	☐ Identifies as independent, stand-alone player ☐ Indifferent to/unaware of issues within community ☐ Focused on core subject matter only	☐ Interested in being more relevant to civic life in the community ☐ Willing to reassess mission and vision ☐ Lacking required resources or clear direction	☐ Acknowledges role as anchor institution in community ☐ Ensures mission and vision reflect civic role ☐ Explores authentic ways to be part of its community and allocates project resources to do so	☐ Embraces and internalizes role as an anchor institution in community ☐ Key civic player with responsibilities and influence used for growth and social justice ☐ Exercises soft power in the community with dedicated staffing and project resources
Institutional Body Language i.e. How the museum embodies empathy through staffing, policies, workplace culture and structure, etc. *Aware of unconscious & unintended messages of white privilege communicated by building., administration, staff, hiring practices, collections, advertising, etc. Values intersectional cultural competency at all levels of staff and governance.* EMPATHETIC MUSEUM MATURITY MODEL	☐ Museum culture embodies privilege (racial, cultural, social, etc.) ☐ Governors, leaders, employees, exhibits, collections, etc. are predominantly single demographic (usually white) reflecting that of founders ☐ Unaddressed issues of pay (unpaid labor, low wages, wage disparity) and employment equity in hiring practices	☐ Token "community coordinator" is hired, or a "diversity function" is added to someone's job to attract "diverse" audiences ☐ "Diversity" initiatives consist of short term "outreach" programs or only overlap with "ethnic" holidays ☐ Some labor practices amended to create more equitable working conditions ☐ No substantial change in internal culture in terms of board, staffing, collections, exhibitions, programming	☐ Enacts formal policies through staff collaborations with community partners, advisory committees, experts on inclusion, equity, etc. ☐ Assesses and reorganizes board, staff, collections, exhibits and programs—its entire ethos—to reflect its community ☐ Hiring practices examined for bias; efforts made to address staff concerns ☐ Parity in representation is prioritized as the responsibility of all staff ☐ Changes from a place of white privilege to a place where all feel welcome	☐ Internalized awareness of privilege communicated by building, leadership, staffing, collections, advertising, etc. ☐ Workplace culture reflects inclusive environment with participation from staff of diverse thought, experience, and cultural competencies at all staff levels ☐ Fully resembles the complex and intersectional community's evolving demographics and values ☐ Recognizes and supports need for staff self-care to limit burnout ☐ Enacts long range plan to ensure sustainability of this transformation

Empathetic Museum Contributors: Gretchen Jennings, Janeen Bryant, Stacey Mann, Jim Cullen, Kayleigh Bryant-Greenwell, Charlette Hove, Nayeli Zepeda, Matt Kirchman, Rainey Tisdale, Elissa Frankle, Jessica Konigsberg, Alyssa Greenberg, and many others who have generously shared their time and expertise. Special credit and thanks to Jim Cullen for the Maturity Model framework.

Courtesy of Gretchen Jennings and The Empathetic Museum.

Community Resonance i.e. How the museum values, relates to, and serves its diverse communities. *Persistent awareness of surrounding community; forges strong, trusted connections with all (often underrepresented) segments of community in terms of race, ethnicity, gender, sexual orientation, disability, socioeconomic status.*	☐ Concerned with "attracting wider audiences" to expand audience base ☐ Uninterested in investigation of institutional connections to exclusion, racism, sexism, oppression, white privilege, etc. ☐ Perception that community issues have little connection to museum	☐ Authorizes research into the history of its building, location, collections in relation to racism, sexism, oppression, and privilege ☐ Examines its relationship with previously ignored or excluded communities ☐ Community connections focus on execution of the museum's mission and vision; relationship is predominantly one way, serving the museum's needs; involves cultural appropriation	☐ Solicits help from experienced facilitators and community partners to address engagement issues from an intentional, structural perspective ☐ Revisits institutional policies (staffing, collections, exhibitions, programming, etc.) to prioritize internal transformation ☐ Secures partnerships with other anchor institutions and local organizations more fully integrated with community issues	☐ Acknowledges complicity in legacy of exclusion, racism, oppression, cultural appropriation and privilege ☐ Implements plan to reverse these connections; seeks reconciliation with affected communities ☐ Nurtures reciprocal, community-driven relationships with local organizations that link the museum and its mission to local/national/global issues relevant to the surrounding community
Timeliness & Sustainability i.e. How, why, and when the museum responds to community issues and events in a sustainable way. *Able to respond to unexpected issues affecting its community due to continuous and sustained relationships & role as anchor institution.*	☐ Rarely acknowledges or responds to local, national, or global events. ☐ Programs are reactive, one-offs and not sustained; do not emanate from prior planning.	☐ Responds and can reallocate committed resources as a plan deviation ☐ Aware that one-off, unsustained responses do not build lasting community engagement	☐ Plans strategically for the future and engages periodically with stakeholders (internal/ external) so that appropriate community/national/global issues can be addressed ☐ Allocates resources to provide responses that are flexible and sustainable	☐ Plans strategically; reciprocal relationships with community members enable museum to anticipate and respond in a timely way ☐ Rarely blindsided, highly nimble and flexible; resources already allocated ☐ Community resources and programs are fully funded and protected in budget
Performance Measures i.e. How the museum measures success in empathetic practice. *Values and commits resources to regular assessment of public impact; shares this with the public.*	☐ Traditional measures focus on outputs, attendance and revenues ☐ Metrics rarely reported to internal/external stakeholders or the local community	☐ Traditional measures supplemented by attempts to gauge community collaboration and impact ☐ Museum reports to internal stakeholders annually	☐ Community impact and effectiveness as anchor institution are included in outcomes to be measured ☐ Annual reviews for all staff include engagement metrics ☐ Museum reports to internal and external stakeholders annually	☐ Museum continuously assesses and redefines its public value impact ☐ Commits resources to continued impact assessment along with attendance and revenue ☐ Reporting is increasingly transparent and widespread

Courtesy of Gretchen Jennings and The Empathetic Museum.

NOTES

1. Chris Taylor, "Inclusive Leadership: Avoiding a Legacy of Leadership." *Mass Action Toolkit*, 73–88.

2. Gail Anderson (ed.), *Reinventing the Museum: The Evolving Conversation on the Paradagim Shift*. Second edition (Lanham, MD: Altamira Press, 2012), 3–4.

3. Jeanne Bell, Jan Masaoka, and Steve Zimmerman, *Nonprofit Sustainability: Making Strategic Decisions for Financial Viability*. First edition (San Francisco: Jossey-Bass, a Wiley Imprint, 2010).

9

Final Thoughts

This book was a professional and personal journey. After decades of thinking about the value of a meaningful mission, and believing I knew what needed to be said, my thinking was challenged yet again, including confronting my own biases, continuing to learn from my colleagues, and realizing the urgent need for change in museums. Writing a book changes the author, and it should. Exploring what were the most inspiring mission statements, talking with colleagues about the challenges of leading change, selecting the mission statements and institutions for perspectives, and refining the Mission Alignment Framework continually tested my convictions and honed my goals for this book. Along the way I gained profound admiration for some of the courageous leaders instigating change in our field. And as the book development process unfolded, so too did the world around museums, most notably the political upheaval and the schisms revealing deeply embedded racism in our country that exclude and harm many of our citizens every day. This was, and is, a reminder that the work ahead for museums requires deep, long-term labor to overcome exclusionary practices to create vibrant museums reflective of and inclusive of the many voices, communities, people, and cultures that surround museums. This work isn't a choice—it is the new mandate.

Every museum has the opportunity to make a difference, to get out of their comfort zone, and to ask what is the *legacy* that I as a museum professional, that we as a museum staff and Board, that our museum wants to leave for the generations to come. Change that benefits more communities, more people and audiences, and the larger world is worth the effort. Change that embraces, reflects, and achieves diversity and inclusion, tackles awareness about our fragile environment, gives voice to the unheard, protects the vulnerable species of our planet, or presents the difficult stories formerly not represented is essential. When so many benefit, we are upholding a new, more relevant, existence. Maybe then more museums will be invited to the table as a vital partner in creating a more just and sustainable world. It is about allocating time for the difficult conversations, changing internal culture, adjusting mindsets, and redefining measurements for success tied to a relevant mission. As a rule, museums are on the treadmill of doing too much rather than focusing on the right scope and emphasis of work for the greater good and greatest impact. The changes ahead will require more than a minor adjustment. These changes will take vision and courage to create museums and missions that reflect what being relevant in the twenty-first century truly means.

In a more perfect world, the building of the book would have included opportunities to visit and see the most relevant museums, missions, and museum practice in action. One recommendation to the field is to invest in the research, study, and exploration of changing ideologies to shore up museum practice, inclusion, and leadership capabilities. Thankfully, some foundations and associations have invested in research and support of individuals committed to contributing to the larger discourse in the museum field and in society at large. There simply need to be more opportunities for the range of leaders of all backgrounds and expertise to support museum field advancements. In the end, if the museum field wishes to advance best practices, then dedicated researchers and leaders should be supported to conduct solid research, analyze findings, and share new approaches and requirements for relevant museums that make a difference.

My deepest hope is that the inspiring stories, leaders, and museums featured in this book contribute to the larger conversation and inspire courage in others to enact change. It is urgent to act now and make a meaningful difference toward resolving and creating more just, safe, and sustainable museums that in turn contribute to a better world.

Bibliography

American Alliance of Museums. *Characteristics of Excellence*. American Alliance of Museums. Accessed December 2, 2018. http://ww2.aam-us.org/resources/ethics-standards-and-best-practices/characteristics-of-excellence.

———. *Mastering Civic Engagement: A Challenge to Museums*. Washington, DC: American Alliance of Museums, 2002.

———. *Museums for a New Century: A Report of the Commission on Museums for a New Century*. Washington, DC: American Alliance of Museums, 1984.

Ames, Michael M. *Cannibal Tours and Glass Boxes: The Anthropology of Museums*. Vancouver, British Columbia, Canada: University of British Columbia Press, 1992.

Anderson, Gail. *Museum Mission Statements: Building A Distinct Identity (Professional Practice)*. Washington, DC: American Associations of Museums, 1998.

Anderson, Gail (ed.). *Reinventing the Museum: Historical and Contemporary Perspectives on the Paradigm Shift*. Lanham, MD: AltaMira Press, 2004.

———. *Reinventing the Museum: The Evolving Conversation on the Paradigm Shift*, second edition. Lanham, MD: AltaMira Press, 2012.

Banaji, Mahzarin R., and Greenwald, Anthony G. *Blindspot: Hidden Biases of Good People*. New York: Delacorte Press, 2013.

Becker, Carol (ed.). *Different Voices: A Social, Cultural, And Historical Framework For Change In The American Art Museum*. New York: Association of Art Museum Directors, 1992.

Bell, Jeanne, Masaoka, Jan, and Zimmerman, Steve. *Nonprofit Sustainability: Making Strategic Decisions for Financial Viability*, first edition. San Francisco: Jossey-Bass, a Wiley Imprint, 2010.

Bergeron, Anne, and Tuttle, Beth. *Magnetic: The Art and Science of Engagement*. Washington, DC: AAM Press, 2013.

Boardsource. *9 Characteristics of a Mission Statement Chart*. 2016. Accessed October 16, 2018. https://boardsource.org/wp-content/uploads/2016/08/9-Characteristics-Mission-Statement.pdf?hsCtaTracking=bcc51ecd-4e67-408c-ba64-47369164a256|f126e742-a74a-4c80-a6c7-0a4d2c4624f8.

———. *The Source: Twelve Principles of Governance That Power Exceptional Boards*. Washington, DC: Boardsource, 2005.

Boucher, Brian. "Outrage at Museum of Fine Arts Boston Over Disgraceful 'Dress Up in a Kimono' Event." *Artnet News*. July 6, 2015.

Boyd, Willard L. "Museums as Centers of Controversy." *JSTOR* 128, 3, (1999). 185–228. www.jstor.org/stable/20027572.

Brophy, Sarah S., and Wylie, Elizabeth. *The Green Museum: A Primer on Environmental Practice*. Lanham, MD: Altamira Press, 2013.

Brown, Tim. *Change by Design: How Design Thinking Transforms Organizations and Inspires Innovation*. New York: HarperBusiness, 2009.

Bunch, Lonnie G., III. "A Place To Come Together On Matters That Divide Us." Interview by S. Goldberg. *National Geographic*. March 14, 2018. Accessed October 16, 2018. https://news.nationalgeographic.com/2016/09/African-American-Museum-real-estate/.

———. "Lonnie Bunch On Telling 'The American Story Through An African American Lens.'" Interview by Ally Schweitzer. *American University Radio*. August 16, 2016. Retrieved September 28, 2018. https://wamu.org/story/16/08/16/interview_lonnie_bunch_african_american_museum/.

———. "New Smithsonian Museum Confronts Race 'to Make America Better.'" Interview by Michele Norris. *National Geographic*. September 24, 2016. Retrieved September 28, 2018. https://news.nationalgeographic.com/2016/09/Smithsonian-museum-confronts-race/.

Chew, Ron. *Museums and Civic Dialogue: Case Studies From Animating Democracy*. Washington, DC: Americans for the Arts, 2005.

Collins, Jim. *Good to Great: Why Some Companies Make the Leap and Others Don't*. New York: HarperBusiness, 2001.

Conley, Chip, and Hsieh, Tony. *Peak: How Great Companies Get Their Mojo from Maslow*. San Francisco: Jossey-Bass, 2007.

Crutchfield, Leslie. R., McLeod Grant, Heather, and Gregory Dees, J. *Forces for Good: The Six Practices of High-Impact Nonprofits*. San Francisco: Jossey-Bass, 2012.

Dweck, Carol. S. *Mindset: The New Psychology of Success*. New York: Ballantine Books, 2007.

Evans, Richard. "Eight Adaptive Capacities." EmcArtsInc. April 18, 2018. Accessed December 2, 2018. https://www.artsfwd.org/eight-adaptive-capacities/.

Fagan, Brian, and Messenger Mauch, Phyllis. *The Ethics of Collecting Cultural Property: Whose Culture? Whose Property?* Albuquerque: University of New Mexico Press, 1999.

Falk, John H., and Sheppard, Beverly K. *The Museum Experience*. Washington, DC: Whalesback, 1992.

———. *Thriving in the Knowledge Age: New Business Models for Museums and Other Cultural Institutions*. Lanham, MD: AltaMira Press, 2006.

Fischer, Daryl, and Roberts, Laura B. *Building Museum Boards*. Lanham, MD: Rowman & Littlefield Publishers, 2018.

———. *The Leadership Partnership*. Lanham, MD: Rowman & Littlefield Publishers, 2018.

Fischer, Daryl, Anila, Swarupa, and Moore, Porchia. "Coming Together to Address Systemic Racism in Museums." *Curator The Museum Journal*, 60, no. 6 (2017), 23–31.

Francis, Errol. "It's Time All Museums Were Postcolonial." *Museum Journal*, 118, no. 7 (2018). https://www.museumsassociation.org/museums-journal/comment/01072018-its-time-all-museums-were-postcolonial?dm_i=2VBX,QLOW,27LLX0,2PUE5,1.

Gilmore, James H., and Pine II, B. Joseph. *Authenticity: What Consumers Really Want*. Boston: Harvard Business Review Press, 2007.

Gladwell, Malcolm. *The Tipping Point: How Little Things Can Make a Big Difference.* New York: Back Bay Books, 2002.

———. *Outliers: The Story of Success.* New York: Back Bay Books, 2011.

Goleman, Daniel. *Emotional Intelligence: Why It Can Matter More Than IQ.* New York: Bantam Books, 2005.

Grace, Kay Sprinkel. *The Nonprofit Board's Role in Setting and Advancing the Mission (Boardsource Governance Series).* Washington, DC: Boardsouce, 2002.

Harlow, Bob. *The Road to Results Effective Practices For Building Arts Practices.* New York: Bob Harlow Research and Consulting, LLC, 2014. Accessed October 16, 2018. https://www.wallacefoundation.org/knowledge-center/Documents/ The-Road-to-Results-Effective-Practices-for-Building-Arts-Audiences.pdf.

Harris, Neil. "The Divided House of the American Art Museum." *JSTOR* 128, 3, (1999). 33–56. www.jstor.org/ stable/20027566.

Hellweg, Eric. "The Eight-Word Mission Statement." *Harvard Business Review*, October 22, 2010. Accessed September 12, 2018. https://hbr.org/2010/10/the-eight-word-mission-stateme.

Henry, Barbara, and McLean, Kathleen. *How Visitors Changed Our Museum: Transforming the Gallery of California Art at the Oakland Museum of California.* Oakland: Oakland Museum of California, 2010.

Heumann Gurian, Ellen. "Choosing Among the Options: An Opinion About Museum Definitions." *Curator The Museum Journal* (May 24, 2010). Accessed September 12, 2018. https://onlinelibrary.wiley.com/doi/pdf/10.1111/j.2151-6952.2002 .tb01182.x.

———. *Civilizing the Museum: The Collected Writings of Elaine Heumann Gurian.* New York: Routledge, 2006.

Hirzy, Ellen C. *Excellence and Equity.* Washington, DC: American Alliance of Museums, 2008.

Holo, Selma, and Alvarez, Mari-Tere. *Remix: Changing Conversations in Museums of the Americas.* Berkeley: University of California Press, 2016.

International Council of Museums. *ICOMS Code of Ethics.* Paris: International Council of Museums, 2004.

Institute of Museum and Library Services. "Museums, Libraries, and 21st Century Skills." Accessed December 2018. https:// www.imls.gov/issues/national-initiatives/museums-libraries-and-21st-century-skills/definitions.

Ithaka S+R. "Case Studies in Museum Diversity." *The Andrew W. Mellon Foundation.* January 22, 2018. Accessed September 12, 2018. https://mellon.org/resources/news/articles/case-studies-museum-diversity/?utm_source=News from the Andrew W. Mellon Foundation&utm_campaign=31fac44ee2-EMAIL_CAMPAIGN_2017_11_03_COPY_01&utm_ medium=email&utm_term=0_75560b415d-31fac44ee2-285822817.

Ivy, Nicole (ed.). "Facing Change: Insights from the American Alliance of Museums' Diversity, Equity, Accessibility, and Inclusion Working Group." *American Alliance of Museums.* 2018. Accessed September 12, 2018. https://www.aam-us.org/ wp-content/uploads/2018/04/AAM-DEAI-Working-Group-Full-Report-2018.pdf.

Janes, Robert. *Looking Reality in the Eye: Museums and Social Responsibility.* Calgary: University of Calgary Press, 2005.

———. "Museums and Climate Change Activism" Alberta Museums Association/Western Museums Association International Conference 2017–Museums UNITE to Improve Communities, Alberta, Canada, September 23, 2017. December, 2018.

———. *Museums in a Troubled World.* New York: Routledge, 2009.

Kakissis, Joanna. "Belgian Museum Looks At Country's History of Colonialism and Racism." *NPR*, September 2, 2018. Accessed December, 2018. https://www.npr.org/2018/09/02/644085214/belgian-museum-looks-at-countrys-history-of -colonialism-and-racism.

Karp, Ivan, and Lavine, Steve D. *Exhibiting Cultures The Poetics and Politics of Museum Display.* Washington, DC: Smithsonian Press, 1991.

Karp, Ivan, Katz, Corrine A., Szwaja Lynn, and Ybarra-Frausto, Tomas. *Museum Frictions Public Cultures/ Global Transformations.* Durham, NC: Duke University Press, 2006.

Karp, Ivine, Mullen Kreamer, Christine, and Levine, Steven. *Museums and Communities: The Politics of Public Culture.* Washington, DC: Smithsonian Books, 1992.

Kinard, Joy, G. *The Man, the Movement, the Museum.* Washington, DC: A. P. Foundation Press, 2017.

Klein, Kim. "Mission, Message, and Damage Control." *Nonprofit Quarterly.* February 9, 2018. Accessed December 2, 2018. https://nonprofitquarterly.org/2018/02/09/mission-message-and-damage-control/.

Korn, Randi. *Intentional Practice for Museums: A Guide for Maximizing Impact.* Lanham, MD: Rowman & Littlefield Publishers, 2018.

———. "To What End? Achieving Mission Through International Practice." Association of Science–Technology Centers. May 16, 2008. Accessed December 2, 2018. https://www.astc.org/astc-dimensions/to-what-end-achieving-mission -through-intentional-practice/.

Koster, Emlyn H. "In Search of Relevance: Science Centers as Innovators in the Evolution of Museums." *JSTOR* 128, 3, (1999). 277–296., www.jstor.org/stable/20027575.

———. "The Relevant Museum: A Reflection on Sustainability." *Reinventing the Museum: The Evolving Conversation on the Paradigm Shift.* Lanham, MD: AltaMira Press, 2012.

"The Legacy Museum From Enslavement to Mass Incarceration." *Equal Justice Initiative.* 2008. https://eji.org/legacy -museum.

Lencioni, Patrick. *The Advantage: Why Organizational Health Trumps Everything Else In Business.* San Francisco: Jossey-Bass, 2012.

Lonetree, Amy. *Decolonizing Museums: Representing Native America in National and Tribal Museums.* Chapel Hill: The University of North Carolina Press, 2012.

Lord, Gail, and Blankenberg, Ngaire. *Cities, Museums, and Soft Power.* Washington, DC: American Alliance of Museums, 2015.

McCambridge, Ruth. "Donors Force a Point at the Met That Never Should Have Had to Be Made." *Nonprofit Quarterly* (October 8, 2018). Accessed December, 2018. https://nonprofitquarterly.org/2018/10/08/donors-force-a-point-at-the-met -that-never-should-have-had-to-be-made/.

Mclean, Kathleen. "Museum Exhibitions and the Dynamics of Dialogue." *JSTOR* 128, 3, (1999). 83–107. www.jstor.org/ stable/20027568.

Monroe, Dan L., and Echo-Hawk, Walter. "Deft Deliberations (1999)." *Reinventing the Museum: The Evolving Conversation on the Paradigm Shift.* Lanham, MD: AltaMira Press, 2012.

Moore, Mark H. *Creating Public Value: Strategic Management in Government.* Boston: Harvard University Press, 1995.

Moore, Porchia. "The Danger Of The 'D' Word: Museums And Diversity." *Incluseum*(blog), January 20, 2014, https:// incluseum.com/2014/01/20/the-danger-of-the-d-word-museums-and-diversity/.

Staff of the Equal Justice Initiative. "The National Memorial For Peace and Justice." *Equal Justice Initiative*. 2018. https://eji .org/legacy-museum.

Ng, Wendy. "Decolonize and Indigenize: A Reflective Dialogue." *Medium* (June 12, 2018). Accessed December, 2018. https:// medium.com/viewfinder-reflecting-on-museum-education/decolonize-and-indigenize-a-reflective-dialogue-3de78fa76442.

Noriega, Chon A. "On Museum Row: Aesthetics and the Politics of Exhibition." *JSTOR* 128, 3, (1999). 57–81. www.jstor.org/ stable/20027567.

Oluo, Ijeoma. *So You Want To Talk About Race*. New York: Seal Press, 2018.

Osterwalder, Alexander, Pigneur, Y., and Clark, T. *Business Model Generation: A Handbook for Visionaries, Game Changers, and Challengers*. San Francisco: Wiley, 2010.

Pink, Daniel H. *Drive*. New York: Riverhead Books, 2011.

Pitman, Bonnie. "Muses, Museums, and Memories." *JSTOR* 128, 3, (1999). 1–31. www.jstor.org/stable/20027565.

"The Power of Board Advocacy: A Discussion Guide for Boards." *Stand For Your Mission*. Accessed September 12, 2018. https://standforyourmission.org/wp-content/uploads/2017/11/S4YM-Discussion-Guide.pdf.

Putnam, Robert D. *Bowling Alone: The Collapse and Revival of American Community*. New York: Touchstone Books, 2001.

Richards, Chip. "Ikigai: Finding your Reason for Being." *UpliftConnect*. May 14, 2016. Accessed September 5, 2017. http:// upliftconnect.com/ikigai-finding-your-reason-for-being/.

Schilling, Mary Kaye. "America Is Racist. So What Do We Do Now? Activist Lawyer Bryan Stevenson Has Some Answers." *Newsweek*, November 29, 2018. Accessed December, 2018. https://www.newsweek.com/2018/12/07/bryan-stevenson -racism-equal-justice-initiative-national-memorial-peace-and-1234169.html.

Simon, Nina. *The Participatory Museum*. Santa Cruz: Museum 2.0, 2010.

———. *The Art of Relevance*. Santa Cruz: Museum 2.0, 2016.

Sinek, Simon. *Start with Why: How Great Leaders Inspire Everyone to Take Action*. New York: Penguin Group, 2009.

Silverman, Lois H. *The Social Work of Museums*. New York: Routledge, 2010.

Skramstad, Harold. "An Agenda for American Museums in the Twenty-First Century." *JSTOR* 128, 3, (1999). 109–28. www.jstor.org/stable/20027569.

Starr, Kevin. "The Eight-Word Mission Statement." *Stanford Social Innovation Review*. Accessed September 12, 2018. https://ssir.org/articles/entry/the_eight_word_mission_statement.

Stevenson, Bryan. *Just Mercy: A Story of Justice and Redemption*. New York: Spiegel and Grau, 2015.

Suchy, Sherene. "Emotional Intelligence, Passion and Museum Leadership." *Museum Management and Curatorship* 18, no.1 (1999).

Sullivan, Lawrence E. and Alison Edwards. *Stewards of the Sacred*. Washington, DC: American Association of Museums Press, 2004.

Taylor, Ron. *The Mission Statement: A Framework for Developing An Effective Organizational Mission Statement In 100 Words Or Less*. Amazon Digital Services LLC, 2013.

Taylor, Chris. "Inclusive Leadership: Avoiding a Legacy of Leadership." In *Mass Action Toolkit*, 73-88. 2017. Accessed November 9, 2018. https://static1.squarespace.com/static/58fa685dff7c50f78be5f2b2/t/59dcdd27e5dd5b5a1b51d9d8/ 1507646780650/TOOLKIT_10_2017.pdf.

Trout, Jack. "'Mission Statement' Words." *Forbes*, August 21, 2006. Accessed October 16, 2018. https://www.forbes .com/2006/08/18/jack-trout-on-marketing-cx_jt_0821mission.html#10ac5d4153ca.

Tschumi, Bernard. "On the Museum of the Twenty-First Century: An Homage to Italo Calvino's 'Invisible Cities.'" *JSTOR* 128, 3, (1999). 333–337. www.jstor.org/stable/20027579.

Weil, Stephen E. *Beauty and the Beast: On Museums, Art, the Law, and the Market*. Washington, DC: Smithsonian Institution Press, 1983.

———. *A Cabinet of Curiosities: Inquiring into Museums and Their Prospects*. Washington, DC: Smithsonian Institution Press, 1995.

———. *Making Museums Matter*. Washington, DC: Smithsonian Institution Press, 2002.

———. *Rethinking the Museum and Other Meditations*. Washington, DC: Smithsonian Institution Press, 1990.

Zimmerman, Steve, and Bell, Jeanne. *The Sustainability Mindset: Using the Matrix Map to Make Strategic Decisions*. San Francisco: Jossey-Bass, 2014.

Index

About the Author

Gail Anderson has dedicated much of her more than forty-year career researching, amassing, and sharing resources and new ideas to advance the museum field. With all the pressures that museum leaders face on a daily basis, her goal has been to make resources easily available with practical and accessible approaches and tools.

Anderson, president of Gail Anderson & Associates (GA&A) works with museum leaders facilitating institutional transformation, building institutional and leadership capacity, and expanding community and global relevance. GA&A works with museums on strategic planning, organizational restructuring, institutional assessment and development, board development, as well as individual coaching. She has worked with more than 65 clients and completed over 105 projects, the majority of which are repeat clientele speaking to long-term relationships.

Prior to launching her own consulting business, Anderson was deputy director of The Mexican Museum; vice president of Museum Management Consultants; chair of the Graduate Department of Museum Studies at John F. Kennedy University in Berkeley, California; assistant director at the Southwest Museum in Los Angeles; and museum educator at the Museum of Northern Arizona.

Highlights of Anderson's professional activities include being a current member of The Museum Group, a past board member of the American Alliance of Museums, an invited member of the committee that produced *Excellence & Equity*, and past president of the Western Museums Association Board of Directors. In 1997, she received the director's chair award for distinguished service and leadership from the Western Museums Association. She is the author and editor of the American Association of Museums publication, *Museum Mission Statements: Building A Distinct Identity* (1997), and this edition entitled *Mission Matters: Relevance and Museums in the 21st Century* (2019). She is also the editor of the first edition of *Reinventing the Museum: Historical and Contemporary Perspectives on the Paradigm Shift* (2004), and the second edition of the Alta Mira Press publication *Reinventing the Museum: The Evolving Conversation on the Paradigm Shift* (2012). Anderson continues her commitment to advancing the field through frequent speaking engagements, writing, and teaching.